STREET STYLE

DRESS, BODY, CULTURE

Series Editor: **Joanne B. Eicher**, *Regents' Professor, University of Minnesota*

Advisory Board:
Djurdja Bartlett, *London College of Fashion, University of the Arts*
Pamela Church-Gibson, *London College of Fashion, University of the Arts*
James Hall, *University of Illinois at Chicago*
Vicki Karaminas, *University of Technology, Sydney*
Gwen O'Neal, *University of North Carolina at Greensboro*
Ted Polhemus, *Curator, 'Street Style' Exhibition, Victoria and Albert Museum*
Valerie Steele, *The Museum at the Fashion Institute of Technology*
Lou Taylor, *University of Brighton*
Karen Tranberg Hansen, *Northwestern University*
Ruth Barnes, *Ashmolean Museum, University of Oxford*

Books in this provocative series seek to articulate the connections between culture and dress which is defined here in its broadest possible sense as any modification or supplement to the body. Interdisciplinary in approach, the series highlights the dialogue between identity and dress, cosmetics, coiffure and body alternations as manifested in practices as varied as plastic surgery, tattooing, and ritual scarification. The series aims, in particular, to analyse the meaning of dress in relation to popular culture and gender issues and will include works grounded in anthropology, sociology, history, art history, literature, and folklore.

ISSN: 1360-466X

Dani Cavallaro and Alexandra Warwick, *Fashioning the Frame: Boundaries, Dress and the Body*

Judith Perani and Norma H. Wolff, *Cloth, Dress and Art Patronage in Africa*

Linda B. Arthur, *Religion, Dress and the Body*

Paul Jobling, *Fashion Spreads: Word and Image in Fashion Photography*

Fadwa El Guindi, *Veil: Modesty, Privacy and Resistance*

Thomas S. Abler, *Hinterland Warriors and Military Dress: European Empires and Exotic Uniforms*

Linda Welters, *Folk Dress in Europe and Anatolia: Beliefs about Protection and Fertility*

Kim K.P. Johnson and Sharron J. Lennon, *Appearance and Power*

Barbara Burman, *The Culture of Sewing*

Annette Lynch, *Dress, Gender and Cultural Change*

Antonia Young, *Women Who Become Men*

David Muggleton, *Inside Subculture: The Postmodern Meaning of Style*

Nicola White, *Reconstructing Italian Fashion: America and the Development of the Italian Fashion Industry*

Brian J. McVeigh, *Wearing Ideology: The Uniformity of Self-Presentation in Japan*

Shaun Cole, *Don We Now Our Gay Apparel: Gay Men's Dress in the Twentieth Century*

Kate Ince, *Orlan: Millennial Female*

Ali Guy, Eileen Green and Maura Banim, *Through the Wardrobe: Women's Relationships with Their Clothes*

Linda B. Arthur, *Undressing Religion: Commitment and Conversion from a Cross-Cultural Perspective*

William J.F. Keenan, *Dressed to Impress: Looking the Part*

Joanne Entwistle and Elizabeth Wilson, *Body Dressing*

Leigh Summers, *Bound to Please: A History of the Victorian Corset*

Paul Hodkinson, *Goth: Identity, Style and Subculture*

Leslie W. Rabine, *The Global Circulation of African Fashion*

Michael Carter, *Fashion Classics from Carlyle to Barthes*

Sandra Niessen, Ann Marie Leshkowich and Carla Jones, *Re-Orienting Fashion: The Globalization of Asian Dress*

Kim K. P. Johnson, Susan J. Torntore and Joanne B. Eicher, *Fashion Foundations: Early Writings on Fashion and Dress*

Helen Bradley Foster and Donald Clay Johnson, *Wedding Dress Across Cultures*

Eugenia Paulicelli, *Fashion under Fascism: Beyond the Black Shirt*

Charlotte Suthrell, *Unzipping Gender: Sex, Cross-Dressing and Culture*

Irene Guenther, *Nazi Chic? Fashioning Women in the Third Reich*

Yuniya Kawamura, *The Japanese Revolution in Paris Fashion*

Patricia Calefato, *The Clothed Body*

Ruth Barcan, *Nudity: A Cultural Anatomy*

Samantha Holland, *Alternative Femininities: Body, Age and Identity*

Alexandra Palmer and Hazel Clark, *Old Clothes, New Looks: Second Hand Fashion*

Yuniya Kawamura, *Fashion-ology: An Introduction to Fashion Studies*

Regina A. Root, *The Latin American Fashion Reader*

Linda Welters and Patricia A. Cunningham, *Twentieth-Century American Fashion*

Jennifer Craik, *Uniforms Exposed: From Conformity to Transgression*

Alison L. Goodrum, *The National Fabric: Fashion, Britishness, Globalization*

Annette Lynch and Mitchell D. Strauss, *Changing Fashion: A Critical Introduction to Trend Analysis and Meaning*

Catherine M. Roach, *Stripping, Sex and Popular Culture*

Marybeth C. Stalp, *Quilting: The Fabric of Everyday Life*

Jonathan S. Marion, *Ballroom: Culture and Costume in Competitive Dance*

Dunja Brill, *Goth Culture: Gender, Sexuality and Style*

Joanne Entwistle, *The Aesthetic Economy of Fashion: Markets and Value in Clothing and Modelling*

Juanjuan Wu, *Chinese Fashion: From Mao to Now*

Annette Lynch, *Porn Chic*

Brent Luvaas, *DIY Style: Fashion, Music and Global Cultures*

Jianhua Zhao, *The Chinese Fashion Industry*

Eric Silverman, *A Cultural History of Jewish Dress*

Karen Hansen and D. Soyini Madison, *African Dress: Fashion, Agency, Performance*

Maria Mellins, *Vampire Culture*

Lynne Hume, *The Religious Life of Dress*

Marie Riegels Melchior and Birgitta Svensson, *Fashion and Museums*

Masafumi Monden, *Japanese Fashion Cultures*

Alfonso McClendon, *Fashion and Jazz*

Phyllis G. Tortora, *Dress, Fashion and Technology*

Barbara Brownie and Danny Graydon, *The Superhero Costume*

Adam Geczy and Vicki Karaminas, *Fashion's Double*

Yuniya Kawamura, *Sneakers*

Heike Jenss, *Fashion Studies*

STREET STYLE

An Ethnography of Fashion Blogging

Brent Luvaas

Bloomsbury Academic
An imprint of Bloomsbury Publishing Plc

B L O O M S B U R Y
LONDON · OXFORD · NEW YORK · NEW DELHI · SYDNEY

Bloomsbury Academic

An imprint of Bloomsbury Publishing Plc

50 Bedford Square	1385 Broadway
London	New York
WC1B 3DP	NY 10018
UK	USA

www.bloomsbury.com

BLOOMSBURY and the Diana logo are trademarks of Bloomsbury Publishing Plc

First published 2016

British Library Cataloguing-in-Publication Data
A catalogue record for this book is available from the British Library.

ISBN: HB: 978-0-8578-5721-7
PB: 978-0-8578-5575-6
ePDF: 978-1-4742-6289-7
ePub: 978-1-4742-6290-3

Library of Congress Cataloging-in-Publication Data
Luvaas, Brent Adam, 1974-
Street style : an ethnography of fashion blogging / by Brent Luvaas.
pages cm. – (Dress, body, culture)
Includes bibliographical references and index.
ISBN 978-0-85785-575-6 (pbk.) – ISBN 978-0-85785-721-7 (hardback) –
ISBN 978-1-4742-6289-7 (ePDF) – ISBN 978-1-4742-6290-3 (ePub)
1. Fashion–Blogs. 2. Fashion writing–Blogs. 3. Fashion photography.
4. Fashion merchandising–Social aspects. I. Title.
TT503.5.L88 2016
808.06'674692–dc23
2015023419

Typeset by Integra Software Services Pvt. Ltd.
Printed and bound in India

For Jessica and Esme, as always.

CONTENTS

FIGURE 1 Marilyn, Pier 57, New York. Photo by author.

ACKNOWLEDGEMENTS

This book would not have been possible without the generous help I received at every step along the way from colleagues, family, fellow bloggers, and photographers. I want to thank Timothy D. Taylor and Brooke Erin Duffy for reading complete drafts of the manuscript. Your advice was invaluable, and it was enormously helpful to know that I wasn't writing into a void. I also want to thank Sherry B. Ortner, Ted Polhemus, Wesley Shumar, Devon Powers, Mary Ebeling, Joseph Hancock, Constantine Nakassis, Keith Murphy, James Hoesterey, Jenny Chio, Heather Loyd, Mark Westmoreland, Jonathan Marion, Janet Hethorn, Heike Jenss, Todd Nicewonger, Stephanie Sadre-Orafai, Joanne Turney, John Bishop, and other colleagues whose opinions, critiques, and thoughts about smaller pieces of this larger work helped shape the final product – whether they are aware of it or not. I am guessing most of them are not. Thanks also go to Anna Wright, Hannah Crump, Emily Ardizzone, Ariadne Godwin, and Joanne Eicher from Bloomsbury for believing in the book and ushering me through the process of its publication.

The list of bloggers and photographers I need to thank is considerably longer. I am really hoping I haven't missed any of you. If so, feel free to leave a nasty comment on my Instagram gallery or something. Thank you Adam Katz Sinding, Alkistis Tsitouri, Amy Creyer, Dana Landon, Dasha Gajic, Emma Arnold, Felicia Nitzsche, Gunnar Hämmerle, James Bent, Javi Obando, Karl-Edwin Guerre, Liisa Jokinen, Lisa Warninger, Michelle Oberholzer, Mordechai Rubinstein, Nels Frye, Putri Soe, Reuben 'Big Rube' Harley, Simbarashe Cha, Yael Sloma, and Yvan Rodic for sharing your time, thoughts, and experiences with me. They were crucial to my writing of this book and also to shaping my own practice as a street style photographer and blogger. Thanks also to Shoichi Aoki and Steve Johnston for the awesome images and great anecdotes. Thank you Magnum Photos, The University of Pennsylvania Museum of Archaeology and Anthropology, and Die Photographische Sammlung/SK Stiftung Kultur der Sparkasse KölnBonn for allowing me to use such amazing images in the history portion of this book.

Shout out to my shooting buddies at New York Fashion Week: Keith Morrison, Tyler Joe, Isaac Harris, Hunter Abrams, Brian Sansivero, Emmy Park, Mark

Iantosca, Ricky Opaterny, Simbarashe Cha, Sam Katz, and Chermelle Edwards. Thanks also to Melodie Jeng, Michael Dumler, Nabile Quenum, Kamel Lahmadi, Eddie Newton, Scott Schuman, Daniel Bruno Grandl, Youngjun Koo, Wataru 'Bob' Shimosato, Jesse Bush, Adam Katz Sinding, and the rest of the black crows with cameras, perched on the sidewalks of New York. I've learned an enormous amount from hanging out with and shooting beside you. I want to express special gratitude, however, to Driely S., who was my tour guide and mentor for my first season of New York Fashion Week and my good friend from then on. I have learned more about shooting street style from her than any other single individual. You can tell how often we shot next to each other just by looking at our photos of the same events.

Thank you, *Racked.com*, *Refinery29*, and *Kenton Magazine* for letting me playact at being a professional photographer for a while. It was fun. I'm glad I did it. But I'm even more glad that I have a tenured position at a university. Freelancing is a rough game. It makes me admire the photographers who play that game even more for managing to scrape together a living through it.

Philly bloggers that deserve special mention for showing me the ropes – and giving me someone to hang out with at parties – include Sabir M. Peele, Ian Michael Crumm, Akief Sheriff, Chaucee Stillman, Fajr Muhammad, Karima Adkins, Alex Delaney, Jacqueline Davis Moranti, Jared Michael Lowe, Melissa Alam, Quentin Washington, Mohammed Shariff, Swabreen Bakr, Anh Mai, Alex Kacala, and Shana Draugelis. Much love, and keep on bloggin'!

Thanks to my wife Jessica Curtaz and daughter Esme Luvaas for all their love and support these past few years, as I have gone through various stages of obsession over this project.

Finally, I want to thank the hundreds of people in Philadelphia and New York, and a few scattered folks in Jakarta, Portland, Los Angeles, and Boston, who have graciously taken time out of their busy lives to stop and pose for me, a total stranger, who could have very well been a homicidal maniac. Being photographed by a blogger is a leap of faith. Thank you for taking that leap for me. I hope you think it was worth it.

INTRODUCTION: ANTHROPOLOGY, STREET STYLE

FIGURE I.1 Akief, Sydenham St, Philadelphia. Photo by author.

Taking it to the streets

It was Monday, 26 March 2012, a windy and unseasonably cold afternoon in Center City, Philadelphia. I was standing on the corner of Walnut and 18th Street, a backpack swung over my shoulders, a Panasonic Lumix GF-1 micro-four thirds camera dangling from my neck. My head ached. My teeth were grinding with caffeine. And my eyes were dry and strained from overuse, darting continually back and forth, as I assessed the outfit of every person passing by. I remember being self-conscious about what I was wearing, though I cannot remember what that was, and I remember feeling restless and uncertain, standing there, fixed in place, like an orange plastic pylon redirecting the flow of traffic. I was beginning to feel like a real creep, and I am pretty sure that at least some of the people moving past me also thought of me as one. It is a feeling I would just have to get used to.

This was my first day out 'on the street' (see Chapter 1) as a street style photographer and blogger. I was looking for stylish 'regular' people to photograph and post on my newborn street style blog, Urban Fieldnotes (www.urbanfieldnotes. com), and though in the abstract I thought I had a pretty good idea of what that meant, out here in the 'real world', it slipped right out of my grasp. What does stylish look like, anyway? I wondered, as I flitted from subject to subject, dismissing each with barely a moment's hesitation. How do I recognize it? How do I sift through the hordes of the dowdy and drab to select the fashionable few? And who was I to judge, in any case, people's stylistic sensibilities? Was I really so stylish myself? Though I had studied fashion as an academic for a number of years and taken occasional pictures of passing pedestrians in other field sites in other parts of the world as part of my work, I was thoroughly outside of my comfort zone. I have no credentials as a fashion critic. I have not earned the right to judge others. I have also never much cared for introducing myself to strangers, and it was becoming abundantly clear that I would have to do so shortly, that is, if I ever found someone who stood out in the crowd enough to warrant my taking their picture. That, it turns out, was by no means certain.

After spending months online reading street style blogs from around the world, taking scrupulous notes, studying their aesthetics, memorizing their look and feel, I had decided it was time to get out there into the city and try it for myself. If they can do it, I can, I thought. That, after all, was the kind of populist rhetoric circulating through the global fashion blogosphere. Bloggers were 'democratizing' fashion – a coterie of journalists, academics, and media critics continually reminded us – using the tools of digital technology to force open a notoriously closed-door industry. 'Anyone' could now go 'out there', take pictures in their respective home cities, and make a name for themselves in the fashion industry as a self-appointed arbiter of style. All you need is a decent digital camera and a little bit of gumption. Or so they say. In practice, shooting street style was proving easier said than done. Now that I was out 'on the street', I had little idea of what I was doing, how I was going to do it, or where I was going to go to make it happen. The city of Philadelphia, once a familiar and comfortable place, had begun to look alien and inhospitable. Its inhabitants blended together into a thick pedestrian soup.

Street style blogs, for the uninitiated reader, are websites, generally hosted by free blogging services like Blogger, WordPress, Tumblr, and TypePad, websites where photographers, in the blog standard of reverse chronological order, post cool pictures of cool people posing in cool locations. That's it. They are not the most intellectually demanding of enterprises nor do they pretend to be. But that doesn't mean they have nothing to offer academics. Street style blogs, I argue in this book, have significant social and cultural value, documenting the look and feel of specific cities at specific moments in time, and expanding the scope of representation of fashion-related imagery, well beyond the traditional boundaries of the global fashion industry. They also have historic value. Collectively, street style blogs make up the largest archive of personal sartorial expression the world has ever seen.

I use the terms 'street style bloggers' and 'street style photographers' almost synonymously in this book, but it should be pointed out that not all street style photographers have blogs, and conversely, not all street style bloggers post their own photographs. Some street style photographers sell their images to magazines. Some keep them for their personal portfolios or files. Others display them in gallery exhibitions or produce books of their images. Conversely, there are street style bloggers, particularly those who use Tumblr as their blogging platform, who 'curate' other peoples' street style photographs rather than generate their own. But I use the term 'street style blogger' in this book to refer specifically to photographers who post their own street style images on their own street style blogs.

It would be difficult to accurately estimate the number of street style blogs there are out there these days, clogging the bandwidth of internet service providers worldwide, providing a new tool of procrastination for students and white-collar workers everywhere. New ones pop up everyday. Others fade away. Others linger in digital limbo, having not been updated for months or years. A conservative estimate would be in the hundreds – my own Excel spreadsheet of current and defunct street style blogs has already topped 300 – but several thousand seems more likely. Street style blogs can be tricky to track down. Most fly under the radar, getting little attention from outside their own hometown and barely registering on Google searches, and not all blogs featuring street style images identify themselves as 'street style blogs'.

What is less controversial, however, is the global popularity of street style blogs. By 2007, they were attracting a huge amount of attention, from both inside and outside the fashion world, drawing in hundreds of thousands of readers per month. Street style blogs had become competitive with major fashion magazines over the course of just a few years, and soon they were attracting those magazines' advertising base. Many street style bloggers were getting big sponsorship deals. Many were having their content featured in print publications. Many were on the invite lists of the biggest fashion showcases in New York, Paris, London, and Milan. Street style blogger, it would seem, had become a potential career path in the fashion world.

Street style bloggers, by 2010, had become a regular presence in the hippest neighbourhoods of Helsinki, Seoul, Buenos Aires, and Beijing (see Chapter 2), and some of the most scrupulous documenters of the events of the major Fashion Weeks in London, Paris, Milan, and New York (see Chapter 6). On occasion, they have even served as some of the fashion industry's most prominent critics – perhaps we might call them 'organic intellectuals' (Gramsci 1971; Williams 1977) – critiquing the industry's representations and entrenched inequalities and putting forward alternative – and more expansive – conceptions of fashion, style, and beauty than those that appear in the pages of magazines and other fashion publications. Street style bloggers have emerged over the past decade as among the most widely viewed content producers of the global fashion industry, even though most of them still see themselves as operating well outside of its bounds.

What makes this accomplishment so impressive – and what adds to the perception of digital democracy that surrounds street style blogs – is that the vast majority of street style bloggers are neither formally trained in photography nor professionally groomed in the fashion industry. Their perceived outsider and amateur status, in fact, is often crucial to their continuing success within the industry, serving as signs of their 'authenticity' and 'realness' within a 'field of cultural production' (Bourdieu 1993) widely perceived to specialize in the fake (see Chapter 1). If mainstream fashion photography is seen as carefully staged, lighted, and retouched, street style photography is understood to be raw, immediate, and spontaneous. If mainstream fashion photographers seek to glamorize the people they depict, street style photographers seek to capture them 'as they really are'. Street style photography serves as a kind of conceptual foil to high fashion imagery, the grit to its glamour, the sidewalk to its catwalk – even, and perhaps especially, when the fashion industry takes inspiration directly from it (Aspelund 2009; Polhemus 1994).

How I became interested in street style blogs

I became aware of street style blogs fairly late in the game, back in the summer of 2010, when they were already well on their way to becoming a fashion world cliché. I had just returned from Jakarta, Indonesia, where I had been working on a long-term ethnographic project on the Southeast Asian country's emerging fashion industry, and as part of that project, I had been taking all sorts of pictures of what 'the kids in Indonesia' (*anak muda Indonesia*) are wearing these days. I had a hunch, as plenty of scholars of fashion have had before me, that personal style plays an important role in a nation's economic development (Gilbert 2006; Jones 2007; Zhao 2013), and a number of shots of assorted Indonesian hipsters in tight T-shirts and skinny jeans that seemed to support the case.

But there I was, now back in the United States, and the research had come to a grinding halt. I needed some way to continue the work from the auspices of my office at Drexel University in Philadelphia, half a world away from my field site. So I did what any minimally technologically savvy social scientist would do in my position in this day and age: I turned to the internet. More specifically, I turned to Facebook and Twitter, where many of my research subjects posted habitually – perhaps even obsessively. And I turned to another source which I noticed many of my subjects mentioning on Facebook and Twitter: fashion blogs, those personal style websites like Diana Rikasari's Hot Chocolate & Mint (dianarikasari.blogspot.com) and Evita Nuh's La Crème de la Crop (jellyjellybeans.blogspot.com), where the authors post images of themselves in various outfits, while posing like amateur models on bridges, in bedrooms, and on rooftops. There were hundreds of fashion blogs in Indonesia alone by 2010, peddling their cosmopolitan daydreams of a borderless fashion world. These blogs attracted tens of thousands of readers daily. I too got quickly hooked. I began to follow about twelve of them.

One day, I was going through my daily regimen of Indonesian personal style blogs – The Versicle, Glisters and Blisters, Afternoon Tea and Living Room, you know, the basics – and one of them had posted a photo of themselves taken by a certain Yvan Rodic, also known as Face Hunter. 'I can't believe I got to meet Face Hunter', she posted, or at least something to that effect – I have since lost sight of the original post and am paraphrasing here – 'and he even took my picture.' Well, I didn't know who Face Hunter was back then, but I was intrigued, or at least, I was intrigued enough to take some minimal form of action – often the only form of action the internet requires of us. So I followed the link that the blogger provided and found myself on Face Hunter's website (www.facehunter.blogspot. com then, now Facehunter.org). It was a stripped down, minimalist affair by website standards, composed of full-length, full-colour images of various stylish individuals posing in alleys and doorways.

Rodic, it turns out, is a Swiss-born, London-based, former advertising copywriter turned photographer. He travels around the world with a point-and-shoot digital camera taking photos in up-and-coming fashion cities, including Jakarta but also Helsinki, Dubai, Rio de Janeiro, Mexico City, and dozens of other places besides. He had already published one book by this time, called, appropriately, *Face Hunter*, and was now working on his second, *A Year in the Life of Face Hunter*. By the time I had gotten around to shooting pictures of the sartorial idiosyncrasies

FIGURE I.2 Yvan Rodic outside the Public School show at Mercedes-Benz New York Fashion Week Fall/Winter 2014. Photo by author.

of Indonesian youth, Rodic had already been through Indonesia doing the same thing – twice. He has been there several more times since.

After a few weeks of frequenting Rodic's blog, a couple of things became clear to me. First, his mission in photographing Indonesians – or Fins, or Jordanians, or New Yorkers, or whoever – was remarkably similar to my own. We were both documenting – albeit selectively – what it looks like for a city, or a nation, to re-imagine itself as a fashion capital. We were both visually chronicling the formation of stylized identities, the rising of new class groups, the falling of the old, and we were both singling out those distinctive individuals in these places that we saw as capable of speaking to larger cultural processes at work. Second, Rodic was doing a much better job of this than I was, capturing a greater variety of Indonesians and presenting them comparatively on a blog that covers numerous other countries as well. I was intrigued. And I was envious.

I started to dig deeper, and through Rodic's site I became aware of dozens of other – largely amateur – photographers doing more or less the same thing, photographing the stylistic idiosyncrasies of various cities well off the fashion map, then posting them online for other people to observe. Some of these websites were devoted to particular cities. There was, for instance, Yael Sloma's The Streets Walker in Tel Aviv, Israel, Dana Landon's It's My Darlin' in Seattle, Washington, and Liisa Jokinen's immensely popular Hel Looks in Helsinki, Finland. Others, like Rodic's website, were more itinerant. Their creators hopped from city to city, and often fashion week to fashion week, to report ground-level trends as they happen.

Some of the best known of these are Tommy Ton's Jak & Jil, Adam Katz Sinding's Le 21ème, H.B. Nam's STREETFSN, and the undisputed most popular street style website of all time, Scott Schuman's The Sartorialist.

Now Rodic, for his part, likes to play down the social theoretical significance of his work. 'I'm not a scientist or a journalist', he writes in his 2010 book with Prestel (Rodic 2010: 41). 'My pictures are not meant to document reality; they are meant to tell you short stories' (Rodic 2010: 41). And yet Rodic is fully aware of the larger cultural significance of those stories. 'Globalization is a myth', he writes in the preface to the book. 'The belief that international brands and pop culture are making the world a standardized society populated by clones is an old-skool science-fiction version of the future, not the reality of the twenty-first Century' (Rodic 2010: 7). He then proceeds to provide numerous examples of the highly individualized 'New Creole Culture' as he terms it that animates global style today. Rodic, I could see, along with the many other bloggers taking on the same task, was something of a popular visual anthropologist, representing through images those irreducible complexities that make up sartorial expression today.

Digital cameras in hand, street style photographers like Rodic are documenting the stylistic sensibilities of real people in real time in cities around the globe. And they are documenting them *over* time, tracing the circuits through which style travels, navigating the aesthetic boundaries between places and periods, challenging the hegemony of one fashion city over another (see Chapter 2). Blogs attest to the continued presence of place, culture, class, and ethnicity within and on the bodies of thousands of individuals worldwide, showing, as only photographs can, the embodiment of lived social difference. And yet they do not reduce the people they depict to these categories. They present them as individuals, fashion singularities (see Chapter 4), whose idiosyncratic sensibilities can only say so much about what is going on in fashion – or culture – more generally. Like anthropologists, that is, street style bloggers document the specific rather than the general, the situated and the contextualized, the fundamentally 'irreducible' (Bogost 2012; Latour 2005).

In the common narrative, circulated through blogs and articles online, street style bloggers are simply lovers of fashion and photography inspired by other bloggers to pick up their cameras and document. The reality, of course, as this book will demonstrate, is far more complex. The reasons for doing street style blogging are nearly as varied as the people who do it, and the position bloggers occupy in regards to the fashion industry are messy and contradictory at best. Nonetheless, bloggers remain in the popular imagination eminently relatable people 'just like you and me', who have been granted inside access to those closed-door events the rest of us can only fantasize about attending. And when they attend those closed-door events, they occupy the position of insider-outsiders. They are participant-observers of the fashion industry, citizen scientists of style.

And there is indeed something 'scientistic' about what street style bloggers do, if not strictly 'scientific' per se. Though most street style bloggers describe their blogs as projects of 'personal passion' (Ortner 2013), a way to collect sources of inspiration from out on the streets themselves, they also draw extensively from a longstanding photographic tradition that can be traced back through alternative fashion magazines like *i-D* and *The Face* all the way to the early anthropological field expedition photographs of the late nineteenth century (see Chapter 1). They cite August Sander and Henri Cartier-Bresson as influences, employ many of the conventions of social documentary photography, and see themselves as the newest wave of street photographers, capturing, with full-frame DSLRs, the aesthetic peculiarities of the present moment.

As a visual anthropologist myself, I felt an immediate kinship with street style bloggers that only grew stronger the more I delved into their work. I knew there was a research project to do about them, but I still had to figure out how to do it.

A method emerges

My first impulse, after years of work in Indonesia, was to study *Indonesian* street style blogs, but there were only a couple of those at the time, Jakarta Street Looks, which stopped producing new content in 2009, and Jakarta Style Journal, which was updated infrequently at best. Street style was not a significant phenomenon there yet, for reasons I have articulated elsewhere (Luvaas 2013) and despite the massive popularity of fashion blogs more generally. Moreover, studying street style in Indonesia would be an arbitrary decision to make, drawing imaginary boundaries around a far more expansive network that extends across the developing and developed world alike. The very thing that makes street style interesting – at least to me – is its global range. It must, I decided, be studied globally.

The only trouble is that I am an anthropologist, and we anthropologists can be rather stubbornly place-ist in our research methodologies. Since Bronislaw Malinowski first set sail for the Trobriand Islands at the outbreak of the First World War, we have been a discipline committed, above all, to 'going places' and 'being there', to encountering people firsthand, rather than depending on secondary accounts and surveys. If I were going to do this project the way an anthropologist would, I would have to find some way of 'being there' appropriate for street style blogs.

But how could I possibly do that? How could I be surrounded by or engulfed within street style blogs? How could I apply the principle of participant-observation, so central to my discipline, to the study of street style? I tend to think of ethnography, the main fieldwork method of cultural (and visual) anthropologists, as the practice of burying oneself beneath a mountain of cultural material one then has to slowly, deliberately dig one's way out of. It should be immersive, overwhelming, saturating one's senses with the material realities of the place and people one is studying. For all of the theorizing in anthropology in recent years about doing ethnography online (Boellstorff et al. 2012; Hine 2000), I knew that online research alone would leave me wanting more, minimizing that firsthand, 'on-the-ground' perspective that I had always depended on in past projects. And how would I study a 'community' anyway that exists largely in concept, that is, as a collective defined by common practice, rather than a group that actually interacts somewhere, either online or in person? How could I engage in a long-term, embedded way with street style bloggers? I could only think of one possible answer. I would have to start a street style blog myself.

Only with my own street style blog would I be able to understand the practical, material realities of street style blogging. Having a blog would teach me, in no uncertain terms, what it takes to produce a blog and build an audience. And it would teach me about the relationship between bloggers and the fashion industry, how tightly knit they are, how mutually implicated, whether the industry held its doors as wide open to bloggers as common rhetoric would imply. I would find out for myself who it is that contacts bloggers, floods their email with spam, invites them – or doesn't invite them – to events. I would find out for myself how deals between bloggers and their various sponsors and partners were forged. Having a blog would teach me the 'howness' and 'whatness' of blogging, the everyday practical constraints, the ethical concerns, the cultural norms in formation. And of course it would teach me what it takes to produce the kinds of images bloggers produce, both in terms of equipment and embodied practical knowledge. Could anyone really become a successful street style blogger, I wondered? And could I? That was the kind of democratic discourse circulating through the blogosphere, the kind of hackneyed sentiment that dominated most reporting on the subject. I wanted to find out if there was any substance to it.

In addition, I saw the blog as a way to interact on a regular basis with other street style photographers and bloggers. I would post my photographs and preliminary thoughts as they happened, invite comments and corrections from other bloggers, link to their blogs, and feature regular interviews with a variety of practitioners of street style photography. I envisioned my blog as a go-to resource for the ethnographic study of street style, an open-access model of visual fieldnotes.

As I put the finishing touches on this introduction, it has been over three years since I started the blog. I have taken tens of thousands of pictures in that time, and I have posted hundreds of them for my readers to view. I have also interviewed and posted my interviews of twenty other street style bloggers, and met and interacted with dozens of others, both online and off. I now count a number of street style

URBAN FIELDNOTES

Street Style Anthropology

Monday, May 26, 2014

Philadelphia Street Style: Shabré, Market St

Follow Urban Fieldnotes

About Urban Fieldnotes

Urban Fieldnotes is a street style blog documenting fashion, style, and dress on the streets of Philadelphia and beyond. It is also a blog about street style blogging, an experiment in auto-ethnographic research and open-source fieldwork that is part of an ongoing project by Brent Luvaas entitled "Street Style 2.0: New Media and the New Politics of Fashion." This blog represents the views, perspectives, and preliminary findings of Brent Luvaas, a professional anthropologist. This blog does not necessarily reflect the opinions and positions of Drexel University, his employer. Your comments and suggestions are welcome, but please note that any comments posted to this blog may be used in future presentations and publications, both print and digital, by Brent Luvaas.

About Me

Brent Luvaas, Ph.D, is Assistant Professor of Anthropology at Drexel University, Co-Editor of the journal 'Visual Anthropology Review,' and author of the book 'DIY Style: Fashion, Music, and Global Digital Cultures.'

FIGURE I.3 Screen Shot of the Urban Fieldnotes Blog (www.urbanfieldnotes.com).

bloggers as close personal friends. In addition, I have been contacted by several hundred companies looking to feature their products on my blog. My blog, in turn, has been featured in *Nylon Magazine*, *The Philadelphia Daily News*, *Drexel Magazine*, *StreetStyleNews*, *The Guardian*, *Mojeh Magazine*, *Harper's Bazaar Brasil*, and several well-known fashion blogs. I have received gifted products, had a stint advertising for American Apparel, 'partnered' with brands including a New York department store, UNIQLO, and Goorin Bros Hats (see Chapter 5), worked freelance for *Racked*, *Refinery29*, and *Kenton Magazine* and watched as my blog's images circulated far and wide through Instagram, Tumblr, and other social media platforms. Blogging has gradually become ordinary for me, part of my routine, part of what I do. It has become a critical part of my practice, both as a researcher of street style blogs and as an anthropologist more generally. I have, that is, become precisely that thing I set out to study. And in doing so, I have taken on a methodology that is sometimes referred to as 'auto-ethnography'.

Auto-ethnography: Using the self as the vehicle of research

Like nearly every concept in anthropology, 'auto-ethnography' is a contested term, with multiple, intertwined histories. When Karl Heider (1975) used it back in 1975 to describe the sixty interviews he conducted with Dani schoolchildren, he was playing with two meanings of 'auto': first for 'autochthonous' in that these were accounts that the Dani generated for themselves, and second for 'automatic' in that the accounts they generated were straightforward and routine, lacking the 'discursive penetration' (Willis 1977) and distanced insight of critical anthropological inquiry (cited in Reed-Danahay 1997: 4). Hayano (1979), Strathern (1987), Dorst (1989), and Pratt (1992) would later use the term to mean something more akin to 'native ethnography', that is, anthropological research carried out 'at home' or among 'one's own people'. For a decade or two, this was the primary meaning of the term. It is only in the aftermath of the postmodern critique of anthropology in the mid-1980s, articulated most famously by Clifford and Marcus in *Writing Culture* (1986), that self-reflexivity replaced earlier aims at outsider objectivity, and auto-ethnographic practice came to mean something more akin to investigating one's 'self' as an embedded actor within a larger social system. Carolyn Ellis has been, perhaps, the most forceful advocate for this brand of auto-ethnography. She defines the method as 'systematic sociological introspection' and 'emotional recall' in the service of understanding 'an experience I've lived through' (Ellis 2004: xvii). Her auto-ethnographic work takes the form of self-reflexive narrative, quasi-literary accounts and stories that connect 'the autobiographical and personal to the cultural, social, and political' (Ellis 2004: xix).

In auto-ethnography self-reflexivity is a mechanism for creating a more honest, situated, and grounded form of social scientific research. Indeed, after the postmodern critique it became a commonplace of ethnographic work to acknowledge how one's own background and experience have shaped the account produced. It can be argued that at least since the late 1980s nearly all ethnography has been auto-ethnographic, as it employs the 'self' as the vehicle of research (Ortner 2006).

But those who have explicitly used the term 'auto-ethnography' have something else in mind. Anthropologists like Ellis use it to describe an additional methodological step of focusing their project in some way on their own direct experience as lived, embodied, and interpreted through 'the self', even while acknowledging that the terms and limits of what constitutes the self are by no means clear or fixed (Reed-Danahay 1997: 03). Auto-ethnography differs from ethnography not in kind, but in the degree of self-reflexivity and focus on oneself: paying particular attention to one's thoughts, feelings, and physical sensations as a form of ethnographic 'data'. Auto-ethnography does not just use the self to do research; it is explicitly about 'the self' as the medium through which research transpires.

In using the term *auto-ethnography* in this book, I am situating my own work within this latter meaning of the term, describing a mode of research in which, not only am I the one carrying it out, but my research takes explicit account of my thoughts, feelings, and experiences as a meaningful form of knowledge in its own right. My understanding of auto-ethnography, however, also makes use of earlier understandings of the term. It relies, for instance, on Heider's notion of the automatic. My process of carrying out fieldwork has gone through moments of conscious self-interrogation and other moments of unconscious acting from the position of, simply doing what a street style blogger does without thinking through what this is or means. In fact, as I argue in Chapter 3, gaining firsthand insight into the experience of bloggers has required this sort of unconscious acting. To become a blogger is to internalize and normalize the practice of blogging to such an extent that it is no longer available to conscious thought. It must become part of one's *habitus* (Bourdieu 1980), one's automatic and embodied mode of practice. Anything short of unconscious embodiment would hardly warrant the title of 'auto-ethnography' to begin with. Nonetheless, a good auto-ethnographer must learn to distance herself from this automatic knowing once it is established, to fluctuate, that is, between embodied modes of practice and critical self-reflexivity.

My work on street style bloggers is also, in a sense, 'native ethnography'. Street style bloggers, like anthropologists, are disproportionately middle or upper-middle class in background, highly educated, and urban in residence. They have a penchant for self-reflection and an interest in sartorial expression in its myriad forms, often prefer the oddball to the mainstream, the off-kilter to the on-trend. Street style bloggers tend to stand in a critical outsider position in relation to the workings of the larger fashion world, and they move through the cities they inhabit like the classic flâneurs of Baudelairean mystique, both a part of and apart from the streets they walk down (see Chapter 1). They constitute, once again, a variety of amateur visual anthropologist. For me to study them is not unlike studying my own people.

So, who are street style bloggers anyway?

There exists in the popular imagination – and, for that matter, in the scholarly imagination – a conception of the fashion blogger as a digital-age shut-in, an isolated teenager locked in her bedroom with a DSLR, an iPad, a full-length mirror, and a pair of shiny red pumps. She – and the use of the pronoun *she* is no accident here; discussions about fashion bloggers in the press and in academic works have been remarkably gendered (Marwick 2013; Pham 2011) – is self-involved and superficial, content to prattle on endlessly about her new thrifted handbag and H&M jumpsuit, the incredible deal she found at the local flea market last Saturday, and the delicious breakfast of spinach frittata and rosemary potatoes she ordered at Sabrina's this morning. She is a living archetype of the Millennial Generation, ambitious, outgoing, and eager to please, with a flair for the dramatic, a taste for the expensive, and a complete lack of interest in anything political, polemical, or otherwise intellectually engaging. But that doesn't mean she has nothing to say. For her, blogging is a kind of compulsion, a 'drive' (Dean 2010) towards producing constant discourse that is apparently outside of her conscious control.

She is tuned in but disengaged, connected but alone (Bauman 2003; Turkle 2011), and seemingly content to live her entire life online where nothing has weight or consequence. She is, in other words, an inflatable doll of a public figure, a 'micro-celebrity' (Marwick 2013) with a seemingly bottomless disposable income and an endless capacity to talk about herself. If you believe critic Andrew Keen (2008), or any number of other nail-biting editorialists, she, and others bloggers like her, is perhaps the single greatest threat ever posed to literature, the arts, or serious investigative journalism. If you believe the fashion magazine editors, in their scathing op-eds in *New York Magazine* or on the *Business of Fashion* website, she is either a thoughtless usurper, taking the places on the front row of runway shows that used to be reserved for people who had 'actually earned' them, or a near messianic figure, ushering in a utopian age of fashion democracy. Either way, she signifies the end times for high culture as we know it. She is rising up out the suburban depths to topple the last remains of a cultural elite and turn the hard-made material industries of previous generations into nothing but digital fluff. She is also, of course, a myth.

According to Technorati's 2011 survey of 4,114 bloggers in forty-five countries, teenagers make up only a small proportion of bloggers worldwide, and that proportion, says Pew Internet Project report, is shrinking all the time, as teenagers migrate from personal blogs to 'micro-blogging platforms' like Twitter and Instagram. The majority of bloggers today are between the ages of 25 and 44, with over a third of them over the age of 44. Some three-fifths of bloggers, furthermore, are male, the overwhelming majority of which (around 75%) have completed at least some college education. Nearly half have post-graduate degrees. This is particularly true of respondents who blog primarily as a 'hobby'. Blogging, it would seem, is an educated adult's pursuit.

But characterizing the goals and ambitions of bloggers with any more precision than that is a dangerous game. Technorati identifies 60 per cent of bloggers as 'hobbyists', another 18 per cent as 'professionals' who use their blog to provide, or supplement, their income, 8 per cent as 'corporate', who blog on behalf of a commercial company or corporation, and 13 per cent as 'entrepreneurs' who blog for a business, company, or enterprise they own themselves. Most (69%) claim to blog primarily for their own personal satisfaction, while a small but significant, minority (13%) claim to blog primarily for profit. These two goals are not mutually exclusive, as I will discuss in detail in Chapter 5. Nor are they easy to tease apart. Even the most hobbyist of street style bloggers is 'professional-like' – if not professional per se. She runs her 'hobby' as if it were a business.

Among all bloggers, the most common topical tags remain 'news', 'business', and 'politics', followed by 'entertainment', 'video', 'sports', and 'music'. 'Fashion' ranks at a humble number eleven on the list of the top thirty most popular blogger tags. The numbers hardly indict bloggers as shallow, self-obsessed fame-seekers. Bloggers are too multifarious a lot for that kind of cheap summation.

As for that relatively small group of bloggers who post about fashion, they too are a varied group, with a variety of motivations and ambitions among them. Some, like Man Repeller's Leandra Medine, came to blogging after a career in fashion journalism, finding the relative freedom of blogging more to their liking. Others, like Tommy Ton of Jak & Jil, launched a career in fashion journalism *through* blogging. Some fashion bloggers came to the practice relatively late in life, like '+40' personal style blogger Bella Q of The Citizen Rosebud. Others, like Tavi Gevinson of Style Rookie, began blogging before finishing elementary school.

Fashion bloggers are also ethnically and culturally diverse. While the majority of fashion bloggers worldwide still reside in North America, Europe, and Australia and are of European ancestry, fashion bloggers are popping up in countries all over the world, from Indonesia (e.g. Diana Rikasari of Hot Chocolate & Mint) to Kenya (e.g. Nancie Mwai of Fashion Notebook). There can be little doubt that the fashion blogosphere is still largely centred around the 'fashion world cities' (Gilbert 2006) of London, New York, Paris, Milan, and Tokyo, with a far greater percentage of bloggers residing in these cities than everywhere else, and yet bloggers are pushing at these boundaries as well, expanding the scope of the industry by redefining its borders and representing style well off its established map (see Chapter 2). And even within the world capitals of fashion, bloggers are a diverse lot. Several of the world's top personal style bloggers, including Aimee Song (Song of Style), Rumi Neely (Fashion Toast), and Nichole Warne (Gary Pepper Vintage) are of Asian descent. In Philadelphia, where I had the most sustained contact with fashion bloggers of all stripes, well over 50 per cent are African American.

But this is not to say that the fashion blogosphere is diverse in every conceivable way. As with bloggers more generally, fashion bloggers tend to be well-educated and middle class. They often work in technology or creative industries and their work as bloggers, whether professional or avocational, requires access to personal computers, an internet connection, and expensive camera equipment out of reach to large portions of the population. By any measure, they are a relatively well-off group. Furthermore, while the blogosphere as a whole skews male, the fashion blogosphere is predominantly female, with a few gay men (Marwick 2013) – and recently, ruggedly straight menswear bloggers with bushy lumberjack beards – thrown into the mix.

Street style bloggers, however, as a smaller subset of the larger fashion blogosphere, are something of an anomaly. Among street style bloggers, the gender divide appears to be closer to 50/50. Of the eighty blogs listed on StreetStyleNews (streetstylenews.com) in mid-2014 of which I was able to determine the gender of the blogger behind them, thirty-nine were male and forty-one were female. Furthermore, most of the male bloggers participating in this study identify as 'straight'. Perhaps this is not surprising. Taking pictures of other people bares all of the familiar tropes of the masculine stereotype: the hunt, the capture (Barthes 1981; Sontag 1973), tracking down subjects, and 'shooting' them. There is nothing 'effeminate' or unbecoming of a heteronormative cis-gender male about street style blogging. The popular conception of blogs as a feminized, youth-dominated space for self-obsessed shut-ins is simply unfounded.

The stuff of street style

The people engaged in street style blogging, then, are a varied lot, but they do have one thing in common: they are part of a still privileged minority, composed of just 39 per cent of the world's population (internetworldstatics.com), the portion of the population, that is, with regular access to the internet. Access to the internet, it almost goes without saying, is critical to the practice of blogging. Just a few years back, access to a personal computer would have been an indispensable requirement for street style blogging as well. This, however, is changing, as much of the world's population, 34 per cent according to the Pew Internet Project, now access the internet primarily through mobile phones and devices. It is no longer necessary to have a personal computer to upload content onto blogs. All of the major blogging platforms, including WordPress, Blogger, Typepad, and Tumblr, have apps available for both iOS and Android mobile operating systems. WordPress, at least, has one for Blackberry as well. Theoretically, this means that a much broader range of the world's population can take part in reading and creating street style blogs than just a few years back, since smart phones have penetrated many areas in the Global South where landlines have not yet been laid. In practice, however, the ascendance of the mobile internet has not 'democratized' the street style blogosphere nearly as much as one might hope. There are a couple of reasons for this. First, the bigger-name bloggers from the western world had a significant head start over everyone else. They established names for themselves at a time when the street style blogosphere was still a relatively open field. Now that the top-name bloggers have secured contracts with major magazines and websites, now that they have saturated the street style blogosphere with their images and amassed a readership in the millions, they have effectively locked out – or at least slowed the momentum of – new competition. New street style bloggers face a steep uphill climb. Although they occasionally rise up out of nowhere, grabbing attention, and inserting themselves into the street style mix, they have to contend with far steeper competition than the early bloggers did. Despite a prominent rhetoric of digital democratization, the street style blogosphere, like every other realm of the internet, has crystalized into a hierarchy.

Second, although it is not mandatory to have a personal computer to create and manage a street style blog, it is enormously helpful, lending one a significant advantage over others who do not. In fact, I know of no street style blogger active today who doesn't depend on one to do their blogging. The personal computer versions of the major blogging platforms continue to have far more expansive capabilities than the mobile app versions, enabling a good deal more personalization and customization and providing readership statistics and analytics unavailable to strictly mobile users. While for many, such analytics feed curiosity more than serve any practical function, for others analytics provide a useful tool for determining which kinds of blog content get traction from readers. Analytics can also be a useful marketing tool when approaching potential sponsors and advertisers. These parties want to see 'big numbers', pageviews in the tens of thousands at least, thousands of social media 'likes' and followers, and other kinds of 'proof' that their content will reach the 'right' kinds of target demographics. As media researcher Van Dijck has argued, online media users are not created equal. They operate in a media 'ecosystem' fraught through and through with the winner-take-all logic of advanced industrial capitalism (Van Dijck 2013). In addition, personal computers enable street style bloggers to use much more sophisticated photo management and editing software than that which is currently available on mobile devices, making their use a necessity for anyone invested in 'professionalizing' their blogs. In the street style blogosphere of today, this would account for just about everyone.

Which brings us to another thing street style bloggers have in common: cameras, the digital kind, and very often of professional, or at least semi-professional grade. In the early days of street style blogging, most bloggers used digital point-and-shoots to do their work. Scott Schuman of The Sartorialist began with a Canon G5. Yvan Rodic of Face Hunter chose a Canon G9. These were not professional photographers. Their owners wanted something easy and compact, a camera that did most of the thinking for them. Not anymore. Street style blogging has suffered from significant camera inflation. Most well-known bloggers today, including Schuman and Rodic, use high-end, full-frame digital single lens reflex – or DSLR-like – cameras capable of producing professional quality images. As of the publication of this book, Phil Oh of Street Peeper was using a Canon EOS 5D, Mark II, as was Garance Doré of her eponymous blog, Reuben Harley of Street Gazing, Driely S. of Pelado Pelado and *Racked*, and Scott Schuman of The Sartorialist. Vanessa Jackman of her eponymous blog used the Nikon D700, the same camera I would eventually use myself for Urban Fieldnotes. Adam Katz Sinding of Le 21ème used a Nikon D4, as did Tyler Joe of Not Your Average Joe. Youngjun Koo of I'm Koo used Sinding's old Nikon D3. The minimum price tag for any of these cameras in 2014 was $2,500. Some, like the Nikon D4, cost over $6,000. When paired with a high quality 85 mm, 50 mm, or 70–200 mm lens – the preferred lenses of street style photographers working today – that price tag moves up to a minimum of $3,000. Street style blogging is an expensive pastime to partake in. It should come as no surprise, then, that so many bloggers are eager to monetize it.

The point of this discussion of the 'stuff' of street style blogging is to suggest that claims of blogging's ability to democratize fashion are overblown. Income still matters online. So do space and place, if only in that they organize our access to online spaces. Not everyone has access to every part of the web in the same way, and no one possesses the linguistic capability or cultural know-how to comprehend or navigate every part of the web they do have access to. It is for this reason that digital theorist Jodi Dean prefers the term 'blogipelago' (Dean 2010) to the more commonly used 'blogosphere'. As Dean writes: 'The term 'sphere' suggests a space accessible to any and all' (Dean 2010: 38). It suggests a unity of interaction, a homogenous social field, and it 'tricks us into thinking community when we should be asking about the kinds of links, networks, flows, and solidarities that blogs hinder and encourage' (Dean 2010: 38). 'Blogipelago', on the other hand, 'like archipelago, reminds us of separateness, disconnection, and the immense effort it can take to move from one island or network to another. It incites us to attend to the variety of uses, engagements, performances, and intensities blogging contributes and circulates' (Dean 2010: 38). I sympathize with Dean's choice of terms and find her description of the diverse range of networks that make up the social worlds of blogging theoretically useful and experientially accurate, but I continue to use the term 'blogosphere' in this book for one simple reason: nobody outside academia, or even outside of Jodi Dean's academic fan base, uses the term 'blogipelago'. I use 'blogosphere' because it is a term in common use among bloggers themselves, and it is bloggers, I would contend, who should ultimately get to decide the meaning, and terminology, of blogging.

Written on the street

This book is an ethnographic study of street style bloggers, based on several years of research, both online and off, as well as my own direct experience shooting and posting street style images for my blog, Urban Fieldnotes (www.urbanfieldnotes.com). It chronicles the curatorial practices of street style bloggers and their common project with visual anthropologists and scholars of fashion. It also documents the increasing incorporation of street style bloggers into the global fashion industry, as well as the insider/outsider, professional/amateur, participant/observer position that they occupy in relationship to that industry. It features the photographic work of many of the most prominent street style bloggers of the last decade – Liisa Jokinen (Hel Looks), Adam Katz Sinding (Le 21-ème), and Günnar Hämmerle (StyleClicker), among them – but it also features many of my own photographs, produced in imitation of and in conversation with the work of these other bloggers. The images – both mine and other bloggers' – are meant to illustrate the themes and ideas presented in this book. They are also meant to complicate them. Images can communicate moods, details, and evidential information that words simply cannot. And unlike written accounts, images are not limited to neat or tidy summations. They produce a superfluity of meaning (MacDougall 1998; Taylor 1996), challenging our pedestrian academic efforts to convert the world into text. The images in this book, then, present their own form of argument, sometimes buttressing mine, sometimes butting up against them, sometimes simply adding a new layer of complication to an already complicated story.

Similarly, my account of street style blogging presented in this book is meant to add to – rather than replace – the already abundant online accounts on the phenomenon of street style blogging produced by journalists, fans, critics, and bloggers themselves. This book is not meant to serve as an authoritative, social-scientific report on what blogging 'really is' or 'really means'. Nor is it an exposé of blogging, revealing the trade secrets of the blogging elite. It is, rather, an engaged, prolonged, subjective encounter with street style blogging, just as street style blogging is an engaged, prolonged, subjective encounter with specific urban environments.

In a very real sense, this book was written 'on the street' (see Chapter 1), through day-to-day interaction with the city of Philadelphia, my home base, as well as less sustained interaction with New York, Portland, Boston, Jakarta, and other cities I happened to visit – and shoot in – while conducting this research. It was written 'on the street' in the same way that street style blogs are produced 'on the street', through strolling through the city, interacting with its inhabitants, taking in its scenes. It was written on the street in the same way that light is written on the sensor of a digital camera or that objects impress themselves upon the minds of their beholders. Its images, ideas, and arguments were forged in the fluid capillaries and central arteries (Sennett 1996) of the modern metropolis. Its photographs, in fact, were produced in direct collaboration with the city, borrowing its light and its alleyways, depending on its moods and conditions, working with its passing pedestrians, who graciously stopped to pose for me. Of course, the book took its final shape on my home and office computers, according to my own personal quirks and idiosyncrasies and my own limited disciplinary position as a cultural and visual anthropologist but not before bearing the influence of dozens of other voices.

In addition to being written on the street, this book was written online, through 'fieldnotes' posted three to seven times a week on my street style blog, Urban Fieldnotes. Most of these fieldnotes were inchoate and unformed at the time they were posted, more seeds of ideas than ideas proper. They then grew into something more developed in conversation with comment threads from other bloggers and blog readers, and through interviews and interactions with bloggers, and, finally, when tested against the practical experience of searching for images back out on the street. *Street Style*, in other words, was written the way street style blogs are written, in a continual dialogic exchange between 'on the street' and 'online'.

Whenever possible, I let the bloggers in this book speak for themselves. They are articulate spokespeople and do not require me to speak for them. I do not presume to know better than they do the social purpose or cultural meaning behind their practice. Most of them, after all, have been doing this a lot longer than I have. They know things – both practical and experiential – I am only beginning to uncover. My goal, from the beginning of this project, was to learn *from* bloggers rather than *about* them (Ingold 2013). As such, I do not translate my findings (Latour 2005) into the academic vernacular of one particular social theoretical framework in this book nor do I cram the complex and conflicting practices of bloggers into one pithy pet argument.

I begin this book with a history of street style photography that starts with the earliest days of the camera and extends into the present moment of street style blogging. I then move into a survey of street style blogs from around the world, exploring the techniques and preoccupations that bloggers, shooting in various urban contexts, share with academic anthropologists. Next, I move on to the insights I have gained from being a street style blogger myself these last several years. Chapters 3 to 6 chronicle my own experiences blogging and relate those experiences to the larger social, cultural, and economic contexts that made them possible. I conclude the book with an assessment of where street style blogs stand today, after a decade of incorporation into the global fashion industry.

If this book reads as too celebratory of street style blogs, I apologize. I have been a street style blogger for over three years now, and I like what I do. I can't help but to want my readers to be infected with some of my own enthusiasm for the practice. If it reads as too critical of what street style blogs have become, unfairly criticizing bloggers for their complicity with global, 'neoliberal' agendas, their digitally enhanced narcissism, or their business-minded pragmatism, I apologize for that too. I have been a street style blogger for over three years now, and I take street style seriously. I am concerned about where street style blogging is headed and hope to have some influence over the course it steers. If however, this book seems to stumble over itself, both critiquing and celebrating at the same time, producing a messy, contradictory portrait of street style blogging, well I don't apologize for that. Street style blogging is a messy, contradictory business. Any honest accounting of it would have to be messy and contradictory too. And, besides, messy and contradictory are what we anthropologists do best. We complicate, complexify, reveal implications, imbrications, and mutual entanglements. A *street style anthropology*, like the one attempted in this book, is an anthropology content to work on and within such 'messiness' (Law 2004). It is one that views from the ground level, where the action is taking place, where the blur of motion obscures too clear of a picture from forming.

1 ON 'THE STREET': A CONCEPTUAL HISTORY OF STREET STYLE PHOTOGRAPHY

What is 'the street' in 'street style photography'?

'On the Street' is the title of photographer Bill Cunningham's long-running weekly column (and now web video series) in the Sunday style section of the *New York Times*. It was also the title of Amy Arbus' photo column in the *Village Voice* throughout the 1980s and 1990s. Midway through the first decade of the new millennium, Scott Schuman began using it as a heading for his posts on The Sartorialist website, followed by a '...', the name of the street in question and his featured image of a particular fashionable individual. 'On the street', in fact, has become a common shorthand for galleries of street style images across a variety of media, from newspapers, to magazines, to websites, narrowly edging out such other notable titles as 'Seen on the Street', 'Street Scenes', and 'Street Smart'. It is a fairly logical title for a street style feature. Street style photography in its most straightforward definition is simply fashion photography taken 'on the street'. Whereas editorials are shot in the studio, under conditions carefully controlled by a photographer, and runway shots are taken in the darkened, stage-lit dreamscapes of fashion shows, street style photographs are produced outside, among the uncontrollable, naturally lit elements of 'the real world'. Street style photographers don't want you to forget that. This is their stock in trade. Natural light. Real people. Real locations. Shot on 'the street'.

'The street', for well over a hundred years in the western world who first covered it with concrete, has been a potent metaphor for that which exists in everyday reality (Polhemus 1994). 'The man on the street' is a frequent guest on local television news, a stand-in for all the other regular folks not currently present. 'The word on the street' is the stuff people are talking about, away from the glare of television studio lights, outside the hype of the political machine. And the clothes worn 'on the street' are those that have somehow slipped out the carefully guarded gates of the fashion in-crowd to become an in-demand item among the urban populace.

But what exactly gets to count as 'the street'? And whose everyday reality does 'the street' represent? Are grand Parisian boulevards 'the street?' Are shopping malls in Dubai? Are Main Street, United States (where most Americans live) and 5th Avenue, New York (where Cunningham tends to shoot) equal in claiming rights to the title? Is 15th Street in Chelsea, just down the block from Milk Studios after a runway event during Mercedes-Benz New York Fashion Week 'the street'? I hope so, because I have spotted numerous well-known street style photographers – including Schuman and Cunningham – shooting models, still in runway make-up, in front of open warehouse spaces and garages on that block. These shots later appear on their blogs and in their columns, labelled, of course, as 'on the street'. Clearly, in these cases, the everyday reality that the street is meant to represent is not the everyday reality of most Americans.

In his 2014 op-ed for the popular *Business of Fashion* website, writer Max Berlinger asks the question on the minds of a lot of street style readers: 'Whatever happened to the "street" in street style?' (Berlinger 2014) 'As interest in street style grows', writes Berlinger, 'there's certainly no dearth of images featuring tony editors, buyers, and other fashion insiders captured at the world's major fashion weeks. But there's a pointed lack of inspiration in these pictures. Too often, they reflect a highly merchandised construct that merely reiterates the seasonal themes dictated, top-down, from the industry to consumers, at the expense of true personal style. Sometimes, they are even part of a premeditated marketing plan'. These images, suggests Berlinger, despite their constant presence on 'street style' websites, and despite their featured backdrops of sidewalks and asphalt, are not 'street' enough to be 'street style'. They are decidedly short on grit. They disproportionately focus their lenses on the white, the well-heeled, and the well-groomed. They emphasize the coming season's trends over the idiosyncrasies of individual style. To be 'street', as Berlinger, and many other fans of street style photography see it, photographs need to capture something 'real' that fashion editorial spreads systematically ignore or Photoshop over. They need to be 'raw' (Edwards 2001), 'immediate' (Bolter and Grusin 2000), still humming with the breath and pulse of lived experience. Somehow, stylized shots of Russian socialites escaping into Lincoln town cars after the DKNY show fail to fit the bill.

It is understandable for Berlinger and many other aficionados of street style photography to lament the loss of 'the street' in its most widely viewed imagery. Street style photography is just not what it used to be. Type 'street style' into an internet search engine these days and what comes up are highly professional images of editors, models, and industry insiders sauntering past a stream of blurred out photographers. Hipsters in Cape Town and Helsinki are buried pages in to search results. 'Street style', it seems, has come to mean more or less the exact opposite of what it meant just eight years before, when bloggers like Liisa Jokinen of Hel Looks and Yvan Rodic of Face Hunter were starting out, no longer the 'authentic' styles of 'the street' in cities off the fashion map (see Chapter 2) but an extension of fashion industry representation into picturesque pedestrian zones.

This chapter chronicles the visual, and conceptual, history of street style photography from one meaning to its near inverse. Using a range of street style images beginning with some of the earliest portrait work of photography as my examples, I interrogate the shifting meaning of 'the street' in street style photography and discuss what it tells us about street style's function in the popular imagination and in the fashion press today. 'The street', I demonstrate, is a highly contested and contextual term, a space of symbolic contradiction. It should come as no surprise, then, that photography's history of depicting 'the street' is as fraught as the very concept of it. From a voyage of discovery into unknown lands to an uncovering of all that is 'real' and 'authentic' in an age of artifice to a glamorous slideshow of the couture-wearing elite, street style photography has served multiple masters, and as it has done so, it has altered the conventions through which it depicts 'the street', from a simple, mood-creating backdrop to a kind of conceptual screen, separating a figure from its context. Nonetheless, in all of its guises, 'the street' has remained a central trope of street style photography. It tells the viewer as much about the image in question as what a model is wearing or how she is wearing it. It carries not just a mood, not just a set of signifiers conveying geographic information but much of the weight of an image's meaning. The street, then, is a *subject* of street style photography, perhaps even *the* subject, a fluid, amorphous entity that accumulates meanings as it snowballs into fashion world ubiquity.

The great modernist promise of 'the street'

A wide variety of historians, literary critics, urban planners, and sociologists have argued that we owe the contemporary conception – and, indeed, the actual physical manifestation – of today's metropolitan streets to the Paris of the mid-1800s. Beginning in 1853, under the authority of Napoleon III, Georges-Eugène Haussmann, the Prefect of the Seine Department in France, carried out a massive programme of urban reconstruction that sought to replace the labyrinthine alleyways and crumbling infrastructure of old Paris with 'broad straight thoroughfares' (Benjamin 2002: 11). Haussmann was a child of the Enlightenment, a firm believer in the power of human ingenuity to engineer a more utopian society. He, like other urban planners of his day, based his model of the modern metropolis on the latest innovations in the natural sciences, and in particular, on ideas in medicine. Haussmann conceived of the city as a kind of living body, complete with a circulatory and respiratory system, one that needs to breathe and maintain movement in order to remain healthy. The roads, in Haussmann's vision, were to become like arteries, the parks like lungs. Planners working under Haussmann 'sought to make the city a place where people could move and breathe freely, a city of flowing arteries and veins through which people streamed like healthy blood corpuscles' (Sennett 1996: 256). The streets became conduits of movement, conductors of flow. Their purpose was to facilitate motion. And they did exactly that. Carriages cut across the expanse of the city with an unfettered conviction only possible with a newly unobstructed roadway.

Pedestrians too meandered through the streets like cells through a vein. They engaged with a much broader portion of the city than they ever had before, strolling the avenues, lingering in the parks, window-shopping in the arcades. It was a new way of life, with its own uniform of top hats and overcoats, one befitting

FIGURE 1.1 Rue Laplace and Rue Valette, Paris. Photo by Eugène Atget. Image courtesy the Metropolitan Museum of Art. The Elisha Whittelsey Collection, The Elisha Whittelsey Fund, by exchange, 1970.

a newly industrialized Europe with a plethora of material goods to display and sell. So basic was the experience of moving through the city to contemporary life that it became necessary to establish a name for the expanding breed of wandering Parisian giving in to its consumerist charms. The poet Charles Baudelaire dubbed him 'the flâneur', and he granted him all the inflated, romanticized attributes of a modernist hero.

'Paris created the type of the flâneur', wrote Marxist literary critic Walter Benjamin in his posthumously published masterwork *The Arcades Project*. A flâneur, Benjamin explained, 'is a walker in the city. He is a connoisseur of the street, someone with an appreciation for its drama that he expressed through his flânerie' (Westerbeck and Meyerowitz 1994: 40). Not that he took much time to express that appreciation. The flâneur kept on moving, pulled by the irresistible currents of the street. The flâneur 'takes on the features of the werewolf', wrote Benjamin, 'restlessly roaming a social wilderness' (Benjamin 2002: 420). In Haussmann's Paris, the flâneur took on a significant social role. He became the 'observer of the marketplace' (Benjamin 2002: 427), a 'spy for the capitalists', (Benjamin 2002: 427), a 'detective' (Benjamin 2002: 453) of modern life, doomed by the architecture of the city to ooze through its cobblestone corridors and pay witness to its consumerist spectacles.

Of course, not everyone had the time, luxury, or disposition to be a flâneur. It took a certain bohemian decadence and a certain bourgeois privilege. 'The attitude of the flâneur', wrote Benjamin is 'the epitome of the political attitude of the middle classes during the Second Empire' (Benjamin 2002: 420). Their brand of consumption occurred through observation. Their brand of participation consisted largely of seeing. This was the new experience of being idle and relatively rich. In Haussmann's Paris the streets were a stage on which the drama of everyday life plays out (Sennett 1974), and the flâneur was there to witness it all, as both audience and critic (Benjamin 2002).

Haussmann's Paris, then, set the conditions for the modern experience of the city, one that sociologist Richard Sennett has depicted as individualistic and, above all, optic. 'Individual bodies moving through urban space', writes Sennett, 'gradually became detached from the space in which they moved and from the people the space contained. As space became devalued through motion, individuals gradually lost a sense of sharing a fate with others' (Sennett 1996: 256). Other people were there to be observed rather than engaged, consumed as they moved past like the flickering images on a movie screen. Along with flânerie, then, Haussmann's Paris gave birth to another popular urban pastime: people watching. 'In the course of the development of modern urban individualism, the individual fell silent in the city. The street, the café, the department store, the railroad, bus, and underground became places of the gaze rather than scenes of discourse' (Sennett 1996: 358).

Perhaps, then, it should come as no surprise that the Haussmannization of Paris occurred in short order after the invention of the camera. Both Haussmann and Daguerre, whose early model daguerreotype paved the way to the camera, held the conviction of a modernist revolutionary. Both were out to change the world. Both believed in the power of technology to fundamentally recreate the experience of reality. The camera and the modern city developed, in a sense, in tandem, the one feverishly documenting the rapid growth of the other. The camera was the natural tool of the modern metropolis, a co-conspirator. It testified to the grand project of modernity in a way that the roaming eyes of flâneurs never could. It cemented into place a vision defined by its ephemerality.

The gaze of scientific realism

The earliest photographers shared with Haussmann a distinctly modern optimism about the ability of humankind to apprehend a clear picture of how the world works and use that picture to create a blueprint for the future. Both the camera and the city were tools of the modernist project. Both served the ends of scientists and reformers. 'The photographer', wrote Susan Sontag in her now canonical essay titled, quite succinctly, *On Photography*, 'is a supertourist, an extension of the anthropologist, visiting natives and bringing back news of their exotic doings and strange gear' (Sontag 1973: 42). He has, that is, something of the disposition of the flâneur, only his project is more concrete than the flâneur's, turning that which is witnessed into that which can be owned, analysed, and manipulated. To photograph, claimed Sontag, is 'to appropriate that thing photographed' (Sontag 1973: 2), to turn it into a 'museum object' (Barthes 1981: 12). And when, by extension, one photographs a person, he turns that person too into a museum object, one 'that can be symbolically possessed' (Sontag 1973: 14), put on display, examined and scrutinized. The history of photography is thus the history of symbolic possession.

Anthropology has played no small roll in advancing this history of symbolic possession. Its own history is inextricably intertwined with that of photography, as it is with the larger projects of colonialism and modernity. As Pinney (2011), Edwards (2001), and Grimshaw (2001) have each noted, the invention of the medium of photography took place at the same historical moment as the establishment of the discipline of anthropology, just as photography took place at the same historical moment as the modernization of the city. This is no accident. The two media follow similar logics, maintain similar ends, indeed were created with similar purposes in mind.

Louis Jacques Mandé Daguerre announced the invention of his direct positive photographic process in 1839 declaring that 'everyone, with the aid of the DAGUERROTYPE [*sic*], will make a view of his castle or country-house; people will form collections of all kinds, which will be the more precious because art cannot imitate their accuracy and perfection of detail' (Daguerre 1980: 12). The same year Fox Talbott independently announced his own process of 'photographic drawing', which fixes into being that which the camera obscura merely illuminated. Both early predecessors of the camera were designed to dramatically slow down the distorting effects of time. They made it possible to freeze a moment of light and thereby gain mastery over it. They made it possible to analyse that which hurls past us without abating.

FIGURE 1.2 'White Eagle and Standing Bear', 1891. Photo by CM Bell, taken in studio in Washington DC to capture the look and feel of Native American life on the Great Plains for the United States Geological Survey. Bell also shot regularly for the American Ethnological Society, whose founding mission, in part, was to document the lifeways and traditions of Native American tribes before they disappeared. Used with permission from the University of Pennsylvania Museum of Archaeology and Anthropology.

The Aboriginal Protection Society, meanwhile, was founded in 1837 followed by the American Ethnological Society in 1842 and the Ethnological Society of London in 1843. All three saw themselves as ventures designed to protect the rights and sovereignty of indigenous people subject to colonial rule. But each also saw themselves as agents of what would later be termed 'salvage anthropology', the efforts to preserve and protect varieties of life that the reach of the colonial empire had doomed to disappear. Photography and anthropology sought to preserve forever those human ventures once subject to the ruthless vicissitudes of time. They captured for the sake of personal, and scientific, preservation.

It is no wonder, then, that proponents of both anthropology and photography saw themselves first and foremost as crusaders for 'truth'. They advocated an 'ethics of seeing' (Sontag 1973: 3) that equated such seeing with the knowing of a fundamental reality. Photography, it was argued, could not lie. It recorded the light of a moment of time. It presented a 'raw history' of events, 'empirical, evidential inscriptions' (Edwards 2001).

FIGURE 1.3 'Naga Hills, India', late 1890s. This image was collected and/or taken on the expedition of Harrison and Hiller as part of their ethnological survey of South and Southeast Asia in the 1890s. Used with permission from the University of Pennsylvania Museum of Archaeology and Anthropology.

But, of course, such an account failed to take note of all of the subjective choices behind producing a photographic image. 'Even when photographers are most concerned with mirroring reality', wrote Sontag, 'they are still haunted by tacit imperatives of taste and conscience' (Sontag 1973: 6). They select apertures and shutter speeds that produce distinct visual effects. They frame a subject within an image in such a way that lends itself to certain aesthetic determinations. They choose where to depict a subject and with what materials visible in the background. And, of course, they choose which subjects are worthy of being captured on film in the first place, selectively weeding out whatever subjects, objects, or inconvenient realities do not fit their conception.

For early anthropologists there was one subject worthy of capture above all others, one subject thought uniquely equipped to encapsulate the scientific interests of the discipline – the human body. It was the human body, notes anthropologist Christopher Pinney 'that constituted the proper terrain for study and for many, anthropology was little more than a form of comparative anatomy' (Pinney 2011: 15). Anthropologists studied the physiognomy of people around the world. They compared skull sizes and body proportions, gleaned 'information' about human universals and differences based on morphology. So when early anthropological field expeditions set out, they often set out with one goal above all others: to capture on film the diversity of human bodies for careful anthropological scrutiny. Anthropologists brought cameras with them into the field in the very earliest days of the discipline. Their mission: to document as visual specimens the myriad morphologies that made up the subjects of the empire. And 'specimens' is the right word. Despite a common rhetoric of humanism, anthropology's early photos are fundamentally reductive and objectifying, casting the world's innumerable peoples into the passive role of objects for analysis. Many of these photos remain in museum collections to this day.

Of course, to serve as adequate specimens, photographs had to appear impartial. One could not compare apples to oranges, landscapes to portraits. If anthropological field photos were to take on the weight of evidence, then they must be presented *as* evidence, as uniform as possible in their depiction. Other social scientists must be able to replicate such photos in other settings. They must be instilled with the same sort of specificity that defines laboratory protocols.

There were a number of efforts to create the appropriate criteria for anthropological photography. Pinney discusses one such effort at length, a paper on 'Photography for Anthropologists' by one Maurice Vidal Portman (1861–1935), a British officer stationed in the Andamans in the late nineteenth century. Portman, explains Pinney, was above all concerned with clarity. 'All aesthetics', he wrote, 'are to be avoided' (cited in Pinney 2011: 41). He continues: 'For ethnology, accuracy is what is required. Delicate lighting and picturesque photography are not wanted: all you have to see is that the general lighting is correct, and that no awkward placing of weapons or limbs hide important objects' (Portman, as cited in Pinney 2011: 41). 'A dull grey or drab background', he goes on to say – as if anticipating the rationale of fashion photographer Irving Penn decades later – 'is best' (Portman, as cited in Pinney 2011: 42).

Edwards (2001) recounts another early effort to establish criteria for proper anthropological photography by Thomas Henry Huxley, a Darwinian biologist who initiated 'a project to produce a photographic record of the races of the British Empire' in 1869 (Edwards 2001: 131). Like Portman, Huxley sought to establish a 'visualizing discourse' (Edwards 2001: 132) that 'sought images uncontaminated by interpretation, aesthetic inference, or fantasy' (Datson and Galison, cited in Edwards 2001: 132–133). To do so, he advocated a strict set of guidelines that 'contained instructions for the precise placing of the body in front of the camera for a somatic visual mapping' (Edwards 2001: 133). The goal was in part anthropometry, the 'science' of taking measures of the relative size of the individuals depicted with the hope of determining something meaningful from their proportions. Anthropometry, in turn, became a mechanism of colonial justification, amassing 'evidence' of Europeans' perceived 'racial superiority'. Subjects, thus, were ideally naked and placed before a background grid. They faced the camera, arms at their side, or stood in profile, no expressions on their faces, no distracting visual information preventing a careful scientific analysis. There was no context presented in the images Huxley or his adherents produced and no activities. 'These photographs', writes Edwards, 'are the most overtly and oppressively scientific, dehumanizing, producing a passive object of study' (Edwards 2001: 139).

In practice, few of the photos produced by the fieldworkers under Huxley managed to strictly adhere to his guidelines. They remained more an ideal than a reality. Many indigenous people – unsurprisingly – objected to being photographed naked. Others refused to stand just so. Others still displayed distress, discomfort, and assorted unsanctioned visual expressions of emotion that compromised the 'integrity' of the images. But criteria were established that would have an impact on social documentation for decades to come: good, scientific images present their subjects in as straightforward and unfussy of a manner as possible, arms at their sides, facing directly to the camera or in perfect profile, all external parts of the body visible, and featured in entirety from head to toe. Innumerable early anthropological photos adhere to this formula, though the obsession with nakedness gradually passed out of fashion. Many anthropologists began including clothing as a critical piece of data worthy of being captured in its own right – tangible, material evidence of culture at work. A subject, arms at his side, would stand in the middle of the camera frame, a minimum of space above and below him (Figures 1.3 and 1.4), a blank expression on his face.

Sound familiar? To the reader of street style blogs it should. The same conventions survive on them today. Their subjects stand the same way, display

FIGURE 1.4 'Arab Merchant in Batavia, Java', late 1890s. Photo collected on the ethnological expeditions of Hiller and Harrison through South and Southeast Asia in the 1890s. Used with permission from the University of Pennsylvania Museum of Archaeology and Anthropology.

the same inscrutable gaze. And the message is simple, if misleading: 'here is a person, just how they were, without any tampering from me'. Looking at early anthropological photographs today, the most striking thing about them to me is how much they resemble contemporary street style photographs, both in composition and sensibility. And this is because street style is the natural progeny of anthropological photography. It has inherited its aesthetics, its photographic conventions, and its visual preoccupation with 'the real'.

From rain forests to 'concrete jungles'

Of course, street style photographers do not tend to cite early anthropological fieldwork photos as sources of inspiration. Most are not particularly familiar with the genre, and even if they were, few are likely to find the comparison flattering. These early anthropological photos are steeped in a colonial-era project of classifying and disciplining that reads as problematic today, if not outright racist. But street style photographers do trace their lineage back to photographers who themselves derived a good deal of influence from this early anthropological work. The most famous of these – and the three that street style photographers cite by name most often as influences – are August Sander, Henri Cartier-Bresson, and Irving Penn, three very different figures within photographic history, operating within different genres of photography. I will consider each of these photographers in the coming sections, along with their respective genres of photography, and their influence on street style photography. But first, a bit of context is in order.

The lens of photography was turned to 'the street' almost immediately upon coming into being. It was a natural transition – an extension of the same logic of classification and control that characterized early anthropology. 'Photographers at the beginning of the medium's history', write Westerbeck and Meyerowitz in their comprehensive history of street photography, *Bystander*, 'sought mostly humble people as subjects' (Westerbeck and Meyerowitz 1994: 71). Fox Talbott, one of the inventors of camera technology, himself produced pictures largely of 'various rustics who worked on his estate' (Westerbeck and Meyerowitz 1994: 71). Charles Nègre, who took up the camera in 1850, photographed 'colorful street types' like peddlers and musicians (Westerbeck and Meyerowitz 1994: 71). For many, photography was an artist's pursuit – an extension of the romantic quest to capture something meaningful about everyday life and attest to the colour and variety of urban dwellers. But for others, it served a more pragmatic end, exposing ruptures in the modernist project that still needed to be attended to.

Cultural theorist Dick Hebdige notes that some of the first subjects to capture the attention of the lens were children and adolescents, especially those poor children occupying the slums of France and the UK, whose stubborn penury stood in the way of urban planners' dreams of a smooth modernization. 'During the mid-nineteenth century', writes Hebdige, 'when intrepid social explorers began to venture into the "unknown continents", the "jungles" and the "Africas" – this was the phraseology used at the time – of Manchester and the slums of East London, special attention was drawn to the wretched mental and physical condition of the young "nomads" and "street urchins" '(Hebdige 1988: 20). Social documentarians treated the slums of Europe to the same combination of critical gaze and aesthetic fascination that anthropologists had lent to distant locales. Both the urban poor of Europe and the 'primitives' of the colonies were viewed, at times, as obstacles to modernization and at times as nostalgic leftovers from a previous era. In either case, they needed to be captured on film. This preoccupation with urban youth would continue for decades to come within social documentary photography, becoming more and more pronounced in the post-war period and featuring more and more extreme examples of 'problematic' youth display, peaking in the 1960s with images of mods and rockers, hippies and skinheads, and lending visual credence to the 'moral panic' (Hebdige 1988) of the older generations about 'the kids these days'. Social documentary and photojournalistic photography of young people in London, New York, and other European and US cities both enhanced popular fears of 'youth gone wild' and gave commentators the tools they needed to categorize and classify such youth and hence gain some kind of control over the threat they supposedly represented. Critical to this modernist project of photographic documentation was the careful classification of urban dwellers according to class, variety, and type.

August Sander (1876–1964) was one such social documentary photographer engaged in a modernist project of enhancing social scientific understanding through capturing contemporary urban (and some rural) dwellers on film (or, more accurately, glass plates). After a stint working in a photo studio in Linz, Austria, in the early 1900s, he did most of his work in his native Germany, during a moment of major social upheaval and historical change. Sander wanted to document that change through the faces of the people who were undergoing it. His best-known series, *People of the 20th Century*, began in earnest in 1910 and continued throughout the duration of his life, producing the book *Face of Our Time* – a sort of preview of the larger project, and thousands of negatives, many of which would be published posthumously. *People of the 20th Century* was an ambitious attempt to document the variety of socio-economic classes and professional categories in the Germany of his time through individual – and some group – portraits, shot in work places and at homes and labelled, typically, with only the profession or social status of the subject in question. In *Face of Our Time* the place the image was taken was also often mentioned. In his posthumously published work, however, his images were labelled with the date but typically not the place. In either case, the emphasis was on social category or professional type. 'Production engineer' reads an undated print of a moustachioed man in a three-piece suit, eyes fixed directly on the camera lens. 'Pastrycook', reads another, of a bald, plump man in a chef's coat with a metal bowl in front of him, facing directly forward in a kitchen. 'The teacher, 1910', reads a third of a bearded, bespectacled man, standing at the edge of a street and turned in three quarters profile towards the photographer. The expression on each man's face is stern, his posture firm and immobile. These are formal portraits shot in informal settings, sociological specimens from the streets and back roads of Germany. Sander's photos are a mixture of bust and full body portraits, and although they are shot *in situ*, there is nothing whatsoever spontaneous about them. Like anthropological field portraits, they are endowed with a heady seriousness testifying to the scientific importance of what they depict.

And yet, his photos conceal as much as they reveal about a person, masking their idiosyncrasies behind formalistic conventions. They strip each individual of personality, reducing him to a body and a set of clothes. Each photograph becomes a representative sample of an entire class, group, or profession of people, as if it were capable of summarizing the complex set of characteristics of each.

FIGURE 1.5 'Painter [Anton Räderscheidt]', 1926, by August Sander. © 2015 Die Photographische Sammlung/SK Stiftung Kultur – August Sander Archiv, Cologne/ARS, NY. The subjects in Sander's work are depicted as representative examples of extant social categories rather than as idiosyncratic individuals. The name of the painter in this image, Anton Räderscheidt, was added posthumously.

The names of the subjects didn't matter to Sander's project, and he didn't mention them within his work. They were, after all, interchangeable. Instead, the people in his photos are meant to serve as 'ideal types' (Weber 1978), individual exemplars of universal categories. In this, writes novelist, essayist, and doctor Alfred Döblin in his introduction to *Face of Our Time*, Sander placed himself firmly in the camp of the 'realists', who believed that generalities and universals 'were actually real and existent' (Döblin 1994: 7). They were not just constructs of social theory but something 'out there' to be observed and documented.

The subjects in Sanders' photographs represent a type more than a person. Hence the ritually enacted realism of their conventions: their stern expressions, their formal poses. Sander's work could easily appear in a museum display next to 'Fulani herdsman' or 'Asmat headhunter'. 'Interior decorator, Berlin 1929' the caption beneath one photograph reads, as if that were all there was to know about the man depicted in it. And yet these images too, like anthropological field photos, contain much of the sensibility of the contemporary street style photograph, the emphasis on expressionless faces and firm postures, and the convention of formal portraiture *in situ*. Street style photographers continue to borrow many of Sanders' conventions for depicting 'the real', even if they have jettisoned his notion of reality.

But they also borrow another concept from Sander and other social documentarians of his time: the idea that reality is in fact to be found, out there 'on the street'. The street, in Sander's work, is the background imagery that places his subjects in a social and historical context. It lends legitimacy to his work. It testifies to Sanders' 'being there' and experiencing for himself. It is the stock source of his image's perceived reality.

The street as romantic idea

Eugène Atget (1857–1927), like August Sander, was committed to documenting everyday life on the streets of his city, in this case Paris, France. He was fascinated by the ordinary comings and goings – the ceaseless activities of street life. His work features the street in nearly every frame, sometimes serving as a backdrop to his portraits, sometimes as a landscape full of buildings and stalls and sometimes as a study of abstract shapes and lines. But if Sander's mission was to categorize and classify the myriad denizens of the contemporary city who occupy the street, Atget's was more altruistic – to preserve.

Like a salvage anthropologist, Atget wanted to document the old world of Paris – its architecture and its alleyways, its bustling mercantile exchange, its quaint peasantry and colourful characters – before it disappeared into the chasm opened up by modernization. Atget was a pioneer of a genre that would later

FIGURE 1.6 'Street Paver', 1899–1900. Photo by Eugène Atget. Image courtesy the Metropolitan Museum of Art. David Hunter McAlpin Fund, 1956.

come to be known as 'street photography'. He spent his days as a proper flâneur, wandering the streets, taking in their charms, seeking out the perfect combination of elements for his artfully composed photographs. Though working with a large format camera, like Sander and every previous generation of photographer, Atget sought to capture those aspects of everyday life that zoomed past us too quickly to be noticed. He stopped pedestrians in their tracks, posed 'authentic' street scenes, then hurried to the back of his camera to get the long-exposure shot his camera necessitated. His photos were thus a hybrid of the candid and the staged. Though posed, they were meant to appear natural, 'real' – no stilted portraits for scientific scrutiny and no stubborn preoccupation with uniformity.

Street photographers like Atget had a different conception of 'the real' than social documentarians like Sander. If Sander was a 'realist', believing in the universality of types, then Atget was something of a 'nominalist' (Döblin 1994: 7), subscribing to the absolute specificity of individual people, places, and scenes. Paris was Paris. No other city could stand in its place. No other photographer, anywhere else in the world, could get the images that Atget was getting there at that time. Both Sander and Atget sought to get at that kernel of truth, buried somewhere beneath the surface of our ordinary experience, but they differed in their conception of truth – 'the nature of that underlying something that black-and-white is able to penetrate' (Scott 2007: 59). The documentary photographer seeks to capture 'the human condition'. He seeks 'truth' with a capital 'T'. The street photographer is after something more slippery and elusive, an immediate and experiential truth, captured in the accidental encounter between photographer and subject. His is a poetic truth, a romantic truth, and it is a truth one finds not in sociology textbooks but in direct, subjective interaction with life 'on the street'.

Street photography, then, is in many ways the opposite of social documentary photography. It is spontaneous and impressionistic. It is aesthetic rather than scientific. It is candid rather than posed. Or at least it takes pains to appear to be. Street photographers value the happy accident, the meaningful juxtaposition, the richly contradictory elements that compose everyday life. They seek out complexity and instil their images with the urgency of the here and the now.

But this is not to say that street photography is haphazard. Anything but. Though street photography in theory can refer to a wide range of photographic styles, in practice it has had a more specific and more constrictive meaning. For the last three quarters of a century, one photographer's conception of street photography has pulled more weight than any other's in establishing the definitions, and setting the standards – the conventions to both flaunt and flout – that street photographers hold to this day. That conception belonged to Henri Cartier-Bresson (1908–2004). Part of the generation of Parisian street photographers after Atget, Cartier-Bresson was a resident of post-Haussmann Paris. He was no longer so hung up on cultural preservation and no longer constrained by the technical limitations of large-format photography. He was free instead to simply wander and encounter, which he did for large portions of his day, exploring neighbourhoods of Paris outside of his immediate purview. Cartier-Bresson was the flâneur extraordinaire, an extreme exemplar of Baudelaire's nineteenth century ideal. Though he worked as a professional photographer, shooting for private clients, newspapers, and magazines, and founded the prestigious photojournalist collective Magnum Photos, Cartier-Bresson considered himself an 'amateur', photographing what he wanted and whom he wanted simply for the love of it.

Cartier-Bresson's tool of choice was a 35 mm Leica rangefinder camera, now considered the gold standard for street photographers everywhere. The Leica was light and portable. It was nearly silent when it captured its images. A street photographer like Cartier-Bresson could take it with him wherever he went, wield it like a concealed weapon, pulling it out at a moment's notice to capture an image of a subject before that subject could even react to its presence. For Cartier-Bresson, then, 'candid' had a very particular meaning. It occurred spontaneously, without his intervention, ideally formulated without even its subject's knowledge. And it arranged itself organically into a semiotic deposition on truth. It was the job of the photographer to notice 'meaningful' moments when they occurred and to react to them as quickly and reflexively as possible. A good photographer could sense them in formation, setting his camera to capture them well before they happened. And when they did happen, he would act swiftly, decisively, capture his subject in a way that laid bare its essential nature, then move on to something else.

'One must seize the moment before it passes', wrote Cartier-Bresson in his treatise on the art of photography, 'the fleeting gesture, the evanescent smile…' (Cartier Bresson, as cited in Westerbeck and Meyerowitz 1994: 157). Cartier-Bresson would dub this preliminary instant of embryonic photographic meaning-making 'the decisive moment', and he would live his life continually seeking it.

Cartier-Bresson had some very specific ideas about the proper protocol for capturing the decisive moment. 'All his pictures were unposed, he never used flash (he considered it "impolite – like coming to a concert with a pistol in your hand") and he rarely cropped his images in the darkroom' (Howarth and McClaren 2010: 12). Photographs, as far as Cartier-Bresson was concerned, were made primarily in camera and in the lived chaos of the street. And then, they were to be left alone. Many street photographers continue to follow Cartier-Bresson's photographic protocol as if it were biblical law. Others have found their own protocols to adhere to. But very few disregard Cartier-Bresson's imperatives altogether. For Cartier-Bresson and his ilk, the 'truth is out there', on the street, flickering past in embryonic moments that only the most attentive and skilful cameraman can capture. And the street, as such photographers conceived of it, is a stand-in for the urban real. It is the gritty, immediate reality of city life.

In street photography, then, 'the street' is an absolutely critical element, both as a visual backdrop and as an accompanying idea, present even in the absence of its explicit depiction. If the street of Haussmann was an artery of the city, the street of Mayhew an ulcer in its gut, and the street of Sander a dispassionate amalgam of social reality, the street of Atget, Cartier-Bresson, and scores of other street

FIGURE 1.7 'The Allée du Prado', Marseilles, 1932. Photo by Henri Cartier-Bresson. 'I was walking behind this man when all of a sudden he turned around', claimed Cartier-Bresson. © Henri Cartier-Bresson/Magnum Photos.

photographers since them, was a kind of religion. They didn't invent this religion. It had been around since at least Baudelaire and likely well before him, but they were among its biggest devotees. The street, for them, 'was experienced as the medium in which the totality of modern material and spiritual forces could meet, clash, interfuse, and work out their ultimate meanings and fates' (Berman 1982: 316). This, Marxist critic Marshall Berman reminds us, 'was what Joyce's Stephen

Dedalus has in mind in his cryptic suggestion that God was out there, in the "shout of the streets"' (Berman 1982: 316–317).

This quasi-religious conception of the street is alive today in dozens of Instagram accounts devoted to 'urban exploration'. It is present in those innumerable tourist selfies shot in the midst of the hustle and bustle of midtown Manhattan. And it is present in the work of contemporary street style photographers, wandering the hippest neighbourhoods of their hometowns in search of visual specimens to attest to their own conception of cool. Street style photographers employ the photographic conventions of Sander and Huxley while espousing the attitude and sensibility of Atget and Cartier-Bresson. Theirs is a medium of social documentary portrait photography built on the chance encounter with the city.

Fashion's own romance with the street

The fashion industry is no stranger to the street photographer's religion of the street. At times it appears to share it, at times simply to plunder its aesthetic riches. Some of street photography's biggest names, including Brassaï, Robert Frank, and Henri Cartier-Bresson himself, have contributed images to fashion magazines (Hall-Duncan 1979: 12), and they have thus helped shape fashion imagery in a significant way. A variety of fashion photographers, working squarely within the industry have also employed street photography's low-tech, stripped down conventions as part of their practice. Street photography's influence is evident in the work of such contemporary editorial photographers as Corrine Day, Jürgen Teller, and Terry Richardson, who shoot their images in ways that emphasize the flaws and quirks of the people they photograph. Street photography's appeal, and indeed the appeal of these niche fashion photographers, lies in its contrast with most fashion photography – a genre that is more 'hyper-real' than realist, flaunting its own falseness as if it were a prized knock-off handbag.

An early proponent of bringing elements of 'the street' into fashion photography was Irving Penn, the celebrated photographer probably best known for his work in US and French *Vogue*. Penn was above all a portrait photographer, as interested in the people wearing the clothes as the clothes themselves. His shots, whether of glamorous models, iconic stars, or chimney sweeps in working-class London, quite knowingly borrowed the conventions of realist portraiture used by August Sander and the emphasis on 'just plain folks' evident in the work of Atget and Cartier-Bresson. He used natural light whenever possible and coached his models to don expressionless faces and stern, rigid postures that emphasized the seriousness of the task at hand. His series entitled 'Small Trades' took an even more direct inspiration from Sander. Featuring 'ordinary people' in London, Paris, and New York shot in their work clothes in the studios provided for Penn by *Vogue*, the images border on homage. They feature some of the same titles and many of the same occupations as those in Sander's work. And yet, there are some startling differences in what, and how, they represent.

For one, in order to shoot his subjects, Penn removed them from the context of their home and work place. He 'transferred his sitters to the neutral territory of the studio, demonstrating that his interest was not in the environmental portrait but in the psychological portrait' (Heckert and Lacoste 2009: 15). He used a muddled grey continuous backdrop for each subject that, in a sense, placed each on equal footing. 'I preferred', said Penn of this practice, 'the limited task of dealing only with the person himself, away from the accidentals of his daily life; simply in his own clothes and adornments, isolated in my studio. From himself alone I would distill the image I wanted and the cold light of day would put it onto film' (Penn, as cited in Heckert and Lacoste 2009: 15). Notice that Penn, like Sander, believed in the ability of his images to capture intact something of the reality of the person he photographed. He believed in the ability of the camera to penetrate beneath veneer. But he did not share Sander's conception of what lies beneath that veneer. For Sander, 'a realist' as Döblin brands him, reality is comprised of universal types observable in the world around us. But for Penn, the individual is what matters. He both subscribes to and defies symbolic representation. He is a member of a group but an *individual* member with his own unique scars and memories. In Penn's work lies an emergent individualism clearly evident in later street style photography. For him, individual differences are not accidental variation from a universal type; they are the defining features of a person.

In no small part because of Penn, 'the street' in high fashion photography was transformed from a space of danger and indifference into a space of intrigue, where upmarket fashionistas could go slumming in search of 'real life'. Representations of fashion 'on the street', claim fashion scholars Agnès Rocamora and Alistair O'Neill, can be 'charted across the twentieth-century history of the fashion media' (Rocamora and O'Neill 2008: 186). As far back as 1926, photographers like Edward Steichen, also working for US *Vogue*, were attempting to recreate the look of the street within their studios as a dynamic setting for their models, a space their on-the-town socialites passed through on their way to the opera, the restaurant, or the theatre. Just a touch of grime was the perfect offset to the glamorous gown. A girl, after all, has to go out when she looks this good.

And yet the street in these images is nowhere that any respectable person, and in particular, respectable woman, would want to linger. In these early fashion images, Rocamora and O'Neill note, the street remains the masculinized space of the urban flâneur, whose gaze, from behind the camera lens, captures the woman of class just as she passes through his field of vision.

It is not until the 1960s that fashion's relationship with the street began to markedly change. The 1960s, a number of fashion historians have argued, marks a critical turning point in the history of fashion. This is when fashion stopped seeing itself as the exclusive sartorial service of the aristocracy and began to reimagine itself as the cutting edge of popular style. The birth of the counterculture, the protests against the Vietnam war, and the changing consciousness brought about by the civil rights movement collaborated to produce a marked shift in fashion's emphasis. Designers like Yves Saint-Laurent and Mary Quant aligned themselves with protesters, artists, and bohemians in a grand project of redefining the visual world. They began to look to the youth subcultures of urban centres like East London and Downtown New York for inspiration for their designs. Youth subcultures leant their power to shock and inspire to the cutting edge couture making their runway debuts at Fashion Week. By the 1970s, traces of punk, mod, and hippie were everywhere on the runways. Fashion, which had for decades been imagined as the exclusive domain of the urban elite, 'trickling down' to the masses once the jet-setters were done with it, was now seen as 'bubbling up' from the streets (Aspelund 2009; Polhemus 1994). The street was being reimagined, not as the opposite of fashion, the place the fashionable fear to tread but as a laboratory of fashion, a bubbling cauldron of sartorial creativity. The industry saw the streets through an 'almost organic' metaphor (Rocamora and O'Neill 2008: 191). This is where fashion gurgled up out of the crevices of the earth like some primordial ooze. The street was pure, dumb fashion potentiality before being shaped by the artful hands of an Alexander McQueen into something chic and sophisticated. It is no wonder, then, that fashion photographers began to turn to the street, like intrepid war correspondents reporting from the hot zones of fashion. 'Coolhunting' and 'trend forecasting' became a mainstream practice of the industry. And it is precisely here where 'street style photography', as we know it today, first enters into the picture.

Bill Cunningham, 'the original street style photographer'

Bill Cunningham is a decidedly likable choice for 'the original street style photographer', and his status as such goes nearly unquestioned in the blogosphere today. He is famously unpretentious and unassuming, wears a generic blue raincoat to some of the most upscale and exclusive of events (see Figure 1.8). He seems to stand apart from fashion, and yet in New York his very presence signals fashionability. Cunningham represents to many New Yorkers a different era of fashion journalism, an era when 'fashion still mattered', and only the chosen few were invited to its dazzling events. Until recently, he shot exclusively with a film camera in a crowd of digital ones. He still laughs giddily when he gets a good image, peppers his speech with antiquated superlatives like 'marvellous' and 'magnificent', and seems to take genuine delight in his job. Not that he doesn't work hard. Cunningham hits the pavement of New York nearly every day – rain, snow, sleet, or shine – shooting the street style action on 57th Street and 5th Avenue. And then, when the sun goes down, he works the party circuit, photographing openings and soirees, the jet set of the Upper East Side. He seems to be nearly always working, and when he is working, he is quiet, focused, smiles politely at the people around him but never stays still long enough for a real conversation. I should know. I have tried more than once to engage him in one.

Cunningham's weekly Sunday column in the style section of the *New York Times* is the longest-running street-style feature of any publication. 'On the Street' began in earnest in 1978 with shots of Greta Garbo in a nutria coat, passing 'practically unnoticed' on Fifth Avenue (Collins 2009). Cunningham, by the way, noticed the coat, not the movie star. He only figured out who she was later. Since then, Cunningham has photographed many of New York's most recognizable faces, alongside thousands of unknown pedestrians whose outfits just happened to catch his eye. There is something almost democratic about Cunningham's column. But 'almost' is the key word here. In theory, anyone could show up in 'On the Street',

FIGURE 1.8 Bill Cunningham at work in New York. Photo by Driely S.

just so long as they happen to be dressed in this season's fashions and be in the right part of New York at the right moment in time.

In 'On the Street', every subject seems to get equal treatment, positioned almost haphazardly on the page to illustrate a particular theme or trend. 'Bag Ladies', a headline might contend, emphasizing the large, clunky bags preferred by the society ladies of the moment. 'Underalls', another might say, revealing the resurgence of a long-dormant staple of work attire. In either case, Cunningham's work is a street-level documentation of changes in fashion as they occur. As such, a 2011 documentary entitled *Bill Cunningham New York* rightly described Cunningham as a 'cultural anthropologist' of style, a continuous presence on the streets of New York, who has forged himself into one of fashion's greatest authorities as well as one of its least likely icons. He is a 'connoisseur of the street', as Benjamin described, a 'spy for the capitalists' (Benjamin 2002: 427). But for Cunningham 'the street' is a fairly constricted place – that narrow stretch of 5th Avenue between Dolce & Gabbana and Louis Vuitton.

There can be little doubt that Bill Cunningham has played a sizable role in making street style photography what it is today, lending it credibility, building its audience, and paving the way for such street style stalwarts of the digital age as Scott Schuman and Tommy Ton. In imitation of 'On the Street', columns documenting everyday fashion popped up in newspapers throughout the major cities of the United States and Europe in the early to mid-1980s. Magazines began their own street style sections, although they didn't call them that yet, and tuning in to see what 'real people' are wearing in the metropolitan centres became a national pastime of the casually fashion-conscious.

But crediting Cunningham with inventing the genre is a stretch. Images similar to his, as I have already documented in this chapter, appeared in street and social documentary photography for decades before 1978. Nor has his style of image-making been particularly influential among the street style photographers working today. Scott Schuman, The Sartorialist, got himself into some hot water when he admitted as much to the 'industry bible' *Women's Wear Daily* in 2012.

'You know, I hate to say it', Schuman told reporter Bambina Wise, 'I'm sure everyone thinks he's a lovable guy, and I'm sure he is. We've never had a conversation. The only conversation we've ever had is when I'm trying to shoot someone and he says, 'Hey, get out'. The only influence he's had on me is that I want to be doing that when I'm 80. That's the only thing. I want to be on the bike, I want to be doing that at 80. His photographs, I think they're nice, they're just a totally different style from me. I don't think they're bad, really just a different style. He's really reportage, shoot, snap, he's just going, going, going…' (quoted in Wise 2012).

Schuman got considerable flack for saying so – the blogosphere momentarily erupting in a chorus of critical comments – but he was merely stating what was already commonly known among street style photographers: Cunningham as an idea has been quite influential but Cunningham as a photographer, maybe not so much. Cunningham, after all, takes snapshots, quick candids taken without the permission of his subjects and without careful attention to composition and aesthetics. For a reporter like him, those elements are beside the point. They get in the way of a cold hard record of 'just the facts'. But they are not beside the point for most other street style photographers working today. Those photographers adhere to a strict set of conventions, immediately recognizable as belonging to a distinctive genre of social documentary realist portraiture. And there is one source, contemporaneous with Cunningham, that was much more influential than he was in disseminating this convention within fashion circles, even if it is less commonly cited as such by the fashion press today. That source was UK alternative fashion and lifestyle magazine *i-D*.

Street style photography, 'straight up'

Terry Jones, the founder of *i-D Magazine*, left UK *Vogue* after a five-year stint as their Art Director between 1972 and 1977. *Vogue*, he was beginning to think, was like a dinosaur in a Chanel dress. They had little of the edginess and ferocity that he could feel fuming up out of the streets of London, and little interest in cultivating it. The late '70s was a moment of economic recession in the UK. Working-class kids were growing disillusioned with the great promise of the capitalist economy and turning to some rather extreme forms of leisure instead (Clarke et al. 1976; Hebdige 1979). This was the golden age of punk rock, that groundswell of youth revolt that produced some of the most iconoclastic street fashions the world had yet seen: safety pins through cheeks, Mohawks elevated to the sky, Vivienne Westwood deconstructed school-girl uniforms reconfigured through the sensibility of BDSM. And yet at *Vogue* it remained business as usual.

Jones had recently met with the photographer Steve Johnston at *Vogue* House in London. Johnston, fresh out of art school, entered his office 'with dyed hair and a ripped jacket, held together with safety pins, worn over a graffitied shirt' (Jones 2000b: 23) and told him he had some pictures to show him. Johnston was shooting head-to-toe shots of punks, teds, and other subcultural types on a white wall he'd staked out across from the fire station on the King's Road (see Figures 1.9 and 1.10). They were 'one-click-per-person' (Jones 2000b: 23) images, nothing fancy, shot on a Nikon F2 camera with a 50 mm normal lens on Kodak Tri-X 400 speed film. Inspired, Johnston told me, by Irving Penn and August Sander, along with an assortment of American and French street photographers, they featured head-to-toe images of assorted young people, blank expressions on their faces, posed with arms at their side, hair touching the top of the image, feet touching the bottom. Johnston had something of an aversion to excess space. He

FIGURE 1.9 'Punk girls in London', 1977, featured in an early issue of i-D Magazine. Photo by Steve Johnston.

wanted his images to look like mug shots, cagey and blunt. Jones took immediate interest. *Vogue* did not. As far as Jones was concerned, this was a much clearer representation of the style zeitgeist than was visible on the pages of high-end fashion magazines like the one he worked for. So when Jones left *Vogue* to start his own project, Johnston was one of the first people he thought to contact.

The first issue of *i-D* was basically a glorified fanzine. Oriented in landscape rather than portrait mode, it was held together with staples, and it featured an assortment of interspersed text and images cut up and reassembled in the style of a punk rock concert flier. Johnston's photographs were front and centre, featuring only a smidgen of text running up the side, explaining, in the subject's own words, what they were wearing, where they got it, and how much it cost. Jones dubbed these photographs 'straight ups', and they became a regular feature of the magazine. They remain so to this day.

i-D, claimed journalist Dylan Jones, was 'essentially an exercise in social documentation; a catalogue of photographs of "real" people wearing "real" clothes' (Jones 2000a: 9). While other fashion magazines featured looks put together by professionals from within the fashion industry, *i-D* focused on the creativity of individuals *outside* of that industry (Lifter 2013: 177). That doesn't mean they featured any ol' person they stumbled upon. Their taste was more particular: punk, club kids, new romantics, the subcultural types left out of mainstream fashion representation. 'Straight ups', as far as editor Terry Jones were concerned, were the best way to capture the 'immediacy' and atmosphere of what was going on in the clubs and on the streets. There was nothing precious about these photos. They had no studio lighting. They were not artfully shot. In fact, for the first several issues, Jones insisted that the photographers shooting for him only use two frames per person (Jones 2000a: 10). Johnston himself preferred to shoot only one. The idea was to thwart the photographer's efforts towards perfectionism, making the image about the subject depicted, rather than the talent of its depicter. And it saved a little bit of money on film besides. Johnston, after all, never made any money off his images for *i-D*. He lived off of welfare while pursuing his artistic passions. As a consequence, notes Dylan Jones, 'the contact sheets became works of art in themselves, a sort of sartorial police file' (Jones 2000a: 10).

The straight up, almost immediately, became a thing. *The Face*, another UK magazine launched just a few months before *i-D*, began its own straight up series shortly after. A variety of other magazines quickly followed suit. Within a couple of years, the straight up had become 'a staple of fashion journalism from the British *Independent on Sunday* to the French *Jalouse* or the aptly titled Japanese *Street*' (Rocamora and O'Neill 2008: 188). By 1985, *The Guardian* newspaper had declared *i-D*, *The Face*, and an assortment of similar magazines, 'the first authentic and original commercial style to make the big time since the 1960s' (Thompson 1985). 'They are street', they declared, 'And the word is style' (Thompson 1985).

FIGURE 1.10 London punk, 1977. Photo by Steve Johnston.

And yet despite the common equation of the straight up with the style of the street, it is curious, looking back at these images now, how absent the streets themselves are from them. In imitation of the dull grey backdrop preferred by Irving Penn, straight ups, as envisioned by Johnston, are almost uniformly shot in front of blank walls. In fact, Johnston's photos are almost all shot in front of the same wall, across from the fire station on the King's Road. Johnston only shot somewhere else, he told me, when there was a car parked in front of it. The background in these photos, then, is intentionally non-descript. They could have been shot anywhere. The street is present in them only as an idea, a site of authentic, grass-roots creativity. The street is that great wellspring of inspiration from which Yves Saint-Laurent got his ideas and where Hood by Air gets theirs today. It is the untidy, uncontrollable version of fashion, outside the sphere of the industry.

Or at least, that's what it was for a while. As the convention of straight ups disseminated throughout the fashion media, its grit began to gradually wear off, so that by the time it reached Main Street USA, the 'street' in its images bore little semblance to the street of i-D. Flowing blonde locks supplanted stiff green Mohawks, casual dresses took the place of black leather bondage gear. The 'regular' people of the straight up, that is, became more and more 'regular'. The street of street style, it seemed, had been tamed.

From the margins to the mainstream and back again

Of course, the term 'street style' itself had yet to enter into the vernacular of fashion. Magazines like i-D and The Face sometimes described themselves as 'street fashion' or simply 'street', but there are few instances of the term 'street style' appearing in newspapers and magazines until 1994. That is when anthropologist and photographer Ted Polhemus put together the photographic exhibition and accompanying book Streetstyle: From Sidewalk to Catwalk for London's Victoria and Albert Museum. For Polhemus, 'street style' was not simply whatever people happened to be wearing in their ordinary lives at some particular moment in time. That was too pedestrian. That was too boring. No: street style, as for Steve Johnston before him, was the style of 'the street' in an older more romantic sense of the term. It was mod, punk, and goth. It was skinhead, rudeboy, headbanger, and hip hopper. It was those 'tribal styles' (Maffesoli 1995; Polhemus 1994) of the modern metropolis that had been capturing the public imagination since first documented by photojournalists in the 1850s. Street style was the kind of style featured on tourist postcards of Piccadilly Circus. It was the kind of style teenagers temporarily adopted in order to scare their parents, the kind of style newspapers documented with headlines like 'the youth menace' and 'riot in the streets'. And it was the kind of style that appeared in *i-D* and *The Face* from its earliest days. Street style, in other words, referred to those 'spectacular' youth subcultures (Clarke et al. 1976; Hebdige 1979) occupying the 'urban jungles' and 'unknown continents' of working-class UK (Hebdige 1988: 20) and downtown New York. Street style was, once again, imagined to be everything mainstream fashion was not.

The black-clad youth featured in the images shown at the *Streetstyle* exhibit were full of piss and vinegar, flair and sass. They challenged the camera with defiant glares, raised middle fingers, ratted their hair to impossible heights. No wonder young people like these had sparked so many 'moral panics' (Clarke et al. 1976; Hebdige 1988) in the 1960s and 1970s, when newspapers routinely published pictures of greasers and teds, mods and rockers, and reported alarming stories of their drug binges and public rivalries. No wonder they made the 'squares' and 'suits' of the high streets and businesses districts so uncomfortable, flaunting their liberty spikes and tattoos, their conspicuous leisure (Willis 1977) and dangerous recreations. And no wonder they had fascinated UK sociologists and cultural theorists for decades. Street style in this depiction was a threat to the bourgeois status quo, an act of 'semiotic guerilla warfare' (Eco 1972; Hebdige 1979) against the UK and US establishment. To the Marxists of the ivory towers, there was something uplifting about such street style images. Street style read as an undergrowth of rebellion, which, given the right nutrients and cultivation, could very well bloom into something bigger. Documenting street style was thus one of the primary occupations of UK cultural studies throughout the 1970s and 1980s.

Polhemus' exhibition helped inject new life into street style photography – for a time. It regained some of the edge it had lost in its transition into the fashion mainstream. It took on a newfound sense of menace. And it reinvigorated its importance to the fashion world. The magazine headlines of the mid-1990s are rife with references to street style. 'Street Style Dances on Couture's Grave', proclaims *The Australian* in 1996. 'High End Designers Would Starve Without the Style and Spirit of Urban Youth', declares *The Washington Post* in 1998. The styles of the street walk the expanse of the runway. Goth, mod, punk, and that favourite fashion punching bag of the popular press, 'heroin chic', infused into the looks of nearly every designer label at some point in the 1990s.

And yet, by the end of the decade, street style had once again lost its fangs. The spectacular looks of the street gave way to the mundane everyday trends of the sidewalk. 'Street Style in the Nineties', declared The Independent in 1998, 'is Less about Shock, More about Blending in.' The fashion press, throughout the 1990s appeared to maintain two simultaneous conceptions of the street:

(1) as the creative stomping ground of fashion outsiders and (2) as the all-too pedestrian zone of the humdrum everyday.

Street style goes global

By the end of the 1990s, street style photography was an established part of the fashion industry, a regular feature in the Sunday style sections of newspapers and a brief detour from the fantasy worlds of magazines towards the end of each issue. It had also gotten decidedly dull. Gone were the days of leather-clad youth with defiant pouts leaning against whitewashed walls. Gone was the sense of menace and mayhem visible at Ted Polhemus' exhibition at the Victoria and Albert Museum. Street style was people 'just like you and me' – assuming, of course, that 'you' and 'me' are white, upper middle-class urbanites with pant sizes somewhere between 0 and 8. Street style may have been more ecumenical than most fashion editorials, but it was hardly exhaustive in its inclusiveness.

Enter *NYLON Magazine*. In 1999, Madonna Badger, Mark Blackwell, model Helena Christensen, and the husband and wife team of Marvin and Jaclynn Jarrett launched the Gen Y-targeted glossy with the intention of bringing the street-savvy sensibility of alternative lifestyle magazines like *i-D* and *The Face* into a more contemporary, and accessible, package. 'One of the major reasons *NYLON* launched in 1999', wrote Eviana Hartman in her introduction to *STREET: The NYLON Book of Global Style*, 'was because other magazines were missing an important point: Fashion doesn't exist in a bubble. To us, it's not only for rich people, models, and the type of people who slavishly adhere to runway trends; we see it as a living, breathing reflection of cultural and social currents, of what's going on in music, art, and on the sidewalks of the communities we live in' (Hartman 2006: 08). Street style was a big part of NYLON's mission. Their 2006 collection of street style images, *STREET*, documented the hip, young populations of New York, London, Tokyo, Berlin, Paris, Melbourne, and Copenhagen in classic, straight-up format: bearded bohemians with cigarettes dangling from their mouths lingered in doorways. Denim-clad waifs feigned indifference to the camera while faux-walking down cobblestone alleys. The images are sharp and simple. The styles depicted are edgy and cool. The subjects are ethnically and culturally diverse, if not exactly expansive in age range or body size. *NYLON* was committed to the sentiment of Polhemus that 'style trickles up, not just down' (Hartman 2006: 8), and they set about to document it on sidewalks throughout the industrialized world. In the pages of *NYLON* we can see the beginnings of an ethos that would become commonplace in the style blogosphere just a few years later, a sense of global interconnection, where the kids in Copenhagen are paying careful attention

FIGURE 1.11 Punk girl in the Harajuku neighbourhood of Tokyo, shot by Shoichi Aoki for *FRUiTs* in the late 1990s.

FIGURE 1.12 Boy in Harajuku. Photo by Shoichi Aoki.

to what's going on in the streets of Melbourne. Street style had become an international buffet table (see Polhemus 1996), a little bit from here, a little bit from there. The days of tribal affiliation to some clearly demarcated subcultural type were over. These days, as *NYLON* Editor-in-Chief Marvin Scott Jarrett put it, it's all about 'what an individual mixes together to create a visible expression of their own personality' (Jarrett 2006: 6). In his *Arcades Project*, Benjamin described the streets as 'the dwelling place of the collective' (Benjamin 2002: 423), but on the pages of *NYLON* it was more like the mobile home of the quirky, cosmopolitan individual.

And no streets gave birth to quirkier or more cosmopolitan individuals than those of Tokyo, Japan. In the mid-to-late 1990s, Tokyo began capturing the fashion world's attention as a place where western subcultures go to get turned into cartoons. Punk was still alive and well in Tokyo, even if re-imagined and re-tooled. As Jarrett put it, the kids of Tokyo dress like 'they're going on stage' (Jarrett 2006: 6). Ripped-up school-girl uniforms were everywhere, liberty spikes were all the rage. Fashion photographers were beginning to take notice.

Self-trained fashion photographer Shoichi Aoki lived in London and Paris throughout most of 1980s and early 1990s. Inspired by the straight ups in *i-D* and *The Face*, he started his own street fashion magazine, *STREET* (not to be confused with NYLON's book *STREET*), in order to document what he saw in these cities. At the time, he explains, he saw 'an energy and a style' there that he had never seen in Japan (personal communication, 2013). 'Japan', he told me, 'was dominated by department store brands and there was no innovation from the consumer'. London and Paris seemed positively otherworldly in comparison. But when Aoki returned to Tokyo in the mid-1990s, he was taken aback by what he saw. 'I saw something happening', he put it succinctly, an explosion of styles so bold they bordered on satirical. The conservatism that had characterized Japanese style for decades was nowhere to be seen.

Aoki founded a new magazine, *FRUiTS* – and later TUNE – to capture those styles he was observing on the streets of Harajuku (see Figures 1.11, 1.12, and 1.13). He eventually compiled many of his images into a hardbound book of the same name that became an unlikely international hit. *FRUiTS* was a new variation on an old formula: an unusually clad teenager stands dispassionately in the centre of the frame with either a street or wall behind her, sometimes a sliver of a smile just slipping through. Arms rest at her side and her vision rests firmly on the lens of the camera. The kids of *FRUiTS* are visual specimens, photographic samplings of the crazy goings-on of the Harajuku streets. This was hardly revolutionary, but the single, Phaidon-published volume made street style elsewhere appear tame. It put the Brit-poppers in the back pages of *NYLON* to shame. When a new generation of self-taught photographers like Liisa Jokinen decided to get into the street style game in the mid-zeros, it was not *NYLON* or *i-D* they turned to for inspiration. It was Shoichi Aoki, testifying, once again, to the more subversive and expressive power of clothing.

FIGURE 1.13 Girl in Harajuku dressed in the Lolita style for which Harajuku became famous in the 1990s. Photographed by Shoichi Aoki for *FRUiTs*.

FIGURE 1.14 An early image on the Hel Looks blog, capturing the influence of the Harajuku style on Helsinki fashion. Photo by Liisa Jokinen.

Street style 2.0

It is impossible to fix a hard date to the advent of street style blogs as we know them today. Predecessors, like Mark Hunter's L.A. party photography blog The Cobra Snake (thecobrasnake.com), stretch back to at least 2003. The Cool Hunter (thecoolhunter.net), which bills itself as 'the world's most read culture and design site', launched in 2004. It posted occasional street style pictures as part of its larger coverage. In fact, Yvan Rodic contributed party pictures to The Cool Hunter prior to starting Face Hunter in 2006. Style Arena, which began its life as the 'Tokyo Street Style' section of the online Japanese lifestyle magazine Coromo.com, began in 2002. The first independent, dedicated street style blogs of the sort we know today began appearing in around 2005. Liisa Jokinen's Hel Looks was likely not the first, though she doesn't know of any street style blogs that came before hers (see Figure 1.14). I also have not been able to identify any. In any case, hers was among the earliest, if it was not in fact the earliest, started in July of 2005. It was followed, in fairly close succession, by Scott Schuman's The Sartorialist in September of the same year. Both blogs took off nearly immediately, attracting tens of thousands of readers within the first months of their establishment. Their success is likely one reason for the efflorescence of street style blogs that followed closely on their heels. By the beginning of 2007, just a year and a half after Liisa Jokinen launched Hel Looks, there were already dozens of street style blogs, reporting on the latest looks walking the sidewalks of fashion capitals (and a few backwaters) from around the globe. In Berlin, Germany, there was Stil in Berlin (stilinberlin.de). In Gothenberg, Sweden, there was Pose and Click (poseandclick.blogspot.com). In Manila, The Philippines, there was Manila Style (mnlstyl.blogspot.com). In Tel Aviv (and Jerusalem), Israel, there was The Streets Walker (see Figure 1.15) (thestreetswalker. telavivian.com).

You already know the story of how these blogs came into being. It has been rehashed in more bestselling books, *Wired Magazine* articles, and online opinion pieces than I can possibly cite here. In the early aughts (or the 'noughties' as the British are inclined to call them), after the first wave of internet investor enthusiasm came crashing against the shores of actual profit capacity, the Silicon Valley began to reimagine itself as an agent of democratization (see Marwick 2013; Van Dijck 2013). They emphasized products based on user-generated content. They marketed interactivity. A revolution was brewing, the internet loyalists shouted from the rooftops of the Oracle Building, and *you* were going to be a part of it. This wasn't just a gold mine, insisted Yahoo, YouTube, and dozens of fresh-faced startups. It was the dawn of a new era, 'Web 2.0', where every consumer is a producer and the old hierarchies of the media establishment are as outdated as an 8-track cassette player. New internet technologies, like social media websites and digital cameras, put the tools of cultural production and dissemination into the

FIGURE 1.15 Cecilia, Jerusalem. Photo by Yael Sloma for her Israel-based, street style blog The Streets Walker, launched in 2007.

hands of more people than ever before. The ethos of Web 2.0 was a do-it-yourself (DIY) ethos (see Luvaas 2012).

'Before [Web 2.0]' Yvan Rodic of Face Hunter told Canada's *The Globe and Mail* back in 2007, 'people were inspiring designers, and then magazines were featuring peoples' clothes, and finally people were inspired by magazines.' The magazines asserted themselves as a critical mediator of style. They were gatekeepers, middlemen, watchers of 'the street' for the rest of us. 'Now the process is more horizontal', says Rodic. 'People are inspiring people' (Villett 2007: L8). By 2007, they no longer needed to turn to the pages of *NYLON* or *STREET* to see what was happening on the sidewalks of New York or Tokyo. They could simply go online, visit the blogs of amateur photographers the world over, and see for themselves.

Moreover, the people who documented style on their blogs in the early days of the street style blogosphere were largely self-appointed. These were self-trained photographers who had bypassed the traditional gate-keeping mechanisms of the fashion publishing industry to bring their images to tens of thousands of people directly. 'I think it's just a great thing', Gunnar Hämmerle of the blog StyleClicker (started in 2006) told me. 'You can reach like the whole world with your work. You don't need any big investment or anything like that. You can just start something, and blog about something that you are passionate about.' No more starting from the bottom and working your way up. No more 'paying your dues' as a thankless intern at a heartless magazine. If you want to blog, just blog already. That was the sentiment of the time.

Nearly all of these early street style blogs used the free blog platform of Blogger (blogspot.com), now owned by Google. Their URLs ended in the '.blogspot.com' designation, and they had the homespun, relatively low-tech vibe of an internet craft project. These were the 'zines' of Web 2.0, low-to-no-cost 'labours of love' (see Duncombe 1997), put together by avid fashion fans for their own, and their readers', amusement. There were no ads. There was no sponsored content. Very few of them even captioned their photos with information about brands or prices (Heffernan 2008: 22), a fairly standard practice today. The images featured were miniscule by today's standards as well, usually no more than an inch and a half by two inches in size. They were almost hard to see, a consequence, no doubt of the dial-up connections most people were still using to access the internet. Larger image files would have slowed internet speeds to a grinding halt.

The format of these early blogs was the standard template supplied by Blogger: a stream of images in the middle of the page, links on the right or left-hand side. And boy did these blogs have links! They linked to their favourite blogs. They linked to other street style blogs. They linked to fashion websites and personal websites. The sense of blogger community was palpable in the very layout of early street style blogs. Bloggers commented on each other's posts, promoted each other's content, and supported each other's practice. There was a feel-good ethos that permeated the blogosphere. Street style blogs displayed the communitarian logic of social media prior to social media even being a thing (see Van Dijck 2013). They were an enthusiastic enactment of the promise and logic of Web 2.0.

As for the images displayed on early street style blogs, they were a lowbrow, no-skill-required, contemporary rendition of the 'straight up'. Their subjects stood on the street or in front of a wall, rendered as clearly and completely as possible. Nothing fancy. No bells and whistles. Nothing you couldn't achieve with a bottom-of-the-line digital camera. The aesthetics of the street style blog were as democratic as the rhetoric that gave birth to them. Anyone with a digital camera could take pictures like this. The camera would practically take them for you.

There was a sense, navigating the street style blogosphere of 2006 and 2007, that street style blogs presented a true alternative to the fashion industry as usual. Here were 'ordinary' people taking pictures of 'ordinary' people. It wasn't about the brands. It wasn't about the trends. It was about the personal style of unique individuals. Street style bloggers, like Schuman and Jokinen, featured young and old, a variety of ethnicities and class groups. They didn't emphasize the high-end to the exclusion of the affordable. They didn't really care much for the trappings of the industry.

'The street' of early street style blogs was the imagined 'public sphere' (Habermas 2001) of a mid-twentieth century Marxist intellectual, a space of the commons made up of diverse, and often quirky, individuals. As broadband internet connections became more widely available worldwide and higher-end cameras became more affordable, the images on these sites got bigger, brighter, and more sophisticated, and the streets featured in the backgrounds retreated more and more into the backgrounds. Photographers like Gunnar Hämmerle (StyleClicker), Scott Schuman (The Sartorialist), Javi Obando (On the Corner), and Felicia Nitzsche (Dam Style) began experimenting with shallow depth of field in their photographs, making the streets behind their subjects fade into a dense field of blur. Between 2008 and 2014, that field of blur only got thicker.

Popping a subject out a scene

The models on Adam Katz Sinding's popular, New York-based street-style blog Le 21ème (www.le-21eme.com) – launched in Seattle in 2007 – often look like they are about to step into – or are just stepping out of – the void. Shot at fashion weeks in New York, London, Milan, Paris, and beyond or on the occasional weekend excursion through the streets of Manhattan, Sinding's candid high-fashion portraits are characteristically opaque. Their subjects, shrouded in couture, stand at the forefront of the image, their visage in crystal clarity, while the background fades into a dense, shadowy blur (see Figures 1.16 and 1.18). Sometimes their subjects' backs are turned to us, the frame of the image cutting off at the waist. Sometimes we see only their torsos or legs, moving detached from the body towards some unseen destination. Other times there is merely a floating head, decapitated from the surrounding scene and situated dead centre in the frame. Cheekbones and shadows dominate the image. The lines of long, lycra-clad legs cut across the length of the frame. There is an aura of mystery to many of Sinding's photographs, both in terms of the subjects they depict and the settings in which they are shot. They share a stark, wintery colour palette, an austere composition that meshes well with the fashion labels Sinding 'allows' to advertise on his site: H. Lorenzo, Vertice London, GrayMarket, merchants of billowy black garments that both cling to and drape off of the body. His photographs are as much about what we don't see as what we do, but what we do see is ethereal and hazy – like streetlights through the fogged up windows of a speeding car.

There is a consistency in mood and sentiment that makes Sinding's photos immediately recognizable as his. Nonetheless, his shooting style bears similarity to a number of the top-name street style bloggers of the second decade of the new millennium: H.B. Nam (streetfsn.com), Youngjun Koo (koo.im), Tommy Ton (Jakandjil.com), Michael Dumler (onabbottkinney.

FIGURE 1.16 Model Lindsey Wixson, Milan. Photo by Adam Katz Sinding.

com), and Nabile Quenum (jaiperdumaveste.com) among them. Each of these photographers has gradually moved away from the street style standard of the straight up towards more dynamic, candid images of various fashion insiders in motion. Sometimes their shots emphasize the details of a garment. Sometimes they focus on the interaction between multiple subjects or the clash of colour palettes and prints. Other times they are a simple homage to a gesture: an inhalation of a cigarette, a lean against a guardrail, a glance at a smart phone, an exhausted sigh from a model, fresh off the runway (see Figures 1.19 and 1.20). Ton and Nam seem to particularly delight in the odd juxtaposition and the accidentally humorous scenario: two men walking at the same pace out of a show at Pitti Uomo, nearly identical jeans adorning their legs, their blazers blowing in the wind at the same precise angle; a couple of editors sizing each other up as they stroll past each other in the Tuileries in Paris, apparently noticing the similarities in what each are wearing; a woman in a stark red dress whose colour just happens to perfectly match the image on a billboard behind her. Many of these photographers, that is, have taken a page out of the Cartier-Bresson handbook. Their work is less about clothing per se than it is about 'decisive moments', those fleeting gestures and haphazard compositions that have long been the domain of street photography. There is often a subtle commentary embedded in this work, even an occasional critique, as when a

FIGURE 1.17 Models and photographers outside the Victoria Beckham show at New York Fashion Week ignoring panhandlers as they go about their work. Photo by Driely S.

photographer catches an image of a dolled up style star strolling indifferently past a panhandler (see Figure 1.17).

There can be little doubt that this new breed of street style photographer has moved away from the domain of 'the everyman' into the glossier, glitzier world of the fashion industry. They capture fewer and fewer of those 'ordinary' but cool denizens of the metropolis that were the stock in trade of *NYLON* and *i-D*. They show little concern for equitable representation. The new breed of street style photographer has focused her lens decisively in the direction of the 'style star' (see Chapter 6), a by-product of the street style blogosphere, which has created an internal hierarchy among choice of subjects.

But in another sense, this same set of street style photographers has helped put 'the street' back into 'street style' photography. This is not 'the street' Max Berlinger bemoaned the loss of in his op-ed for *Business of Fashion*. It is not the street of social documentary photography, the street that stands in as a metaphor for a base-level reality. And it is not the street of Ted Polhemus's exhibition at the Victoria and Albert Museum, a fantasy of youth menace in the minds of the suburban bourgeoisie. This is the street of the poetic moment, the street of romantic possibility, of happy accident. This is the street, that is, of street photography. Anything that doesn't fit that conception dissolves into a field of lens blur.

FIGURE 1.18 Blogger Natasha Goldenberg, Paris, a style star of 2014. Photo by Adam Katz Sinding.

FIGURE 1.19 W Magazine editor Giovanna Bataglia taking a smoking break outside the Ralph Lauren show at New York Fashion Week, a rare moment of tranquility amidst the madness. Photographer Driely Schwartz had to motion another photographer out of the frame to get this shot. Photo by Driely S.

FIGURE 1.20 A candid moment at New York Fashion Week. Photo by Driely S.

From street style to street fashion

The years 2009 and 2010 saw the entrance of a substantial number of new street style blogs into the fashion blogosphere. Competition increased among bloggers – an issue that grew only more acute as more and more bloggers found inroads into the industry, selling their photos to magazines and commercial websites. More blogging platforms, like WordPress, TypePad, and Tumblr, gave bloggers more options for configuring their blogs and greater upload and download speeds, provided by the broadband and satellite internet connections that were rapidly replacing dial-up, meant bloggers could post vastly larger images at a far greater resolution. Newer, more sophisticated digital cameras saturated the market, and their lowering price points made them affordable to a broader range of people. Quite predictably, as the number of bloggers increased and the professionalism of their work became more pronounced, the communitarian vibe of the early days of Web 2.0 began to decrease. Bloggers were becoming less of a network of impassioned amateurs than a field of dynamic competitors.

In hindsight, one of the first signs that the street style blogosphere was changing occurred all the way back in 2007, when Style.com, the glossy website created by fashion magazine goliath Condé Nast, paid Scott Schuman, The Sartorialist, to shoot editors and buyers outside the fashion week events in Milan and Paris. Street style had entered into new terrain. Though Schuman had shot at fashion weeks previously, it was a small part of his larger street style practice, which primarily revolved around combing the streets of Lower Manhattan. When Style.com got involved, fashion week style became a substantially bigger component of his street style portfolio. Soon Schuman was shooting for Style.com regularly, traveling from fashion week to fashion week, until he landed a monthly feature in the men's fashion publication *GQ*, also owned by Condé Nast. Budding street style photographer Tommy Ton, already shooting outside fashion weeks himself, and amassing a significant following for his blog Jak & Jil, stepped in to fill Schuman's Style.com shoes. That same year, 2009, Schuman released his first book, sharing the name of his blog, through Penguin Books. It did well, and Schuman released a follow up book in 2012. Both books featured a range of subjects, from Lower East side skateboarders to noted menswear designers. But the obvious stars of the book, and the ones who got the most attention, were industry insiders – whether unknown editors or celebrated menswear tailors. Schuman's work made street style stars out of hard-working industry folks, who had once kept a relatively low profile.

The message to the street style blogosphere was clear: If you want to be a big deal, get the fashion industry to pay attention to you, and get magazines to buy your work, start shooting outside runway events. Make your subjects people with influence within the industry. Numerous photographers heeded the call, from

Phil Oh of Street Peeper to Tamu McPherson of All the Pretty Birds. By 2012, many street style photographers were shooting fashion weeks as their primary venues (Yarhi 2012: WP6). The sidewalks outside fashion shows were crowded with photographers, whom Mary Fellowes of UK *Vogue* dubbed 'bloggerazzi' (Safe 2012: 12). And they were also crowded with other fashion bloggers and wannabe style stars, hoping to be shot by up-and-coming street style bloggers. 'Bloggers and photographers', wrote David Yi for *The New York Times* 'camp[ed] around [the fashion week main venue of] Lincoln Center' (Yi 2012: 4), scouting for style, shooting the latest looks before they hit the stores. Yvan Rodic summed up this change when he told Rohaizatul Azhar of *The Straits Times*, '[Street style] used to be a romantic idea – you walk around the streets and find a stylish subject by chance. And it can take days before you get to shoot someone. These days, it's more like speed dating. You just need to camp outside some Fashion Week venue; everyone wants to be photographed' (Azhar 2013).

'Street style' in much of the blogosphere today has become a synonym for 'street fashion', perhaps even, suggests Sinding of Le 21ème, 'off-runway fashion'. 'Street' is still an important conceptual element of these bloggers' work, but the question remains: Just what is 'the street' of street style today? Is it the concrete runway? The circus outside fashion shows (see Chapter 6)? Is it the chance encounter between a famous model and a wannabe-famous blogger? Is it the faint promise of ground-level authenticity buried beneath the artifice of the fashion industry? Or is it just another form of artifice, contrived to hock ready-to-wear to a growing online audience?

These are not mutually exclusive categories, and I would suggest that 'street' now means 'all of the above'. The tensions between the historically accumulated meanings of 'the street', documented in this chapter, are all still evident in street style photography. None has become truly dominant over the others, and none has completely erased the others as it gains salience. What we see in street style photography, instead, is an ongoing struggle between contradictory and overlapping meanings: the street as a space of movement and flow, a place to see and be seen; the street as an ordinary pedestrian reality, and a hard scientific 'fact'; the street as a romantic ideal, a bubbling cauldron of creativity; the street as the last vestige of authenticity in a commodified culture; and the street as the stage on which that very commodified culture performs some of its most ostentatious displays. The 'street' of 'street style photography', that is, is no static thing. It doesn't just stand there posing like an aspiring street style star waiting to be photographed by Sinding or Schuman. It is continually made and remade through the practice of photography. The next few chapters explore that practice in greater depth, beginning with a survey of street style bloggers from around the world who helped make street style – intentionally or not – into a fashion industry phenomenon. I will then move on to recount my own experience of becoming a street style blogger.

2 TRAVELLING THE STREET STYLE BLOGOSPHERE: AMATEUR ANTHROPOLOGY FROM AROUND THE GLOBE

FIGURE 2.1 Eetu, Helsinki, Finland. Photo by Liisa Jokinen.

Helsinki, Finland

'People watching has always been my obsession and my hobby', Liisa Jokinen told me, as we chatted in June of 2012 via the voice-over-internet protocol of Skype. 'I've always been interested in peoples' clothes, why [they] wear certain things, and the reason behind their outfits, what kinds of stories [go into them]. So it was kind of natural to start also taking pictures of those people.' At first, she says, she took pictures of her subjects on the sly, capturing other people's sartorial idiosyncrasies when they weren't paying attention. It was like a hidden vice, a quirk of her otherwise ordinary life. She would keep the photos for herself as a source of inspiration and amusement. But beginning in 2005, Jokinen started to bring her hobby out into the open.

She was at the Accelerator music festival in Stockholm, Sweden, with her partner Sampo Karjalainen, and 'it was crowded with really good-looking people'. Jokinen found herself wishing she had brought her camera with her. This was, after all, still a few years before smartphones were the baseline of telecommunication. Bringing a camera along still had to occur to someone beforehand. But then, on the second day of the festival, Jokinen had a realization: 'The Swedes were really not all that interesting [anyway]. They were more into fashion than individual styles, were sharing the same rules [of] what looks good and what does not. It somehow started to seem a bit boring.' What she really wanted to capture, she realized, was something 'more colourful', more 'crazy and individual', like those images of Harajuku kids in school girl skirts and pink pigtails that photographer Shoichi Aoki had made famous through his magazine, and subsequent book, *FRUiTS*, just a few years before. Jokinen was a big fan of Aoki. She appreciated his eye for oddball individualism. She too wanted to attest to the playfulness and possibilities of style. And what better place to do that, she figured, than her own hometown of Helsinki, Finland.

Helsinki, explained Jokinen, has 'a strong punk rocker culture'. It's got 'heavy metal rockers, and gothic style. And you can see a strong influence from Japan [there as well]'. Situated at the crossroads of Scandinavia and Eastern Europe but removed by water from the mainland of each, it has evolved its own stylistic sensibility out of other peoples' subcultural pasts. 'All the trends have come very slowly to Finland', Jokinen said. There are 'many Lolita girls still in Helsinki', long after the elaborate, Victorian-influenced outfits went out of style elsewhere. But it is not as if people in Helsinki are stuck in some narrow, outdated conception of urban cosmopolitanism. In Helsinki, said Jokinen, 'You can wear what you want.' There are 'many people who are really into fashion', but there are also 'other subcultures' with their own stylistic points of view (see Figures 2.1–2.4). 'That's something special that we still have.'

FIGURE 2.2 Karoliina, Helsinki, Finland. Photo by Liisa Jokinen.

So after returning from Stockholm, she and Karjalainen took to the streets of Helsinki, digital single lens reflex (DSLR) camera in hand, looking for people to stop and photograph. Their shots were posed but straightforward, naturalistic in their artifice (see Chapter 1). Jokinen didn't have any formal training in photography or much experience using an SLR camera, but her photographs didn't really require it, and Karjalainen showed her the basics of shutter speed and aperture in any case. The rest she learned from experience. And she has, in fact, had a lot of experience since then. Karjalainen and Jokinen launched Hel Looks (www.hel-looks.com), their own photo-based weblog devoted to documenting the everyday styles of people on the streets of Helsinki on 16 July 2005. The term 'street style blog' had not yet been invented. Karjalainen handled the backend. Jokinen took most of the pictures. It was meant to be just for fun, Jokinen claimed, just a new extension of her people-watching hobby into the digital realm, but it soon became something more.

When they had ten or twenty pictures posted on the site, Jokinen and Karjalainen started sending out links to it to their friends. One of those friends, in turn, passed on the link to one of his friends, Cory Doctorow, a tech journalist and one of the founders of Boing Boing (www.boingboing.net), a website devoted to geek curiosities and technology news. Boing Boing just happened to be one of the most popular websites anywhere at the time. Doctorow then posted a link to Hel Looks on Boing Boing. 'Finnish kids are actually a pretty well-dressed lot', he wrote in the post, 'and don't seem to dress in highly stylized flocks.' It was a simple enough statement and hardly a ringing endorsement, but it sent droves of readers to Jokinen and Karjalainen's newborn site. Hel Looks immediately took off. 'It took only a couple of days', recalled Jokinen, 'and we had many, like tens of thousands of visitors.' Their readership has stayed pretty consistent since then, around 6,000–12,000 pageviews per day.

Jokinen and Karjalainen are not interested in growing the site any further than that. They call it a 'slow blog' on account of the measured steady pace they have maintained with it after all these years. They shoot in their spare time, post once a week, refuse to give in to pressure to accelerate or expand. Besides, they have already achieved all they wanted to with the blog. They have used it to feed Jokinen's passion for people watching and demonstrate Karjalainen's acumen for web design. They have used it to launch their respective careers in the Helsinki fashion and software scenes. Jokinen now does freelance writing and styling for a number of Finnish publications. Karjalainen works as a product designer at Facebook. What's more, they have used the blog to help put their hometown of Helsinki, Finland, on the global fashion map, drawing the eyes of the style cognoscenti to a region of the world they had previously ignored.

FIGURE 2.3 Atte, Helsinki, Finland. Photo by Liisa Jokinen.

FIGURE 2.4 Mariannlinn, Helsinki, Finland. Photo by Liisa Jokinen.

The insularity of the fashion world

Fashion may be a global industry, but it is also a remarkably insular one. Its creative production is centred around a few select cities – London, Paris, New York, Milan, and, more recently, Tokyo (Gilbert 2006: 4). These cities have become so identified with fashion, so intimately sewn into the fabric of fashion, as to have become 'transparent sign[s], only noticed when disrupted' (Gilbert 2006: 4). It is in these cities where fashion is almost universally imagined to take place, on the narrow medieval alleyways of Milan, down the grand boulevards of Paris, beneath the gothic highrises of New York City. This, despite the fact that such cities are less and less frequently the places where the garments of the fashion industry are actually manufactured. Fashion, these days, is made in the 'third world', but it is dreamed up in London, New York, Paris, Milan, and Tokyo.

Fashion magazines, for their part, have tended to support the dominance of fashion's world cities. They compose vivid hagiographies of Milanese designers, praise the innovativeness of Japanese couture, effuse about the effortless chic of Paris. When somewhere outside of these places is depicted, it is usually for its exotic value, its symbolic otherness, a set of signs worn on Western garments as a kind of embellishment or flair. Fashion magazines have become, in other words, something like the ideological arm of the established fashion world, justifying its emphases, making its focus on fashion's world cities seem natural and inevitable. They reinforce the global status quo, representing an entrenched elite of designers, models, stars, editors, and photographers, and acting as if they are all we ever wanted to see in the first place.

Enter street style photography. When it first began appearing in fashion magazines in the early 1980s (see last chapter), its focus was on the quotidian, the everyday, on what pedestrians on the backstreets were wearing, even if those backstreets remained firmly housed in the usual fashion capitals of New York, Milan, Paris, and London. Street style became a window from within the industry into a world beyond its own. There was no doubt something voyeuristic about street style photography, but there was also something empowering. People without industry credentials were being granted the elusive quality of 'cool'. You didn't have to be a fashion model to be noticed by a street style photographer. You didn't have to be beautiful with flawless skin and the body dimensions of a mannequin. You just had to have *something*, some indefinable spark or energy that could be translated to film (see Chapter 3). It should come as no surprise, then, that starting in the mid-2000s, amateur photographers from cities well off the fashion map would use the street style model as a way of drawing attention to the unique creative contributions of their own home cities. Street style bloggers documented styles that the industry was indifferent to or unaware of, and in doing so, they expanded its narrow scope and insular gaze. Street style blogs drew the eyes of the industry – at least temporarily – into unforeseen directions.

In this, the role of street style bloggers within the fashion industry has been not unlike that of anthropologists within the social sciences. Ask the average undergraduate student what the difference is between sociology and anthropology, and after perhaps, a little hemming and hawing, they are likely to come up with something like the following answer: sociology studies people in the industrialized West, and anthropology studies everyone else. Fair enough. For the first hundred or so years of the two disciplines' intertwined histories, this division remained more or less intact. While sociologists sought out those social universals, capable of making sense of the entrenched inequalities, tensions, and power relationships of advanced capitalist systems, anthropologists travelled to far off lands in search of exceptions to those universals. Where sociology studied the large-scale, anthropologists focused on the small. When sociologists took on European Protestantism, anthropologists took on Azande witchcraft.

Things, of course, have gotten more complicated in recent decades. Plenty of anthropologists now focus their critical lenses on their own societies, and sociologists do work far beyond the traditional confines of the Western world. Nonetheless, something of the original inclinations of both disciplines remains in place. Anthropologists continue to pride ourselves on speaking for those left out of the conversation, championing the people on the margins, and offering up critiques of Western thought (Clifford and Marcus 1986), based on the diverse worldviews, beliefs, and practices of those populations unaccounted for in the mainstream of social science.

This chapter is about street style bloggers on the frontiers of the fashion industry. It features full-body portraits by street style bloggers based in cities as far afield as Buenos Aires, Argentina, Beijing, China, and Cape Town, South Africa, as well as the personal stories of those amateur anthropologists who took them. You can see this chapter as a curated collection of street style anthropology in all its lived diversity and idiosyncrasy. Or you can see it as a mash up of various bloggers' stories and experiences. There are overlaps between these stories, common themes and elements that emerge, just as there are commonalities in the images these bloggers produce. But they do not match up entirely, and the bloggers featured here do not necessarily represent the 'typical' stories of one class or variety of people. Like the subjects of their photos, many street style bloggers refuse to succumb to type (see Chapter 4).

Rather than categorize street style photographers popping up in cities throughout the world in the standard typologies of the social sciences, imposing categories from above, I have attempted here to use the photographers'/bloggers' own words to tell their stories. In this, I follow the lead of Bruno Latour (2005), Tim Ingold (2013), Stephen Tyler (1986), and many other proponents of a cooperative, nonhierarchical model of ethnographic fieldwork (Pink 2006), wherein the interlocutors of social science are elevated from the domain of 'subjects' to that of 'collaborators'. I do not presume to know better than the bloggers featured here the meaning and significance of the work they do. Nor do I weave their stories together into some convenient common narrative. There is no narrative here or at least no single narrative. There are only overlapping and intersecting ones. The effect is no doubt somewhat disjointed. It is meant to be. Otherwise each blogger's voice would be subsumed into my voice, a top-down dictation overriding whatever individual messages would be embedded in each section. I would prefer each section to retain a certain autonomy. I do, however, offer some further clarification and extrapolation, and piece together these stories into something of a loose montage. I hope this isn't already too much interference.

Buenos Aires, Argentina

Javi Obando and Flora Grzetic are not all that interested in 'fashion'. Sure, they run a modelling agency, Crudo, based on their popular street style blog On The Corner (onthecornerstreetstyle.blogspot.com), and sure, they work with plenty of fashion companies, shooting ad campaigns, supplying talent, lending their own distinctive brand of urban edge to their clients' products. But it is not *fashion* per se that interests them. Fashion is just not that *interesting*. It is a business, an industry, a commodity-producing enterprise that runs on contrived novelty. As the duo behind Latin America's best-known and longest running street style blog, Obando and Grzetic get their share of invites to fashion events, and they go to some of them, when they must. 'We do go to Buenos Aires Fashion Week', Obando told me, as an example. In fact, it is Buenos Aires Fashion Week where the two of them got the idea for their blog in the first place.

'Flora and myself met at Palermo University', Obando explained. 'I am from Ecuador, and she is from a place called Rio Gallegos in the extreme south of Argentinian Patagonia. We both came to Buenos Aires for our studies, and as foreigners – or at least people who did not grow up in the city – people caught our attention, the way they dressed, the costumes that they wore. We were finishing our studies, and neither of us wanted to work at an agency. I was working already with internet stuff. She was working with fashion, and we were working together at [Buenos Aires] Fashion Week, and we thought, "Ok, we can take pictures of these people and maybe sell them to some magazines or something."' That was 2007. They started On The Corner shortly thereafter.

'But every time we go [to Buenos Aires Fashion Week]', Obando confessed, 'it's more boring for us. It's the same people. They are all very dressed up for the occasion. [But] we don't want to [capture] people all dressed up for the occasion. That's why we don't go to bars or parties or places like that [to shoot]. We try to get people in their quotidian life. We try to get you going to buy bread.' It is this basic impulse, to capture the everyday, to portray something meaningful about a person

FIGURE 2.5 Andrea, Buenos Aires. Photo by Javi Obando.

FIGURE 2.6 Gabriel, Buenos Aires. Photo by Javi Obando.

in those moments when they are not consciously constructing meaning at all, that Obando and Grzetic share with anthropologists.

'We've always wanted to believe that we are on the opposite side of the world of fashion', Obando explained. 'Even though we are part of the fashion scene here, we are trying to rescue *style* from *fashion*' [emphasis mine]. 'Style', he went on – reinforcing a longstanding conceptual divide in Fashion Studies between 'fashion', or the relentless cycle of planned obsolescence intrinsic to the mass selling of garments (Pink 2006), and 'style', the expression of personal or group identity through choices of dress (Lipovetsky 2002) – is about 'trying to be original, trying to be yourself, instead of following this trend we all know.'

The main idea of On The Corner, he went on, is 'to show anonymous people the way they dress'. There are no celebrities on their blog. There is no conscious attention to spectacle or fad. What there is instead is a continual attentiveness to the irreducibility of the individual – the uniqueness of a single person in a single place at a particular moment in time (see Chapter 4). For Obando and Grzetic, being 'cool' and being 'yourself' are one and the same thing.

Not that Obando and Grzetic photograph just any old person they come across. Of course not. That wouldn't be street style; it would be documentary (Polhemus 1978). A good street style photographer doesn't just produce images; she curates them. 'We take the time to go out looking for someone special', Obando said, every day, when time allows, combing the streets for a couple of hours at a time. And it is their ability to find those special individuals that has made Crudo sought-after as a modelling agency. Rather than look for exemplars of international trends, Obando and Grzetic focus on those distinctive styles one can only find in Buenos Aires. 'And what is it?' I pursued further, 'that makes Buenos Aires [style] unique?'

'At some point in the middle of the last century', Obando explained, 'Buenos Aires was a rich and kind of important city. But now it's not anymore. It's like an old lady, who once was a millionaire, but now that her husband died, tries to be in high society but can't. So I believe that there is a kind of heritage from that time that lives on in porteños [residents of Buenos Aires, a port city], something that their grandfathers and grandmothers once had, and now they try to keep alive. Young people have to be very creative to do so. They don't have Chanel stores. The only kinds of luxury brands that we find on the streets are ones our grandmothers bought back from a trip, or which we found at the Salvation Army. I always like the creativity of porteños, the way they mix old luxury garments with bad quality, new stuff from China or somewhere.'

Obando's photos portray this creative, stylistic bricolage (Luvaas 2010; Polhemus 1996) in characteristically austere fashion. Their subjects stand in the middle of the frame, sometimes smiling, sometimes scowling, sometimes with no discernible expression on their faces in the grand tradition of social documentary photography (see previous chapter). The backdrops are carefully chosen, an intersection, perhaps, with a decaying nineteenth century apartment building in

FIGURE 2.7 Lian, Buenos Aires, Argentina. Photo by Javi Obando.

FIGURE 2.8 Belu, Buenos Aires. Photo by Javi Obando.

FIGURE 2.9 Fernando and Jasmine, Buenos Aires. Photo by Javi Obando.

the background, a parking garage, or a wall covered with graffiti, or even more typically, directly in the middle of the street, whether concrete or cobblestone, at a calm moment when no traffic zooms past (see figures 2.5 to 2.9). There is something eerie about such pictures, as if Buenos Aires, where, Obando says, 'everyone is in a hurry', had just for a moment come to a standstill. And in a sense it had, a moment of its light captured on the surface of the digital sensor of Obando's Canon 5D. Looking through these images, it is hard not to feel that one is learning something meaningful about Buenos Aires – its mood, its flavour, its clash of European and indigenous elements, its grubby, stubborn idiosyncrasy – that one is peering into a world not ordinarily visible to us.

Taiwan, Hong Kong, Tokyo, Seoul, Bangkok

Obando and Grzetic's photo-documentation of Buenos Aires comes from a conceptual space quite familiar to anthropologists – that of the outsider looking in. Ours is a discipline of the displaced. We do our work as academics living in temporary, self-imposed exile in the hopes that such a vantage point may lend us the ability to see those things that are too habituated and too normalized to stand out to people actually from the place in question. Though neither travelled a great distance to reach Buenos Aires, their position as outsiders nonetheless informs every aspect of their work. They *notice* those individuals who break type, defy conventions, and set trends rather than follow them. And they *notice* those unique details of porteño culture that locals simply take for granted. Such is the advantage that being an outsider can afford, and it is one that James Bent, a self-described 'conservative Englishman' living in Singapore, knows all too well.

'We [my wife Stacey and I – also a blogger for Style Sophomore at www.stylesophomore.com], lived in Australia and New Zealand before [coming to Singapore]', he told me, 'and I try to think back now to what Australia was like in terms of what people wore, and I have absolutely no idea. I just didn't look. It's not something you really consider until you start consciously looking at it.' For a street style blogger, 'consciously looking' is key. And it takes time, Bent explained, at least two weeks of sustained effort in each new place he visits. It must be cultivated, honed, and developed like any other skill (see next chapter). Bent started cultivating it himself back in 2010, after accepting a position as a business consultant for an Australian enterprise software company and moving to Singapore. His business was mostly elsewhere, and there was no real need for him to stay in one location, so he and his wife took to taking long sojourns to other countries in the region, snapping photos of people on the streets and posting them

FIGURE 2.10 Red, Tapei. Photo by James Bent.

on their respective blogs (see figures 2.10 to 2.14). He named his blog La Mode Outré (lamodeoutre.com), or 'fashion also', as a nod to Asia's place outside the conventional limits of the fashion industry. He has recently rebranded it as 'Asian Street Fashion', now that he has produced a book of street styles images of the same name for the British publisher Thames & Hudson.

'I came into it from a totally non-fashion perspective', said Bent, echoing the sentiments of Obando and Grzetic. 'I studied English and Creative Studies at University, and I was using pictures of people to create characters for short stories. I was finding these pictures off the internet, like through Google searches, and it was just getting difficult to keep finding pictures. So I went into a bookshop, hoping to find a book that was just of regular, modern people, and I came across The Sartorialist's book, without knowing anything about it or anything about street style, and it was just perfect. 500 pages of pictures of what I thought were pretty, not perhaps "regular" people, but people who would make for good characters. And then about three months later when we shipped up to Singapore, Stacey [my wife] suggested to me, "Why don't you just go out and take your own pictures to write your stories from?" So I did that, and straightaway I went from having a website that I put the stories up on that was getting like ten hits a day that basically nobody wanted to read it, to suddenly getting maybe two, three, or four hundred people a day looking at them. I was like, forget the stories! Besides, this was around three and a half years ago when street style really started to take off, when The Sartorialist and Face Hunter had just done their books, and so I realized that it's the photographs that are the popular things. It just kind of grew from there. I'd say it took a good couple of years to really get my head around it.'

In a sense, he is still 'getting [his] head around it'. Street style has been a long strange journey for Bent, one intertwined with other, much more literal journeys. 'Considering your background in fiction', I asked him at this point in our conversation, 'do you find yourself interested in the stories behind the people you shoot? Do you get into conversations with them?'

Bent considered for a moment before answering, then responded: 'Well actually, you know, sure. It's nice if you can chat with someone, although half the time we just can't speak the same language, so that [doesn't] happen. Right from the start, I realized that what I'm interested in is more the sense of character that these photos show than the stories behind the people in them. I realized that street fashion photography is just not the right forum for getting into their story. It is what it is, and I don't want to dress it up too much more than that.'

And what it is for Bent is a sort of street style travelogue, a document of the persistent differences between places and his own encounters with them. He has to train his eye for each new city he visits, he told me, taking time to 'go and sit and just look at what people are wearing and try to get a feel for what you can and can't see there'. It can take a couple of weeks, he said. 'But even after

FIGURE 2.11 Ted, Hong Kong. Photo by James Bent.

three months, I think there's always going to be something new and something different to see.' Plus, there is no way to simply sit idly, he explained, like a stone in a stream, and just watch the styles float past. His own perspective is also continually shifting, drawing his eyes in new and different directions. 'There are things that I might have photographed two years ago that I wouldn't photograph now', he said, 'or that I'm no longer interested in. So it's not just how long it takes you to figure out what's on the street, but it's also about how you grow as a person.' What he has found is that, 'every city [he visits] is interesting and exciting for different reasons. Even Singapore, which sometimes we can criticize quite heavily for being a little boring or lacking culture or being centred around the business world, it's still a fascinating place. You walk around the streets and there's a real mash of culture.' That mash of culture is evident in his pictures, a mix of blasé alternative styles from the west with a brand awareness and nouveau riche sensibility commensurate with Singapore's hard-won place as an Asian Tiger economy.

But if it's 'Fashion' with a capital 'F' that you're looking for, said Bent, there are really only two destinations in Asia: Tokyo (Japan) and Seoul (South Korea). Both have seen an exponential growth in their fashion industries in recent years, and this growth is evident in the creativity and diversity one sees in the looks on the streets there. Bent had been documenting them with a kind of passionate fervour for the past eighteen months before I spoke with him, going out to shoot practically every day. And he hasn't been alone. These days, where there is fashion, there are street style bloggers to document it.

'Korea [in particular] is a fascinating place to me', said Bent. 'We went there twelve months ago, and it was really difficult to communicate with people. We'd go up to people and ask for their photo. I'd have it on my iPad, and I'd just ask in English and show them that, and they'd just run away or laugh. To some extent they just didn't get it. Whereas now, [only] twelve months later, it's gone crazy. There are so many people doing street fashion there. You know, you walk through parts of Korea and there are like fifty or sixty photographers on the street, and if someone fashionable is walking down the street, then they're going to spend two hours getting photographed by everyone. It's only when you go to the smaller places like Singapore, or even Hong Kong, or say Thailand or somewhere, where people are a bit shy. But I don't know. It's actually really fascinating to me how people everywhere now seem to get the whole thing. It's like an international thing of "Can I take your photograph?" And to be honest I still find it amazing that people, complete strangers, will let you walk up to them and take their photograph. I actually find that in some way quite nuts. And it's amazing how easy it is. It's almost stupidly easy.'

Even in Kuala Lumpur, where the women often dress modestly in Muslim headscarves and maxi-dresses, posing for pictures has become as natural as chatting with a friend or stopping for a spot of tea. Bent's website is a compendium of Asian

FIGURE 2.12 Mika, Tokyo. Photo by James Bent.

FIGURE 2.13 Novo, Seoul. Photo by James Bent.

FIGURE 2.14 Matina, Bangkok. Photo by James Bent

style today: young Korean men with slicked back hair and long, androgynous black shirts and skirts Harajuku girls in bright floral print and eight-inch heels, and scruffy long-haired Malay guys in tank tops and cut-offs. The backdrops in Bent's pictures are varied but nondescript, vaguely urban locales that could be just about anywhere. But the styles in them are unmistakable. When one gets accustomed to looking at them, it is easy to guess where each individual is from, their city's unique stylistic mood impressed upon them like a tight-fitting T-shirt.

Beijing, China

It has never been James Bents' intention to focus his blog on the cultural differences between places. That has happened as something of an accident of his shooting. His photos document such differences with or without his conscious intent. Bent is quite clear that he documents simply what interests him, with full awareness that his perspective sharply influences what he finds.

'I think who I am and where I'm from has a big bearing on what I do', he told me. 'I don't go to Japan and think, "Right, I'm in Japan, so I want to photograph someone in a kimono." Although, interestingly, now that I'm back in Singapore [after a number of months travelling through Japan, Korea, and elsewhere] I do think it would be interesting to look more at the cultural aspects of this place and take photographs focused on the more cultural stuff that you really can't find unless you come to these particular countries. But up until now it's been very much about going somewhere and looking for the things that are pleasing to my eye, irrespective of where I am.'

For Nels Frye, however, the US expatriate and also former business consultant behind China's biggest street style blog, Stylites (www.stylites.net), chronicling local style with all of its nuances and flavours, has been the intention almost right from the start (see figures 2.15 to 2.19). 'It started out quite accidentally', Frye explained to me. 'It was really more of a personal blog.' He was shooting the quirky looks and sundry curiosities he found on the streets of Beijing largely for the amusement of his friends and family back home.

'And then, very soon after I started doing it, one of the local English magazines asked that I start contributing street style pictures for them.' They wanted work that showcased Beijing's emergent style, emphasizing its fashionableness, its capacity to hold its own in the international arena. 'And that's really what did it', he went on, 'because I hadn't necessarily intended to make it into such a big thing. But with the pressure coming from the publication deadline I was sort of forced to generate more content, and that's how it developed.' Like Obando and Grzetic, Frye started his blog in 2007. It was a good year to be a street style blogger. Street style blogs were just getting popular and yet there was still relatively little competition among bloggers, particularly in China. 'The blog, as its own address',

FIGURE 2.15 Fashion photographer Joy Island, Beijing. Photo by Nels Frye.

FIGURE 2.16 A couple on the streets of Beijing. Photo by Nels Frye.

he said, 'is sort of a dying form in China.' In fact, Frye went on to say, 'I don't know that [blogging] ever had its peak [here]. Nobody here has ever been in the habit of having their own URL and having a blog. I think there were more blogs associated with larger blogging platforms that were very successful [when I started], but [since then] everything has really transferred to Weibo (www.weibo.com)', the Chinese language social networking/micro-blogging platform often referred to as 'China's Twitter'. His uniquely carved-out niche gave Frye a significant voice in the budding fashion industry in Beijing, and he was soon invited to more events than he could manage to attend. 'I mean', he said, 'there's probably no other individual figure associated with it here aside from me.' Nonetheless, he admitted, his blog has probably always been more popular internationally, among the curious fashion set looking to find out what's going on in China, than among China's own population. 'Chinese people', he reiterated, just 'don't go to independent URL blogs.'

Frye's unique position, as a foreigner both to China and to fashion, operating 'in a sort of peripheral zone, which is neither/nor', framed his approach to street style photography, just as it has framed the perspective of generations of anthropologists. Street style photography was never an easy, obvious, or 'natural' thing to do for him. It required considerable thought and concentration to pull off. The simplest decision demanded forethought. Where, for instance, was one to even go to shoot street style photos in Beijing? 'When it started out', said Frye, 'I tried to go out just street combing, but that's just too time consuming, and maybe I'd get one person after four hours that I wanted to take a picture of. And the thing is, Beijing, you know, is not the Lower East Side [of Manhattan]. Beijing doesn't really have a place like the Lower East Side or Kreuzberg in Berlin. You don't have these walking areas, nearly so much in Beijing, not even compared with Shanghai, which has the French Concession. Beijing isn't really a walking city. There are some very touristy areas. But really, it's a driving city. People that have money drive.'

So in a sense, I suggested to him, '[street style] is already a misnomer [for what you do]. It's not on the street'.

'To some extent', Frye conceded. But, he went on, 'I shouldn't say that it's a complete misnomer. There are certain very small pockets where it exists. I think street style exists wherever stylish people walk. And there are certain pockets. I think in Beijing the place where you're most likely to see those people is Sanlitun, only because a major outdoor mall was constructed there. I don't even know if I would call that "street style".' 'The point is that', he continued with his explanation a bit later on in our conversation, 'the traditional conception of Beijing is as these islands of development – or I should say islands of affluence – separated by streams of undeveloped grunginess. And you would kind of jump from island to island.'

Shooting street style in Beijing, in other words, has made Frye keenly aware of the fact that street style, at least as it is popularly conceived, holds an implicit Western bias. It assumes a European-style pedestrian zone where fashionable people stroll. And it assumes a variety of conspicuous display that would enable a photographer to

FIGURE 2.17 Fashion designer Ivy Hu, Beijing. Photo by Nels Frye.

FIGURE 2.18 Chinese bass player, rock star and socialite Zhen Yang, Beijing. Photo by Nels Frye.

separate out the stylish wheat from the ho-hum chaff. Neither assumption necessarily holds true for Beijing. As with any street style blog, what Frye captures in his images is not just any old resident of Beijing. It is a very narrow slice of its population, a select few, who may very well be the fashion forebears for the rest of the city but also may very well not be. They may just be a niche group, running along a parallel course that will never quite intersect with or even make sense to most people. 'I think what I've captured on my blog', he said, 'is a segment that is rather distinctive to Beijing, a sort of bohemian group in a very broad sense.' 'I'm using the word "bohemian"', he clarified, 'in (way that) encompass(es) hipster and rock musician and even fashion types.' But defining them more precisely than that has its difficulties. Frye conceded that most of them come from relatively affluent backgrounds, and hence constitute something of an emergent elite, perhaps China's 'creative class' (Florida 2002) or 'new petite bourgeoisie' (Bourdieu 1984), but even that is a relatively hard thing to determine. 'There are some of them that might come from a less affluent background, no doubt', he told me. 'I think it's even more difficult to tell in China what kind of background somebody's from, in fact, than it is in other places. Sometimes you can judge it based on the way they speak and such. But remember, the Cultural Revolution screws everything up. And the fact that wealth is generally off the records makes it so that if you ask somebody what their parents do it isn't necessary going to give you a very good notion of whether they're affluent or not.'

'People both want to downplay and show off their affluence', he explained. This is especially true of the type of people Frye photographs. Although he concedes that some portion of his photographic subjects may be 'the artsy children of wealthy people', he shies away from shooting the indisputably rich. 'What we don't have [on the blog]', he said, 'is the sort of wealthy, luxury-brand-buying, brand-obsessed person, that has, without a doubt, money.' He is just not interested in them. Their taste is predictable. Their sensibility is garish. And they are usually safely tucked away behind the locked doors of automobiles anyway. He is more comfortable describing the subjects of his blog using a term borrowed from *New York Times* columnist David Brooks (Brooks 2000), 'bobos', or 'bourgeois bohemians'. He takes his pictures at fashion events, art events, and music festivals. He eschews the streets themselves in favour of places pre-selected by the stylish and the chic. 'I think the people that I photograph for my blog are inherently more aware', he said, comparing them to China's nouveau riche, 'a little more international, a little more savvy.' His blog, then, has served as something of a chronicle of the rise of this small but influential group in China. It documents, not just style on the streets of Beijing but the emergence of a new cultural sensibility, China's distinct brand of 'cool'. And as such, it should come as no surprise that Stylites has been of such interest to the Chinese fashion industry. It attests to the existence of a much sought after entity, that elusive, not-for-sale quality that lends international cachet to one's city, and which Beijing desperately needs if it wishes to convince the other, bigger players in the fashion industry that it can play the game too (see also Zhao 2013).

FIGURE 2.19 A stylist at Bazaar, Beijing. Photo by Nels Frye.

Cape Town, South Africa

While Nels Frye's Stylites blog chronicles the rise of a very specific socio-cultural category in China, Michelle Oberholzer's Cinder & Skylark testifies instead to the sheer diversity of stylistic perspectives and possibilities in a single locale, her hometown of Cape Town, South Africa (see figures 2.20 to 2.23). Oberholzer takes a decidedly ecumenical approach to street style photography. 'I love interacting with different people on the street', she told me. 'The cultures in South Africa are so diverse, and there are such diverse people that I come across all the time … that I discovered after I started [doing this] how interested I am in people.'

On any given week, her blog might feature a blonde woman in a straw hat and black dress, a dapper black gentleman in a bow tie and tailored jacket, an Asian woman in a Che Guevara T-shirt, military fatigues, and short floral shorts, and a dark-skinned hip-hop head in kente cloth and camouflage. No doubt, she admits, there is an observable bias on her blog towards casual dress. But that is largely a function of where and how she shoots, she explained.

'Cape Town is the kind of place where a lot of people just get in their cars and drive', Oberholzer told me. 'They'll leave home, get out at point B, and just get straight back in [their cars] and go home, so I do know that there's a huge part of the population that I never see on the streets. And I wanted to keep my blog very authentically "street", so I don't really like going to big places like malls, where there's a different kind of person going out, because to me that's not true street. Cape Town is definitely not like it is in European cities, and American cities, where there's a lot of people walking on the street all the time, so the kind of people I meet on the street tend to be quite young. They tend to be using public transport. So what I photograph is usually quite casual.'

Unfortunately, Oberholzer admitted, this tends to give people the false impression that this kind of style, locked in an older conception of 'street' (see the previous chapter), is all that Oberholzer is interested in. In her words: 'I think a lot of people have the perspective that that's [a reflection of] my style. That that's what I want to photograph. Whereas [in fact], I love diversity, so if there [were] more diversities available on the street, I would be photographing [them].' But the streets of Cape Town, as with streets the world over, yield their own processes of self-selection. Not just everyone is out 'on the street' parading their style for all to see. It is the cool kids and the hipsters, the dapper dandies and the stylites, those who want to be seen, noticed, observed. And with Beijing, it tends not to be the truly wealthy out and about, showing their stuff. They are locked away behind the tinted glass of automobiles. And it's not the working poor, who have to spend their days earning a living. No, as anthropologist Ted Polhemus has claimed, fashion is for those people 'in between' categories (Polhemus 1978), for the upwardly mobile, the young and transitioning. It is for those people obsessed with self-invention,

FIGURE 2.20 Yolisa, Cape Town, South Africa. Photo by Michelle Oberholzer.

FIGURE 2.21 Nhuthuka, Cape Town, South Africa. Photo by Michelle Oberholzer.

FIGURE 2.22 Pfano, Cape Town, South Africa. Photo by Michelle Oberholzer.

FIGURE 2.23 Lindi, Cape Town, South Africa. Photo by Michelle Oberholzer.

who use their clothes as testimony to their own creative potential, and by proxy, their city's creative potential.

'I really respond to the individuals I meet', said Oberholzer. 'And having a great love for style, as opposed to trends, or fashion, or what's on the catwalk, I love seeing how people interpret their own way of dressing. And [I say that as someone who has] a diploma in fashion design. [Street photography took] my love of fashion and it brought it closer to who I am as a person.' She has found it the most creatively fulfilling thing she has done so far in her life, and this after thirty-odd years of searching for something that would be the right fit.

'I would say [that] deep down inside I'm a creative', she said. 'I've been creative since I was a small child, always painting and drawing and knitting and crocheting and making things, and exploring different ways of being creative. And over years of trying different things and enjoying some of them more, some of them less, I never really found something I could actually continue doing without getting bored, until I started [doing] street photography. With street photography, from the very first day I just loved it. The very first day I went out, I was very insecure about it. I didn't even know how to use a camera or anything. [But] when I got home I [realized], "Whoa! I really really love doing this." It was quite a surprise to me.'

It is interesting, I would add, that Oberholzer has found her own creative outlet in documenting other peoples' creative expression. And it is worth pointing out at this juncture too, if it were not already clear, that street style photography is creative, not just in terms of how one composes a shot or uses various photographic techniques but in terms of choosing whom to identify and represent on one's blog in the first place. Oberholzer's choice of subjects has become testimony to her own style and taste. It as if she were displaying the divergent aspects of her own self on the blog. Cape Town has become Oberholzer's canvas, and on it she has pasted hundreds of distinct images of her own intricate self-portrait.

Athens, Greece, Los Angeles, California

Alkistis Tsitouri doesn't know how to describe Athens style, but she 'can recognize it from miles away'. It has something distinctive about it, she told me, that she and her friend Aris Karatarakis weren't seeing on other blogs when they started their own, Streetgeist (streetgeist.com), back in 2008 (see figures 2.24 and 2.25). 'Nobody was doing [Athens]', she said. She and Karatarakis recognized an opportunity, both to occupy a vacant niche, and to help put Athens, Greece on the fashion map. 'We thought there were many interesting stylish people out there, and we felt that we could do it nicely', she said. 'So we did it.' Seven years later, as I was putting the finishing touches on this book, they were still doing it, Tsitouri the photographs and Karatarakis the site design and management. Their audience has grown considerably since then, from a few

FIGURE 2.24 Dafni, Athens, Greece. Photo by Alkistis Tsitouri (www.streetgeist.com)

dozen pageviews a day to hundreds, and they have had numerous opportunities made available to them in the process, from small ad campaigns, to freelance deals. They are not, however, any closer to pinpointing what it is that makes Athens style Athens' style.

'Athens has good taste', Tsitouri explained. 'The people I photograph, the ones who are actually making the effort, are very [well-dressed].' But for a more precise depiction of Athenian style you would have to look at her pictures, posted once a week at www.streetgeist.com. It is a simple website. Like Hel Looks, it is minimalist in design, with little text and few ads to distract the reader's eyes. The background is plain white. The script is bold black. 'We don't want to take away from the pictures with any text', Tsitouri told me. '[So] it's very clean.' Each subject is depicted as close to the centre of the frame as possible, arms at her side, no evident expression on her face. A street, staircase, or sidewalk leads to a clear vanishing point behind. The overall feeling is naturalistic and unpretentious, reflecting the Western ideal of realism as closely as any portrait could (see Scott 2007; Sontag 1973). 'Here is a person in an everyday outfit', her images seem to say, 'make of it what you will'. 'Unlike fashion photography', where 'everything is set up in advance [and] staged', Tsitouri said, her own photography 'is very much a matter of [going] out into the world and hunt[ing] for the right person, the right moment, the right light.' Like the Parisian street photography of Henri Cartier-Bresson, her photos are a product of the chance encounter (see Scott 2007; Westerbeck and Meyerowitz 1994). They freeze a random instant into a meaningful moment (Scott 2007: 43), capturing one individual's fashion sensibility at one specific juncture in her life. To look through her images of the last several years is to sift through the subtle shifts in sensibility that have animated Athenian fashion more generally. It is hard not to ponder those shifts, to add one's own insight and experience to the photos, as if they tell us something meaningful about the larger shifts in consciousness, culture, and context that we are all undergoing.

Between October 2008 and May 2010, Tsitouri and Karatarakis posted, in the blog standard of reverse chronological order, close to a hundred images of Athenian men and women 'on the street' as they went about their daily lives. They were posed in the same way, shot from the same perspective, presented in the same tidy trope of photographic realism. There were women with carefully coiffed hair, men with intricately groomed beards. There were military epaulets on structured trenches, blouses that extended off the shoulders like unfurling flowers. There is no one consistent theme or trend to these images, no dominant look or style, only a record of Athenian stylistic diversity as perceived by Tsitouri. Tsitouri feels no need to assign any specific attributes to these looks. She can see what makes Athenian style Athenian, even if she cannot quite articulate it. That is enough for her. But she, like any other street style photographer, hopes that by photographing that thing, whatever it is, 'the viewer can recognize it [as well]'. Especially now that she is no longer shooting in Athens.

FIGURE 2.25 Jim, Athens, Greece. Photo by Alkistis Tsitouri (www.streetgeist.com).

FIGURE 2.26 Zoe, Los Angeles, California. Photo by Alkistis Tsitouri (www.streetgeist.com).

FIGURE 2.27 Kooly, Los Angeles, California. Photo by Alkistis Tsitouri (www.streetgeist. com).

In late 2010, Alkistis Tsitouri relocated 6,989 miles away to Southern California to be with her new husband. These days she shoots primarily in Los Angeles, West Hollywood, and Santa Monica, very different cities from Athens with a very different stylistic sensibility (see figures 2.26 and 2.27). In Tsitouri's words, 'The first shock I had [upon moving to Los Angeles] is how people can wear the same clothes all year round. I don't like that. For me flip flops are for the ocean – for a day at the beach or maybe if you're running errands and don't go far from your house. But that's it. I was surprised by how casual everyone dresses. Here in LA, it's very very very casual. There's nothing wrong with that. That's just how it is.'

The other thing Tsitouri notices about L.A. fashion is the lack of layering in peoples' outfits. 'I miss layering', she says, 'because layering is an opportunity to play with and be more creative with clothes.' This perceived lack of creativity in L.A. clothing is an issue for Tsitouri, because she wants her pictures to be inspirational to her readers. 'We don't care if their jeans are this [brand] or another. You see pictures. You like it. You get inspiration out of it. And maybe [what they're wearing] finds [its] way into your closet.' It is a decidedly humble ambition for a photographer of fashion and one Tsitouri shares with many other bloggers like her. She is now continuing this goal on the streets of Los Angeles. The last several years have seen routine weekly updates, the structured blouses and coats of Athens giving way to the loose-fitting tank tops and board shorts of Southern California. The mood or 'affect' (see Barthes 1981) of the photos has changed, and in the transition, the blog has become an even stronger testimony to the specificity and irreducibility of place. She still has a hard time explaining what the difference is between Athens style and L.A. style, but it is apparent to anyone who has ever visited her blog. Street style just isn't available to such easy articulation. It is identified, both by blogger and reader, through something else: a kind of stylistic intuition, which the next chapter takes on as its explicit subject.

It is perhaps in this nebulous zone of the undefinable and the unclassifiable that street style blogging has the most to contribute. For if there is one thing – if only one thing – that the social sciences and the fashion industry have in common it is a penchant for classification. Both love to isolate types and assign them geographic coordinates. Go to Paris for boho chic, instructs *Vogue*. Look to the Kalahari for the prototypical egalitarian band, says the anthropologist. Street style bloggers present an alternative geography, a visual depiction of individuals in a wide array of cities who fail to conform to an obvious type. And in doing so, they both draw the eyes of the fashion world to new terrains and refuse to show them, once there, what they think they want to see.

3 STYLE RADAR: ON BECOMING A STREET STYLE BLOGGER AND KNOWING WHOM TO SHOOT

First day out

Let's go back to that day in late March of 2012, where we started this book, my first time out 'on the street' as a street style blogger. I had brought my camera and a stack of photo release forms, a notebook for jotting down thoughts, and an iPhone for posting Twitter updates to a non-existent set of followers. I was anxious and over-caffeinated, with little idea of where to go and even less of what to do when I got there. So I went to the first location that popped into my head, South Street. South Street is Philadelphia's most famous nightlife destination and one of its bigger tourist draws. Situated just over a mile south of Independence Hall and Philadelphia's other colonial era attractions, it serves as something of an urban playground for New Jersey suburban teenagers, a place to show off their new pink Mohawks without getting laughed out of the mall. South Street is crowded with shops selling sneakers, sex toys, and accessories, anarchist panhandlers harassing tourists for change, and a motley crew of bohemians, artists, and frat boy partiers, all occupying the space in different ways. I figured it would be a good place to capture some of Philly's more lively sartorial flavours. But on that Monday afternoon in late March it was quiet, and I didn't see anyone who caught my attention. With only a trickle of shoppers passing by, a few retail workers on smoking breaks, a few tourists with cameras three times the size of my own, it gradually became clear to me that it would take hours to find anyone to shoot there. Street style, after all, is not just people on the street in clothes. It is a relatively rare aesthetic (Johnson-Woods and Karaminas 2013; Woodward 2009), a photographic documentation of exceptions. Most people, I learned that first day, and have had driven home for me every time I have gone out shooting since, are just not that stylish – at least by the standards of street style photography – nor do they seem particularly interested in becoming so (Hill 2005). The myth that the street is some gurgling cauldron of sartorial creativity, as described in the first chapter, is just that – a myth (Woodward 2009) – promoted by fashion magazines and trend forecasting companies. It does real conceptual work, selling clothes, inspiring designers, giving teenagers something to aspire to, but it does not correspond with a ground-level reality. Most people passing down the city's concrete corridors are more interested in fitting in than standing out (Miller and Woodward 2012), or more likely, just getting on with their lives. They are not there to be judged by a cadre of photographers working the blogs. Consequently, I soon discovered, I would need to observe far more people than South Street had to offer that day in order to pick out appropriate subjects for my pictures. So I headed over to Passyunk Avenue, the retail artery of South Philadelphia and allegedly one of the hippest destinations in the city. It too seemed dead, its residents cooped up behind closed doors. No one was parading their weekend chic on a sleepy Monday afternoon. I stood there feeling foolish for a while with my camera dangling from my neck. That feeling would never entirely go away.

James Bent of the Singapore-based street style blog La Mode Outré would explain to me, months later, that standing around wondering where to go and who to shoot is one of the primary occupations of the street style blogger. 'You've really got to go to a place for quite a long time, two or three months, before you start really getting your head around where you want to go, and where the good spots are,' said Bent. 'And in some places, I don't think there is anywhere in particular to go. Even in Japan, in areas like Harajuku, Aoyama, and Omotesando, which are all right next to each other [and are world famous for their street style], there are a lot of nuances you need to learn: what time of day is the best time to shoot, the movement of people, where they're coming from. It's not enough just to find the area; you also have to find the exact street and the exact time, the exact day that you need to go.' I never worked out an exact formula of where and when to go in Philadelphia. Street style, as Michele Oberholzer of Cinder & Skylark explained to me, can pop up anywhere. It thwarts our best efforts to predict it. But there are certain basic rules I would discover. Friday afternoons are often better than Tuesday afternoons. Summer days are better than winter, calm days better than windy. Those brief periods of warmth in the midst of a cold stretch are the best of all. It is like people have been waiting impatiently to wear their coolest clothes and jump at the opportunity to do so. This all seems obvious to me now. But back on my first day of shooting, it wasn't. I just thought I would go out and shoot. Where and when were afterthoughts.

Finally, I got back into my beat up Honda Civic and drove over to the only other place I could think to go, Walnut Street, the upscale shopping district right in the heart of Center City, Philadelphia's metropolitan core. It is nearly always busy, with no shortage of pedestrians passing through. I had been hoping to avoid Walnut Street up until this point, thinking that what it would have to offer would prove too mainstream for my taste, but after my experiences in South Philly, I wanted somewhere with enough people present that it was numerically impossible not to find someone interesting to shoot. And I wanted somewhere where I could be effectively anonymous. I was already tired of feeling like a creepy guy with a camera lurking on a street corner.

Ultimately, Walnut Street came through for me, and I would end up returning there again and again to shoot over the next couple of years. It is within walking distance of my office at Drexel, and for largely practical reasons it became my default field site, the place I went to shoot when there were no other events going on, or when I wasn't so painfully bored of it, I just had to wander elsewhere. It wasn't a sure thing. There are no sure things in street style. But it would become my safest bet, one I made again and again throughout this project.

This chapter chronicles my early efforts to go out 'on the street' and forge myself into a practicing street style blogger. This was not an easy task, as this chapter attests. I had to refresh my lagging camera skills, learn to compose a shot the way a street style blogger does. I had to figure out the best times and places to go out. But most of all, I had to determine whom to shoot in the first place. Street stylistas do not line up to have their photos taken. They are an elusive bunch. One has to give them plenty of time to show up, and one has to be able to recognize them when they do. This chapter focuses most attentively, then, on that process of recognition, the carefully cultivated visual intuition that I describe, with only a minimum of tongue in cheek, as *style radar*.

Knowing whom to shoot

Standing on the corner of Walnut and 18th Street for what felt like hours, I couldn't at first bring myself to approach anyone. I had the same kind of nerves I had experienced years before, canvassing for a peace activist organization. I imagined being eyed suspiciously by agitated passers-by. I imagined being turned down rudely by those who just couldn't be bothered. I imagined beat cops harassing me. 'Just what do you think you're doing out here?' they would ask, and I, a befuddled academic, would have no readymade answer. All of these fears turned out to be unfounded. No cops have ever questioned me, and only around one out of every twenty-five people I stop turn me down. When I first started, it was about one in seven, but the more confident my pitch has become – 'Excuse me. I do a street style blog called Urban Fieldnotes. Would you mind if I took your picture for it?' – the better my success ratio.

Then, when I finally worked up the courage to stop someone for their photograph, I couldn't decide what I was looking for in a street style subject in the first place. Was I after a street-smart cool kid in spikes and black leather of the sort who might have appeared in *i-D Magazine* circa 1981, a quirky individualist in a puffy coat and overalls a la Hel Looks, or perhaps a rakish middle-aged gentleman in a tweed jacket and foppish scarf of the sort Scott Schuman might have stopped for The Sartorialist? Philadelphia is not exactly overflowing with any of those categories. I would have to settle for someone who was simply 'cool'. But how does one *know* that a subject is 'cool'? Is it an objective quality, a certain observable aestheticized indifference, itself born from the racialized streets of urban America (Leland 2004)? Or is it a measure of one's own background, one's accumulated taste as a member of a particular group (Bourdieu 1984; Thornton 1996)? I have come to think of cool, after shooting on the streets for over two and a half years now, as a performance of stylized autonomy (see Warren and Campbell 2014), a steadfast commitment to being and displaying 'who one is', regardless of what is 'in' or 'trendy'. Cool is not showy or pretentious. It does not try to be something it is not. When a cool person wears a particular trend, she occupies it, becomes it. It appears natural on her, inevitable. She looks comfortable, that is, in her own skin, and her clothes become an extension of that skin rather than something she puts on it. But there are lots of people who are cool in this way, who are nonetheless not *my* cup of tea. Their being who they are simply does not correspond with my own sense of style. Face Hunter's cool is not the same as The Sartorialist's cool, which has little in common with the cool of Hel Looks. Whose cool, I wondered, is closest to my own?

Bloggers tend to answer the difficult question of how they isolate appropriate models for their blogs with the conversation-stopping 'I just shoot what I like.' Javi Obando of On The Corner says, 'We just look for someone who claims our sight, who commands our attention. If we like it, we take a picture, and that's it.' Mordechai Rubinstein of Mister Mort says, 'For me, it's normally that I like something. There has to be something about them that interests me. I'm not looking for cookie-cutter beauty or style.' Adam Katz Sinding of Le-21ème told me: 'I just take photos of things that I like. And things that inspire me. I don't even want to say inspire me, things that intrigue me. Things that catch my attention.'

But what do *I* like? I wondered, wandering the streets that day, and many days after. What catches my attention? What intrigues me? I thought I knew once. I thought, in fact, I had a fairly decent sense of my own tastes and interests. I had obsessed about them at various points in my life, wondering what they said about me, wondering how they made me appear to others. But in the heat of the moment, stalking the streets of Philadelphia with a micro four-thirds camera around my neck, I couldn't seem to remember what they were. How does one know what they like in the first place? The more directly you look at your likes, I discovered, the more they seem to disappear.

The sociologist Herbert Blumer in his classic 1969 article in *The Sociological Quarterly* argued that fashion industry buyers have little ability to articulate what it is they are looking for in a clothing item (Blumer 1969). They simply *know* an item they want for their brand or their store when they see it, and when asked afterwards what it is they saw in that item, they defer to the vague yet decisive descriptive term of 'stunning'. They choose dresses that are stunning, blazers that are stunning, weed out anything that is not stunning, as if stunning were an objective, intrinsic quality of a piece of clothing rather than a culturally produced and historically specific attribute, as if anyone, properly trained, could learn to see it, and as if all qualified buyers, past, present, and future would also recognize that item as an example of stunning. And yet what is considered stunning to industry buyers constantly changes. This season's stunning is next season's bland. That's what makes it fashion. It operates on a series of momentary collective agreements. Fashion is an industry built on the ephemeral (Lipovetsky 2002), the constant production of novelty (Polhemus 1978). Nothing can stay stunning forever.

In her more recent study of fashion models in New York and London, sociologist Ashley Mears (2011) discusses a similar phenomenon. When a model walks into a room, a casting agent simply *knows* she has the right look for the client. It is not something articulable. It is not something they can describe. It is a felt reaction to something perceived as intrinsic to that person, a special quirk or quality. Talent scouts and model bookers can be trained over time to spot 'the look', subjected to a rigid regimen of fashion magazines and runway shows, but they can never adequately explain what 'the look' is. If they could, their alleged expertise would be rendered irrelevant. Anyone could pick it out. Anyone could do what they do. Their job depends on a relatively rare ability to simply *know*, a sort of sixth sense for style. Out on the streets of Philadelphia, my own ability to simply *know* was repeatedly put to the test.

After several hours of exhaustive looking, analysing every person who walked by, clicking off mental 'no's like boxes on a survey, I sauntered past the Zara on Walnut Street, and right then I made a decision. Or was it a realization? That guy, right there, in the blue blazer, high-necked sweater, and newsboy cap. *He* is the person I want to photograph (Figure 3.3). There was no hesitation. There was no questioning of my motives. I just *knew* I wanted to photograph him. After hours of relentless thinking, second-guessing, even third-guessing, that simple *knowledge* was an incredible relief. The chatter in my head went mute, if only for a moment. I walked up and talked to him before I had time to change my mind.

Later on I would analyse my own intentions in identifying that first photographic subject, a man I would come to know by the name of Erik Honesty. He looks a little like someone who might appear on The Sartorialist. He has the dapper black gentleman vibe of a Ouigi Theodore or a Sam Lambert, a Brooklyn vintage shop owner and London tailor respectively, both commonly featured on street style blogs. He has the polished, put-together look of someone who wants to be singled out for attention. His clothes fit well. His cap is tilted ever so perfectly to the left. He captures, that is, a sensibility I had encountered previously on street style blogs and menswear websites, one I had already begun to internalize and identify with, even if I could not quite give it a name. Suffice it to say, he fit neatly into the emerging menswear *zeitgeist*, a *zeitgeist* I had painstakingly familiarized myself with over many months of consuming street style online. He conformed, that is, to my own emergent conception of cool. But in that moment, I was not thinking of any of those things. I saw, and I reacted, and that would become my street style recipe from then on. Thinking, it turns out, just gets in the way.

Here is what I posted on Urban Fieldnotes, my nascent street style blog, that night:

> My first day of street style blogging was a qualified success. I spent three hours out and ended up with several good images. Of course, they were all of the same guy, Erik, a photogenic vintage shop owner, who seemed utterly unphased being asked to be photographed for a street style blog. I got the impression this wasn't his first time. Here are some of the lessons I learned from my first day of

FIGURE 3.1 Erik Honesty, a vintage-clothing store owner and my first photographic subject for this project. Photo by author.

shooting: 1) most people aren't all that distinctive. It can take hours just to find someone interesting to shoot. Plus, it took me close to two hours just to work up the nerve. 2) Street style shots are best done in high traffic areas. South Street and Passyunk on a windy Monday afternoon = not so good. Walnut St and Rittenhouse Square proved more fruitful, even if less populated with hipsters. And 3) if you want to get a good shot, you have to stop moving. The more you move, the less you see and the slower your response time. Better to become a fixture.

Street style photography, at the end of that first day, seemed like an exercise in Zen big game hunting – if Zen and big game hunting were in fact compatible things. One must be calm and collected, let go of self-doubt, and act without hesitation. One must, in other words, become 'cool' oneself (Mentges 2000), exemplifying a bodily discipline of aloof stillness. And the biggest obstacle getting in the way of that goal: mental chatter. The trick is to stop the chatter in one's mind, so that it doesn't cloud one's judgement or slow one's reaction time. This is a difficult trick to master for anyone, but it poses a special challenge for an anthropologist used to taking constant mental notes. I struggled to be quiet and receptive, open to whoever came my way. Form too clear an understanding of who I was looking for, and I would miss out on the actual interesting subjects right in front of me.

Case in point: Mandi, my next photograph for Urban Fieldnotes, taken the following day (Figure 3.4). Mandi and Erik have little in common with one another other than my recognition that both were people I wanted to shoot. That is enough commonality for a street style blogger. After practically giving up that second day, standing on Walnut Street, assessing everyone who came by, I let go of my expectations. I would either find someone or I wouldn't. Either way I would post about it on my blog. And then along came Mandi. I saw something in her and reacted to it – gut-level, thought-free – and I am glad I did. Her picture remains my most widely 'pinned' image on Pinterest, a perennial virtual corkboard favourite.

There can be little doubt that what I recognized in Mandi has a precedent elsewhere in the street style blogosphere, as it does in magazines and on runways. There is a simultaneous cuteness and hardness to her look that would be right at home on Streetgeist or Hel Looks, a certain brand of urban angst and post-adolescent alienation that alternative lifestyle magazines like i-D and Dazed and Confused made their bread and butter back in the 1980s. And she embodies a defiant yet feminine look often sought out by high fashion brands. Mears (2011) refers to this quality as 'edgy'. Mandi is edgy in the sense often used by modelling agencies, both 'unique' and 'strong', 'sitting on the border between beautiful and ugly, familiar and strange' (Mears 2011: 42). Not everyone would like her look, and that is precisely its appeal. To be one of the select few who can appreciate it testifies to one's credentials as a legitimate curator of style. She is also, however,

FIGURE 3.2 Mandi, my second photographic subject, has little in common with Erik other than me. Photo by author.

'cool', maintaining her own stylistic autonomy (Caleb and Campbell 2014). On the streets of Philly she stood out, not just for looking different but also for appearing not to care that she does. But once again, this is not what I was thinking about when I stopped Mandi. I just *knew* that I wanted to photograph her. That was already enough.

Cultivating your style radar

People, when they find out about my street style project, often ask me if I am continually assessing the outfits around me, evaluating every person who wanders past whether I am shooting or not. Turn on the fashion attention switch, the assumption goes, and it is hard to turn it off again. Suddenly the world looks as if it were populated by slobs and oafs. That guy, ugh! That lady, what was she thinking? Him, that would be a big 'no'. 'Are you evaluating my outfit right now?' people – especially academics – want to know. 'And, more importantly, have I passed the test?'

I have gotten used to assuring people that I am not judging their outfits, and, for the most part, it's true. I am not. I have other things on my mind. But I have to admit that for the first few weeks of shooting street style, that is exactly what I was doing. I stood on the corner, rapid-fire rejecting some 500 or so people before I would spot that one person in the crowd I wanted to shoot, and then, when I had finished shooting for the day, my mind just kept carrying on doing the same thing, with or without my consent. I noticed what people were wearing on the subway, in the classroom, at the supermarket, at academic conferences, just about everywhere, and the verdict was not good. Cool, it turns out, is a relatively scarce resource, and like other scarce resources, it is all the more valued because of it. I couldn't stop chasing cool. I dreamt about cool, daydreamed about cool, stood helplessly by while my eyes darted from person to person seeking it out in public places. But this phase, thankfully, passed. It had to pass. Otherwise it may very well have driven me crazy. I thought about throwing in the towel nearly every day of the first few months of shooting street style. It was too taxing. Evaluating everyone's style left me feeling cold, cruel, and exhausted. Besides, it is not a very effective way to scout street style. It simply takes too much time. As Javi Obando of On The Corner put it: 'If we take time thinking and all that, people go on. They are always walking. It's a fast style of living here [in Buenos Aires].'

Rather than evaluating everyone that passes, actively eliminating all the *wrong* people from contention, experienced street style bloggers assume a stance of active reception, waiting for the *right* person to come into their view. They then evaluate that person and that person alone. It feels something like gazing at an object in soft focus until it comes into sudden, sharp relief. The crowd is a continuous blur punctured by tiny holes of light.

It is no accident that the terminology we use for photography is so similar to that of hunting – 'shooting', 'aiming', 'capturing' on film (see Sontag 1973). My interviews with street style bloggers have been rife with such terms. Both photography and hunting are steeped in a discourse of stoic masculinity. Both are disciplines of self-mastery. Both require acting without hesitation or self-doubt. Both place a premium on instantaneous bodily action. And yet both, perhaps in contradiction, also depend on an almost mystical kind of attentiveness, an openness, a receptiveness, a near thoughtless state of self-transcendence. I would revise my formula for effective street style photography again and again after that first day – sometimes standing in one place, sometimes wandering restlessly, other times methodically moving between predetermined points – but I always came back to the same basic equation: Thinking + street style photography = no photos, or at the very least, thinking + street style photography = bad photos. In the end they amount to the same thing, having no usable material.

Street style photography is a project of honing one's intuition into a sharp visual focus. It is a project of automatic thinking. A good street style photographer cultivates her own distinctive *style radar*, a delicate mental instrument that works only when conscious thought gets out of the way. As Emma Arnold, blogger for the Chicago-based Trés Awesome, put it, 'I'll know if I want to take their picture almost immediately, but then sometimes I hesitate because I'm nervous or [because of] whatever sort of circumstances are happening inside my head.' Reuben 'Big Rube' Harley of the Philadelphia-based blog Street Gazing told me, 'It's totally instinct. Because if I run around thinking "I'm looking for a Gucci bag" I'll drive myself insane, and pass up some other greatness that walked right past me. So it's all reaction to what I see. A certain swagger, the way a person walks.' Adam Katz Sinding expressed a similar sentiment when he told *Redmilk Magazine*, 'The picture will come when I'm not even thinking about it. Otherwise I'll think the photo over and over and become critical and I might break it apart ... so I'll say my attention is catch [*sic*] by not letting my mind get in the way ... that is when I get the best pictures.'

Another case in point by way of a contrast: my third day out shooting I got stuck on the idea that I was looking for certain 'punkish' iconoclasts in the same vein as Mandi, my second photographic subject. This, after all, is 'real street style', the kind of stuff that got the whole photographic genre going in the early '80s. I fixated my gaze on said brand of would-be rebels. Two guys, dressed like my high school self's idea of punk rock passed by. I didn't feel my style radar light up. I didn't feel much of anything. And yet, the second or third time they passed, I made the conscious decision (not wise, I would later realize) to take their pictures. Aren't they 'street style' enough for my blog, I asked myself? Wouldn't Liisa Jokinen take their picture for Hel Looks? I ended up with pictures I hated so much I never posted them on the blog. They were awkward, stilted, like clumsy snapshots at a school dance. I still feel bad for those two guys. They did their part for me, but I couldn't do mine for them. For reasons I cannot quite articulate, they just were not what I was looking for at that moment, and I could not, as such, depict them in the right way to make them into effective street style photographs. To put it in the (all too) self-conscious vernacular of the street style blogger, 'they just weren't me'.

Street style bloggers have a number of ways of talking about this delicate mental instrument I am calling *style radar*, but their descriptions all suggest a similar underlying form: a dependence on instinct or intuition, a sense of simply *knowing* whom they want to shoot, and a feeling of internal coherence between their own self-concept and the stylistic sensibility of the subject in question. *Style radar* links photographer and subject. It places them into the same pre-articulate category, the photographer standing in for the subject, the subject standing in for them. And the pre-articulate part is important. *Style radar* operates outside of articulation. It is felt rather thought, and it adheres to a variety of unfiltered bodily experience cultural theorists often describe as '*affective*'.

'Affect', write Gregory J. Seigworth and Melissa Gregg in their introduction to *The Affect Theory Reader*, consists of 'those forces … beneath, alongside, or generally *other* than conscious knowing, vital forces insisting beyond emotion – that can serve to drive us toward movement, toward thought and extension, that can likewise suspend us (as if neutral) across a barely registering accretion of force-relations, or that can even leave us overwhelmed by the world's apparent intractability' (Seigworth and Gregg 2010: 1). Affect describes felt realities that are not translatable into any known lexicon. But their un-pin-down-able, affective nature makes them no less keenly felt.

What is perhaps most interesting about *style radar* as street style photographers describe it is that it is perceived to pick up on something intrinsic to a person, something not available to description but there nonetheless. *Style radars* react to something that another person possesses, something that they emanate or project – even if other people, including other street style photographers, cannot see it. It is, as Seigworth and Gregg describe it, a kind of 'force'. Street style photographers describe being able to see this force from a distance, often being able to tell whether or not someone possesses *it* before being able to identify what a person is wearing or even how they look. I myself, after a few months of shooting, began to experience it as such, very often *knowing* from several hundred feet away whether or not I wanted to photograph someone. It comes through in one's walk, one's movement. It has something to do with how a person displaces the air around them. It is an 'aura', to use Benjamin's Marxio-mystic term, that shimmers in their wake (Benjamin 1955), a force field of affect that surrounds and engulfs them.

Michelle Oberholzer of Cinder & Skylark describes what she is looking for in a subject as an 'energy'. Simbarashe Cha of New York's Lord Ashbury uses the same term. 'For me', said Cha, 'the energy of the person is really what attracts me to even decide if I want to take their picture, [and] if I can take their picture. And there are some people on my site that are admittedly not [even] that fashionable, but there was *something* about them that sort of compelled me to want to shoot them in a fashionable way' [my emphasis]. Dana Landon of Seattle's It's My Darlin', similarly, describes what compels her to take someone's picture as a 'spark'. 'I don't know what happens', she told me. 'I just get a really great feeling'. Alkistis Tsitouri of Streetgeist described how she experiences this intuitive recognition when she told me, 'Sometimes I instantly know. I mean, it doesn't even go through my brain. My body just runs up to them, and I start talking to them, and then I realize, "Oh! I just did that!"'

Eddie Newton, the photographer behind one of New York's best-known street style blogs, Mr. Newton (www.mrnewton.net) perhaps gave the most evocative description of *style radar* in the short documentary he shot for GILT Groupe at the Spring/Summer 2014 collection of Mercedes-Benz New York Fashion Week. When asked by Gilt Groupe's producer: 'So there are a lot of people out here. What's most likely to catch your eye in this sea?' Newton responded, 'You know it when you see it. I've heard forensic experts talk about looking for fiber evidence. It's very small, and they say once you know what you're looking for it looks like glow worms … It's almost like that. There's this sea of people, and the ones I want to shoot are just glowing to me.'

Street-style *Habitus*

I find street style photographers' descriptions of how they isolate their subjects rather compelling and true to my own experience of being out on the streets shooting. Style radar is an immediate sort of *knowing*, felt 'in the gut' more than in the head. It is pre-articulate and often quite unpredictable, applied to a variety of subjects who seem to have little in common with one another other than their ability to trigger a photographer's intuition. It is a measure of affect, aura, charisma, cool. It speaks to some shared internal reality of which we cannot quite speak. I frequently find myself trying to justify the feeling, why it sparked or didn't spark for some particular passer-by, but I cannot effectively force it, and when I adhere to its internal, logic-less logic, its apparent whims and flights of fancy, I almost uniformly agree with its sentiments, once I have time to look back and reflect on the images produced. While intellect may be more useful for isolating examples of a particular look or trend, *style radar* is critical for detecting those less tangible elements: edge, coolness, grit, all more affective than precise characteristics. Style radar has proven more effective than any sort of formula or checklist for finding pictures that please both me and my readers – a determination that gets blurrier and blurrier over time as we develop our tastes in tandem. It is the one thing I seem to be able to rely on for producing blog content with impact. What street style photographers are looking for is just too nebulous a thing to be easily categorized. Yvan Rodic, Face Hunter, described it to me as 'a global package of uniqueness'.

Nonetheless, when I present my street-style material to other social scientists – say, at a conference or a guest lecture – I am almost always offered up the advice from one colleague or another that I may want to find some way to rephrase this experience through the vocabulary of social theory. I am not opposed to the practice. I too find social theory to be a useful framework for distanced reflection that enables us to forge connections that may not be immediately obvious. At its best, theory gives academics a common language to talk about a variety of subjects and situations. It clarifies our thinking. It places our work in conversation with other people's work. At its worst, however, theory threatens to bury the lived insights of direct experience beneath an occult and opaque language our subjects would neither understand nor relate to. One set of terms, those preferred by the people we study, is replaced by another set of terms, preferred by social scientists, and we remain in our understanding exactly where we were before. Like anthropologist Tim Ingold, I find something unethical about such an act (Ingold 2013: 3) of academic superposition. It seems disingenuous to me, like a bait and switch. We ask people to let us into their lives and tell us about their experiences, and then, once they are out of our sight, translate their narratives into ones that correspond with trends in social theory. We rewrite and rework the statements they provide us, finesse them into 'data'.

The one single social theorist who comes up more than any other in my conversations with social science colleagues about this project is a certain deceased French sociologist by the name of Pierre Bourdieu. Bourdieu, who died in 2002 after an illustrious and productive career, has held a celebrity status in anthropology circles for the last few decades, rivalled only by the philosopher/ historian Michel Foucault. I have a genuine affection for Bourdieu's work, as I do for Foucault's. It is elegant and all-encompassing, sometimes dazzling in its brilliance, and for the sake of humouring my colleagues, it may be worthwhile taking a short detour into the some of his insights here.

Bourdieu, to grossly oversimplify an immense body of work, was concerned primarily with 'practice', or the ways in which we act within the social world, which he refers to as a 'field'. Bourdieu is widely considered one of the largest contributors to the body of social theory known, appropriately, as 'practice theory'. In short, as Sherry Ortner writes, practice theory 'is a theory of history. It is a theory of how social beings, with their diverse motives and their diverse intentions, make and transform the world in which they live' (Ortner 1996: 193). The practice theory framework asserts that all human action 'is constrained by the given social and cultural order', or 'structure' (Ortner 1996: 2). We make sense of and act within the world according to shared 'interpretive schemes' or 'schemas' (Ortner 1989; Sewell 1992) that are specific to a particular social and historical location. Our actions, similarly, are always constrained and limited by the positions we occupy within a given social field. For Bourdieu, the class structure of modern western societies is a particularly important structure operating within that field, defining our place within it, and thereby determining a great deal about how we act, think, and engage with those around us. In fact, class structure is little more than the accumulated consequences of practice within a field.

Now, the important thing to understand at this point in our discussion is that for Bourdieu, the structuring of our practices is largely unconscious. It happens not at the level of conscious thought, but at the deeper more embodied level of 'practical consciousness' (Giddens 1979), which Bourdieu's describes as 'bodily hexis'. We act without knowing why we act or the structural components that have necessitated such action. Bourdieu calls this kind of automatic, pre-structured practice '*habitus*'. In Bourdieu's terms, *habitus* describes '[s]ystems of durable, transposable dispositions, structured structures predisposed to function as structuring structures, that is, as principles which generate and organize practices and representations that can be objectively adapted to their outcomes without presupposing a conscious aiming at ends or an express mastery of the operations necessary in order to attain them. Objectively 'regulated' and 'regular' without being in any way the product of obedience to rules, they can be collectively orchestrated without being the product of the organizing action of a conductor' (Bourdieu 1980: 53). I can imagine the brains of my undergraduate readers shutting off in the middle of Bourdieu's first sentence. Like many of Bourdieu's descriptions, this one is an acquired taste, an odd mixture of in-jokes and technical precision. To put it in simpler, if less precise terms, *habitus* is culture as embodied practice. It is the product of one's accumulated experiences, and once accumulated, determines one's future actions without any necessary intervention from one's conscious mind. To put it in yet another way, *habitus* is the crystallization of past actions into habits.

Like other practice theorists, Bourdieu sees such 'structuring structures' as products of our personal history. We are born as a member of a particular group (or class), occupying a particular position in a larger field, and through occupying this position, we begin to act in a way that mirrors those actions of other people, occupying similar positions in that field. Together, we form the *habitus* of a particular group, expressing a common set of tastes, likes, values, understandings, and behaviours. These tastes, likes, values, understandings, and behaviours then lead us to act in certain, predictable ways in novel situations. But perhaps more importantly, they lead us to NOT act in some other way, for to do so would define us as members of some other group, potentially further down the social totem pole, a group with whom we would, all things considered, rather not be confused. Our *habitus*, then, does not only define us as members of a particular group, it marks us as distinct from other groups. It enacts an unconscious mode of social distinction (Bourdieu 1984).

You can probably already see where I am going with this. From Bourdieu's point of view, our tastes and likes are by no means arbitrary, even if we are unaware of their origins. They define us as a member of a group and mark us as different from other, less desirable groups. Plus, they happen without us thinking about them or even necessarily being aware of them. We do not have to be consciously working to set ourselves apart from others to nonetheless be actively setting ourselves apart from others. We simply *know* what we like and don't like.

Now, let's return to the case of street style photography. Using Bourdieu's terminology, it is the *habitus* of a street style photographer/blogger – as a member of a particular group, operating from a particular position in a larger social field – that she interprets as a simple 'knowing'. She is not consciously scrolling through her likes and dislikes when deciding whether someone is worthy of being photographed. She is relying instead, on a deeper, more embodied form of awareness – an awareness that simultaneously identifies her as a member of one group and not as a member of any other.

The lines of inclusion and exclusion

And what is that group to which the street style blogger is aligning herself, consciously or not, by singling out certain people for her attention and ignoring all others? Let's stop for a second to take a look at the kinds of people who show up on street style blogs. Javi Obando describes the typical subjects of On The Corner as 'creative people', because, after all, 'a lawyer will not have the same liberty to dress as a creative person, because of the environment they work in'. Nels Frye describes the people he shoots for Stylites as 'bourgeois bohemians', using a term borrowed from *New York Times* editorialist David Brooks to describe an emergent group of cultural creatives popping up in today's China. A quick glance through the occupations listed on Gunnar Hämmerle's StyleClicker will yield a disproportionate number of artists, stylists, and designers. On Emma Arnold's Trés Awesome it is mostly musicians, bloggers, and designers.

Yvan Rodic of Face Hunter, when I asked him if he thought there was any commonality among the people he stopped told me: 'They tend to be working in creative industries, but not necessarily. I mean, it's almost like interesting to see, for example, in Scandinavia, where style is really something that everyone is interested in, you will meet someone who is studying science, and they will still have a really awesome style. And in many countries where style is still limited to like the fashion industry, the majority of people have some sort of connection with something creative. And I guess I would say, [are] kind of like middle-class. I would say it's some kind of middle-class phenomenon, because people who are too extremely poor or extremely wealthy tend to like be stuck into some stereotypes. I think that they're middle-class kids who are more into reinventing themselves and being more, "I don't have an obligation to one type."' Fashion, as Polhemus claims, is for the in-between (Polhemus 1978), and as such, the truly poor and truly rich go largely unrepresented on street style blogs, along with a broad array of less style-oriented occupations, from fast food workers to corporate financial officers.

As for my own blog, the most common occupations of the people I have stopped to photograph are fashion designers, graphic designers, artists, art students, photographers, videographers, musicians, hair stylists, and retail clothing store employees. Of course there is also the occasional lawyer or accountant, even a Presbyterian minister or two, who have somehow found themselves in the mix, but the tendency is strongly towards those in more 'cultural' or 'creative' occupations (see Hesmondhalgh and Baker 2011). The street style blogosphere, in other words, is largely populated by what Bourdieu has termed the 'new petite bourgeoisie' (Bourdieu 1984), those workers in the cultural industries who sell intangible and often immaterial products. To use Richard Florida's more popular term, they are the 'creative class'.

I am guessing this comes as little surprise to anyone. It is precisely this group that has the most to gain from dressing in a way that signifies hipness, stylishness, creativity, and an awareness of larger currents in fashion. The typical subject of a street style photograph is identifying herself as part of an emergent sector of the transnational economy, a new elite who trades in culture the way previous elites traded in goods. And the street style photographer, of course, to be any good at her game, needs to be able to recognize such people – the more immediately the better – for to recognize them is to categorize herself among them. 'It takes one to know one', goes the old playground jibe, and bloggers count on its truth to demonstrate their own hipness, awareness, and established place within the emergent cultural elite. This cultivated skillset has led a number of street style bloggers to eventually leave behind the practice to become stylists, marketers, or journalists within the fashion industry. A good street style photographer, like any of these other occupations, has to be able to distinguish the stylish few from the unbranded masses. She knows them so immediately that it is as if they were a part of herself.

Style radars, then, can be read as a kind of class-based instant alarm that goes off when one – who is equipped with the disposition to receive it – is confronted with the presence of 'style'. And like *habitus* in general, style radars work best when they are left to do their own thing, no thinking getting in the way. As Yael Sloma of Tel Aviv's The Streets Walker describes the process: 'It's only when I see someone that I know he is right. Only afterwards can I try to understand why I found him interesting'. But one can imagine all sorts of mechanical gears working beneath the surface of style radar. A photographer sees someone who conforms to some set of ideals accumulated over a lifetime, a set of ideals that marks her as part of an emergent cultural elite. She judges, in an instant, based on a shared conception of style. The more deeply she buys into this conception of style, the more instantly she recognizes it when she sees it. A good photographer may not be able to tell you why one person makes for a good photo and not

FIGURE 3.3 David, Chestnut Street, Philadelphia. Photo by author.

FIGURE 3.4 Gabriella, off 17th Street, Philadelphia. Photo by author.

another, but they *know* who does and who doesn't. It has become a part of their own make up. And in acting on these embodied standards – learned from blogs and magazines and a lifetime of class-structured experience – the photographer works to both establish her position among those who *know*, and reinforce what gets to count as stylish in the first place. The cycle perpetuates itself. The stylish stay stylish, and the stylish of the street style photographers remains the model of stylishness for everyone else. Hence the oft-noted absence of 'plus-size' models on street style blogs, or the bias towards younger women. Hence the general lack of accountants and lawyers, not to mention factory workers and fast-food employees. Stylish has never pretended to be inclusive. It is the invidious logic of those with the power to control representation, the 'dominant class' of the digital age, imposing their own vision of how to be and how to appear on everyone else.

From an experiential point of view, however, the photographer simply acts – no rhyme, no reason, no articulated set of standards to which she is adhering. Hence, the following pictures of two very different people, taken by me, many months after my first day of shooting, on the same day. They are united only by my automatic response, by the triggering of my style radar, the springing into action of my *habitus* as a street style photographer. I cannot tell you my reasoning behind taking these pictures, because there was no reasoning involved. But aren't they both just cool as hell? And aren't I awesome for recognizing it?

The problem with convenient social categories

It is this pre-articulate quality of *habitus*, this affective, experiential quality, that led Bourdieu's protégé, Wacquant (2004) to decide that the only way he could understand boxing, that is, *really* understand boxing, was to become a boxer himself. He couldn't depend on other boxers being able to describe their own experiences to him. Such insight would likely not be available to them. He couldn't depend on his own observations as an outsider either. There would always remain a practical barrier between their *habitus* and his own. What boxers do is fundamentally, and irreducibly experiential. Boxing is lived and felt rather than theorized or articulated. It is carried out bodily, and as such, requires a 'carnal sociology' (Wacquant 2004) for its study. And it is for this reason as well that I decided I could only understand street style blogging by becoming a street style blogger, by walking the streets, day after day, with a digital camera clenched in my fist.

Yet there is a limit to the utility of the concept of *habitus* for describing the practices of street style bloggers. For one, it depends on a conception of one's social position as a relatively stable point within an essentially static social field (Massumi 2002). Working-class people share a working-class *habitus*. Boxers have the *habitus* of boxers. But do bloggers share a common *habitus*? They operate in very different cities around the world, often with no direct interaction with one another. To suggest they operate according to the same shared set of bodily dispositions, the same set of inherited rules and standards, seems absurd just on the face of it. Yes, most come from positions of relative privilege. Yes, most occupy a position within that nascent social structure sometimes called 'the creative class' or the 'new petite bourgeoisie'. But what kind of structure is that, compared to, say, the entrenched social positionalities of the British proletariat or the New Delhi Brahmins? How strong and enduring can such an emergent sociality hope to be, at this early point in its existence?

The rabble rousing sociologist Bruno Latour – perhaps best described here as the 'anti-Bourdieu' – has argued that groups are in fact remarkably difficult to maintain (Latour 2005). They are fragile, tentative things that overlap with other competing ones, modes of sociality that only exist so long as their constitutive members perform and maintain them. Street style bloggers barely constitute a group at all. In fact, they often openly defy efforts to categorize them as one. When I asked Yvan Rodic, for instance, whether he saw himself as part of a community of street style bloggers, his answer was blunt and to the point: 'No. Not really'. He knows a number of other bloggers, he explained but seldom interacts with them. He prefers, as he said, to 'do his own thing'. When I asked Adam Katz Sinding the same question, he told me he was too busy taking pictures to worry about making friends. The expectation that bloggers would share a common culture at a bodily or structural level is suspect at best.

Moreover, although Bourdieu himself borrowed the concept of *habitus* from such theoretical heavy-hitters as Mauss (2000) and Merleau-Ponty (2013), an early anthropologist and phenomenologist philosopher respectively, who borrowed it, in turn, from Aristotle (1999), he seemed to have let slip a fundamental component of the concept for its earlier theorists. For Bourdieu, *habitus* is acquired gradually, without awareness, by a simple process of accretion that one undergoes as a member of a group. But for Aristotle and his successors, the crucial characteristic of *habitus* is that it is *cultivated* through one's deliberate actions. If we wish to become a virtuous person, we must act virtuously until we do so without trying. If we want to be a good photographer, we must take lots of pictures until it becomes second nature, until we cannot stop taking pictures in our heads, until photography is simply who we are. In other words, Bourdieu puts forward a view of a *habitus* as something of a steady state, something that has already happened to us. It is the product of history, and history is located in the past.

To understand street style blogging, however, is to understand a *habitus* in formation, a *habitus* that is as multifarious and heterogeneous as the people who subscribe to it. It is to understand what theorists Deleuze and Guattari would have called a *becoming* (see Deleuze and Guattari 1987). Street style bloggers are not defined by a single shared *habitus*. They are not one type of *being* at all. Rather, street style bloggers, like any subject position whatsoever, are a variety of *becoming*, or more specifically, many varieties of becoming, ones that share certain moments of intersection but never quite overlap. And as such, the *habitus* of a blogger is fundamentally incomplete. It is singular, personal, and irreducible to the *habitus* of any other street style blogger. My *style radar* is not the same as yours, even if we happen to occupy a similar rung in the street style hierarchy. Once again, Face Hunter's cool is not The Sartorialist's.

Perhaps, then, it is simply too convenient to label the practice of street style blogging as stemming from the *habitus* of an emergent social class. It makes tidy and simple what it is intrinsically messy and complex. Perhaps in the final analysis, a better description of what street style bloggers do is scour the streets, looking for people to photograph who have some sort of ineffable quality about them, an 'energy', as so many bloggers describe it, that somehow reflects or characterizes the times and places in which we live and yet also testifies to the singularity and irreducibility of one individual's sense of style. Perhaps, that is, the descriptions that bloggers themselves provide are already accurate enough for our purposes. Bloggers document an individual's affective presence, their *effect* on others, their 'energy', their 'spark' rather than a minute range of stylized expressions of an emergent class *habitus*.

Perhaps street style bloggers are not perpetuating one small elite set of tastes at all. Perhaps they are expanding them, opening up new realms of stylistic possibility. Even if bloggers have cultivated their *style radar* by looking at fashion magazines, and even if they are highly selective about whom they choose to depict, there is a marked difference between the aesthetics of these magazines and the aesthetics of street style bloggers. Whereas fashion magazines depict models ranging between a size 0 and a size 6 (Mears 2011), street style bloggers depict a range of body types somewhere between a size 0 and a size 16. Whereas fashion magazines focus their lenses on a narrow age range, between around fifteen and thirty years old, street style blogs like The Sartorialist and Hel Looks frequently depict people in their 50s and 60s. Advanced Style, the blog project of Ari Seth Cohen, in fact exclusively depicts people aged 50 and above. Whereas fashion magazines look for the 'on trend' or about to be, bloggers look for the off-kilter and the idiosyncratic – the individually cool. Subcultural style has a strong place within blogs. So do a variety of uncategorizable styles seldom, if ever, depicted in print. Whereas fashion magazines depict a disproportionate number of white models, bloggers, like Michelle Oberholzer and Liisa Jokinen tend to value the diversity of their own representations. People of African, Latin American, and Asian backgrounds are frequently depicted on blogs. Some blogs, like Singh Street Style out of London, focus on ethnicities like Sikhs underrepresented in fashion.

Street style blogs, that is, are widening the possibilities of style. They are expanding its parameters, not simply reinforcing the standards of an emergent elite. Bloggers' perspectives on what constitutes cool, I have found, are quite expansive, if not entirely inclusive. There is no one 'right' way of dressing. There is no one single set of trends that deserves representation over all others. Instead, bloggers gesture in a number of directions. If they are representing and reinforcing the perspective of an emergent class group, then that class group they are representing is a diverse and unwieldy lot. And in fact, not all bloggers are comfortable asserting themselves as representatives of that group at all. Many bloggers don't want to see themselves as part of any group, including that of 'bloggers'. What a mess this makes of our efforts to understand them as a neat and tidy social category!

Being a blogger vs. having a blog

In the summer of 2013, an article posted on the website of Independent Fashion Bloggers (heartifb.com), perhaps the single largest network of fashion bloggers online, posed the classic question of identity authenticity applied to blogging: 'Are you a blogger', asked Ashley 'Ashe' Robinson of the blog Dramatis Personae (http://www.mischiefmydear.com/dramatispersonae/), 'or someone who has a blog?' The difference is not academic, Robinson claims in the article, nor, she goes on to say, is it a question of a right path and a wrong path. 'Both bloggers and people who blog', writes Robinson, 'have a place on the internet.' But it is no secret which of these Robinson aspires towards. 'Deciding that you will BE a blogger', writes Robinson, 'is dedicating a portion of your life consistently to blogging.' 'It's about dedication, focus, and consistency, whether you make money or not.' 'More than anything', Robinson goes on to say, 'I believe the difference between being a blogger and being someone who has a blog is a personal philosophical decision and choice.' 'To have a blog means having the freedom to pick it up and drop it as you please,' but to *be* a blogger is something of an existential burden. 'At the very least it's a passage that lights a fire under me, inspires me and pushes me in my creative pursuits to make a conscious decision and a choice about where to direct my energy, my passion, and my enthusiasm.'

To 'be' a blogger, as opposed to simply 'having a blog', is to make blogging a significant portion of one's everyday life. It is to routinely set aside time to blog, as if it were an exercise regimen mandated by a heart doctor. It is, indeed, to habitualize the practice of blogging, to make it so engrained and so embodied that one feels its absence when going a few days without doing it.

But one does not blog in isolation. Being a blogger also means to participate in a larger network of bloggers, like Independent Fashion Bloggers or some local equivalent. It is to communicate with other bloggers, leave comments on their posts, encourage their activities, and perhaps even attend the occasional face-to-face meeting, such as IFB's own IFBconn, held just prior to New York Fashion Week in September and February or Alt Summit in Salt Lake City, Utah. Most importantly, it is to *identify* as a blogger, to take pride in having a blog, and to see blogging as a legitimate enterprise, if not quite on par with magazine publishing, then at least worthy of respect in its own right. For the self-identified blogger, having a blog is an end in itself. It is not just a pathway to something else.

Not all people with blogs, of course, do become bloggers in this sense. Scott Schuman, The Sartorialist, for instance, often complains about being labelled as a 'blogger'. For him, occupying a space more or less on the inside of the fashion industry, his status as a blogger has often read to him as a kind of black mark, something to scrub off rather than own. In a famous, and oft-cited incident in 2009, fashion label Dolce & Gabbana seated Schuman in the front row of their Spring/Summer show, alongside other well-known fashion bloggers, including Schuman's then partner (and fellow blogger) Garance Doré, Tommy Ton (of Jak & Jil), and Bryanboy (Bryan Grey Yambao of the eponymous bryanboy.com). Each was supplied with a laptop computer on a tiny podium before their seat. The fashion press picked up on the incident as 'a paradigm-shift moment', 'the first time anybody had ever given up that kind of real estate in Anna Wintour territory to the insurgents from the internet' (Pappademas 2012). Schuman, however, saw things differently. He told Alex Pappademas of *GQ Magazine* that he felt like he had been seated at the kids' table.

'They got a humongous amount of press', said Schuman. '"*Look, we brought the bloggers in and gave them the front row. Look at the dancing-monkey bloggers!*" I could barely bring myself to sit down' (emphasis in original). In the picture that often accompanies the fashion press coverage of the event, Pappademas notes, Schuman looks as if he is trying to escape. 'Like, "Ugh, I don't want everyone looking at us."' Schuman told Pappademas. 'Like, *Oh, look at the cute bloggers! Isn't that cute! Are they playing Angry Birds?* When you've got Ron Frasch behind you going: 'I spent two fucking million dollars on D&G's last collection, and I'm sitting *here*? For these little schmucks?' (Pappademas 2012, emphasis in original).

Schuman, thus, refers to The Sartorialist as a website'. It is a portal peering in to the fashion world, not a 'blog' as such. He describes himself as a fashion 'photojournalist' or just a 'photographer', preferring to reserve the term 'blogger' for those further down the fashion food chain. Everything about Schuman's rhetoric announces that he is a 'professional', not some cute little amateur with a Digital Rebel camera. Adam Katz Sinding, similarly, announces quite boldly at the top of his blog page for Le 21-ème, 'THIS IS NOT A STREET STYLE BLOG', despite all evidence to the contrary. The word just rubs Sinding the wrong way. He too prefers the more mature 'website'. In French, Sinding pointed out to me in our interview, 'blague', a homonym with 'blog', means joke. Sinding, like Schuman, isn't so interested in being labelled as one. He wants to be taken seriously by the fashion industry, and all signs point to his success in this regard. In 2013 he quit his day job as a concierge at New York's W Hotel, because it was getting the way of his making money. For photographers with blogs, like Sinding, blogging is a means to an end. It is not something you do just for the sake of doing it.

Yvan Rodic, Face Hunter, on the other hand, has few qualms about identifying himself as a blogger. It is part of his low-key, casual persona. He resisted getting his own domain name for some seven years, using the URL of Facehunter.blogspot. com until he finally made the leap and grabbed 'Facehunter.org' in 2013 when he joined Condé Nast's commercial blogger collective NOWMANIFEST. He was too late to claim the better internet real estate of Facehunter.com. His blog links to other blogs of a similar ilk. It features frequent photos of other bloggers, often labelling them as such. And unlike the bulk of bloggers of his stature, Rodic continues to use a compact camera (albeit a full-frame Sony RX 1 these days) rather than giving in to the increasingly common expectation of DSLR. Like Mordechai Rubinstein (mistermort.com – mistermort.typepad.com until a few months into 2013), Shot by Shooter (shotbyshooter.blogspot.com), Mark 'The Cobra Snake' Hunter (thecobrasnake.com), or Susanna 'Susie Bubble' Lau (of stylebubble.typepad. com), Rodic has avoided the pretence of professionalism, preferring instead to portray himself as a fun-loving adventurer, living his life outside the strictures of formal employment.

As for myself, I have had a number of moments of identification with the term 'blogger' but have never entirely adopted it as a permanent aspect of my self-concept. I admit to feeling a twinge of pride at my first Philly Style Bloggers meeting, a meeting sponsored by Google+, who used the event as an opportunity to promote the use of their video conferencing tools among bloggers, when one of the attendees asked me if I was with Google+, and another whom I had already talked to, intervened, saying, 'No. He's one of us.' I also admit to feeling some spasms of shame at New York Fashion Week, clustered around the entrances to runway shows, as various fashion editors and journalists struggled to get by the crowds of photographers out front. You could hear some of them mutter under their breath. 'Damn bloggers!' Or 'Jesus, there are a lot of fucking bloggers out here.'

But whether one identifies as a blogger or not, all parties are agreed that being a success as a blogger (or simply someone with a blog), requires cultivating a broad skillset and knowledge base. And it involves being tuned in – by means of one's *style radar* – to the larger currents in fashion. A street style blogger, however, is no one without the people they photograph. *They* are the real stars of their blogs, the people, once identified and captured, who attest to a blogger's value as a curator and arbiter or style. It is worth spending some more time talking about them. The next chapter turns to the subjects of my own street style images, the people I selected for my blog, and what they have to tell us about the current moment in fashion. If street style bloggers are slippery subjects, not easily captured within a single class or group designation, it should come as little surprise that the people they photograph are slippery too, who tell us as much about what we can't know about fashion as what we can.

4 THE SUBJECT(S) OF STREET STYLE: STREET PORTRAITS AS FASHION SINGULARITIES

A visual argument

What does street style photography 'reveal' about its subjects? What does it show us about who they are, where they are from, and the times they are living in? What hidden meanings does it unearth from the clothes they wear and the styles they embody? What kinds of anthropological knowledge, in other words, can we glean from a street style photograph? If the realism of street style photography is largely performative, a construct of the conventions photographers employ (see Chapter 1), and if the subjects of street style photography fail to cohere into a single group or category (see Chapter 3), then what 'genuine' insights can we expect to gain by shooting or looking at them? Are we not just fooling ourselves into thinking they show us anything at all?

This chapter addresses these thorny epistemological questions through the only kind of argument street style photography is equipped to make: a visual argument. I present here a small selection of the thousands of street style photographs I have taken in Philadelphia since beginning this project, along with excerpts from my brief interviews with the people photographed, and some of my thoughts about what these images tell us – or fail to tell us – about the nature of style in Philadelphia today. I do not presume that these images are able to reveal some universal truth about style. They are too singular in their focus, too insular in their gaze. I shot them in Philadelphia, a city of around 1.5 million people in the mid-Atlantic region of the United States, between 2012 and 2015, according to the dictates of my own *style radar*, which was itself formed out of years of looking at other peoples' street style images. I do, however, hope that these photographs show *something* of value – about Philadelphia, about style – that my textual descriptions alone are unable to pin down. Certainly they reveal something about the ethnic composition of Philadelphia, where African-Americans retain a slight majority over whites and Asian and Latin Americans constitute a further 18 or so per cent of the population, as well as Philadelphia's regional idiosyncrasies, its proximity to New York, Washington, D.C, and other major East Coast cities, its penchant for hip hop, punk, and other 'urban' subcultural styles, its post-industrial grit, its long working-class tradition, and its colonial origins, still visible in the architecture of its streets.

But photographs are ambiguous. We understand their meaning differently based on the context in which they are presented. Presented as anthropology, they become anthropological. Presented as marketing material for clothing brands, they become advertorial. And we understand their meaning differently based on who we are: our cultural capital and visual literacy, our life experiences, personal background, attitude, and mood. Photographs do not *contain* meaning; they facilitate its production. When we look at photographs we read things into them, things which were not necessarily what their photographers intended. There are

FIGURE 4.1 Khalia, Sansom Street. So much of style is inscrutable. It is a presence a subject exudes, a stance or an attitude, not an item of clothing one wears or a category to which one belongs. The kind of understanding street-style photography produces, then, is singular. It is not universalizable. It is not 'typical'. And it remains stubbornly visual. Photo by author.

FIGURE 4.2 Aldo, 19th St. I wouldn't know how to categorize Aldo's style, just as Aldo didn't know how to categorize it. Does it gesture towards hipsterdom? Probably. Does it say something about the influence of bicycles on today's urban culture? Perhaps. But more than that, it testifies to the singularity of Aldo's style, its unique configuration that may overlap with other peoples' but fails to map on completely. Photo by author.

details in photographs the photographer herself did not notice when taking the photo and elements in them that were not under her direct control: people walking by in the background, reflections and imperfections of light, a hint of strain around the eyes, accessories peaking out from beneath a coat. That is precisely the utility of photographs for anthropologists and other observers of style. They say more than a written argument, without the false clarity of a thesis. They refuse to conform precisely to our descriptions and classifications. They generate an excess of meaning (Taylor 1996), and in doing so enable a range of interpretations that texts often prematurely foreclose (MacDougall 1998).

In the case of street style photography, I argue in this chapter, photos do more to complicate our social theoretical schemes than reinforce them. The subjects they depict remain stubbornly out of focus, even in the sharpest of images. They elude our best efforts to 'place' them as members of a particular category or type, and testify instead to the 'singularity' of style.

The subjects of street style, then, like the subjects of any sustained gaze, are slippery subjects, evasive subjects. Their style, self-presentation, attitude, and stance say a good deal about who they are and where they come from. Or rather, they *show* a good deal about who they are and where they come from, an affective truth we recognize but cannot quite articulate. But they only show so much. As soon as we put into words what it is these photos show us, some portion of their meaning slips out of our grasp.

A question of style

In the absence of some universal scheme for making sense of the images I generate as a street style photographer, I have turned to the subjects of my photographs themselves for insight into what their style 'means' or reveals about them. Once I grew comfortable approaching strangers on the street and detaining them for longer and longer periods of time, I began asking a few basic questions: (1) What are you wearing?; (2) How would you describe your style?; and (3) What kinds of music are you listening to these days? I often followed up these questions with further clarifying inquiries, taking my subjects' lead, following their streams of thought, and paying attention to their emphases.

I didn't pull these questions out of thin air. They are not my attempt to impose some artificial or foreign meaning on street style photography. The first question – 'What are you wearing?' – is more or less standard issue for street style photographers, who, like the subjects of their photographs, tend to see it as having exactly one possible interpretation: 'What *brands* are you wearing?' Many bloggers list the brand names of a subject's outfit below their image as if they were doing a fashion magazine editorial spread. Some bloggers, like Vanessa Jackman (vanessajackman.blogspot.com), and Garance Doré (garancedore.fr), provide links to the websites of the brands featured, often accumulating link-through commissions from an affiliate marketing company like LinkShare, Reward Style, or Commission Junction in the process. Some blogs, including Where Did You Get That Street (www.wheredidugetthatstreet.com) and Candice Lake (www.candicelake.com), provide corresponding images of clothing items similar to those worn, along with links to where readers can purchase those items. They are often labelled with the consumer imperative of 'Shop This Look'. Whether links are provided or not, however, bloggers are aware that any mention of a product's brand name could reach the attention of the company who makes it and, thus, make possible future sponsorship deals and 'collaborations' (see next chapter). Understanding this potential, many bloggers list brand names on their sites habitually. But courting brand partnerships is only one reason to do so. Other bloggers do so out of personal interest or to 'educate' their readers, who often draw inspiration from the looks they see. Still others do so as a practice of near-archaeological classification, approaching street style with the meticulous eye of a curator. As for myself, I never got over a deep ambivalence towards the practice. Brand information on blogs may serve as a kind of social scientific data, but it is always also a *defacto* advertisement. As such, most of the time I asked, but sometimes, on my more cynical days, I did not.

The second question ('How would you describe your style?') is somewhat less common among street style photographers, but it shows up in various guises on street style blogs as well. Nigel Hamid of TorontoVerve (torontoverve.org) asks the question directly of his subjects, posting quotes from them below their image. Liisa Jokinen of Hel Looks asks hers about 'style inspirations', achieving more or less the same effect. Amy Creyer of Chicago Street Style frequently describes and discusses her subjects' styles in depth though seldom draws her descriptions from the subjects' own words. I asked the question myself because I wanted to learn the vocabulary of style meaningful to the subjects of my photographs rather than presume to know it. I wanted to let them speak for themselves on my blog, providing the interpretations and analysis of their outfits and looks that they found appropriate.

The third question I was inspired to ask by Michelle Oberholzer of Cinder & Skylark. In my interview with her, she explained to me why she asked it of her subjects. 'Music being one of my great loves', she said, 'it [was] sort of a way of relating to people.' She realized that music was a significant point of identification for her subjects. It *meant* something to them, something descriptive about who they are as a person. Frequently, what a subject listens to has a good deal to do with how they present themselves to others. Musical taste is often expressed through fashion, a fact subcultural theory has taken so much for granted it is often implicitly assumed through the body of its work. Punks dress punk. Metalheads dress metal. How else could it be?

FIGURE 4.3 Camilla, Walnut St. I don't know precisely what Camilla is wearing in this picture. Does it matter? Is it important? Are you missing a crucial piece of information in interpreting it without knowing? This day, I decided you were not. What seemed important to me was the mood she created with her look, not the brands she utilized to do so. Photo by author.

FIGURE 4.4 René, Walnut St. René and I bonded over our affection for 1990s gothic rock and industrial music. The imprint of these genres is visible in her fashion sense and likely has something to do with why I stopped her. But so is something else besides: a pin-up, retro sensibility, equal parts Betty Page and Siouxsie Sioux. She likes school-girl uniforms and aprons, like the one in this picture. It was a gift from a friend. Photo by author.

Nonetheless, this doesn't mean that music definitively classifies someone as this or that kind of person nor is a preference for a certain kind of music necessarily legible in a person's choice of attire. In fact, Oberholzer and I talked about how unpredictable peoples' musical tastes often turned out to be. 'Obviously if someone is dressed in a very gothic way, they [probably] listen to goth music', she told me. 'You kind of know what they think. But most of the time there's no way of telling, and I love that element of surprise.' I found something similar when I asked this, along with the other two questions, of my photographic subjects on the streets of Philadelphia. I got a range of answers to each, a catalogue's worth of brand names and band names, adjectives and adverbs, and the ones my subjects used to describe themselves were often quite different from the ones I would have used to describe them. It, like the other two questions, was a valuable lesson in academic humility. And for that precise reason I think it is worth considering my subjects' answers to each of these questions in more depth. Their answers will frame the structure of the remainder of this chapter.

Question one: What are you wearing?

I can usually tell which of the people I stop on the streets of Philadelphia read street style blogs. These are the people who nod knowingly when I explain to them what I'm doing, then immediately assume the 'straight up' pose, standing arms at their sides with an indeterminate expression on their faces. They are the ones who inquire immediately after the URL of the blog and vow to 'like' its page on Facebook or follow it on Instagram. And they are also the ones most likely to interpret the question of 'What are you wearing?' as 'What brands are you wearing?' Many people can rattle off the brands on their body as if they had consciously memorized them that morning as they put on their clothes, just in case someone might stop them for their photograph. These days, after all, you never know.

'The jacket is Burberry', said Jamele, nonchalantly. I had stopped him as we approached an alley on 3rd Street in the neighbourhood known as Old City. After I took his photograph, we immediately switched into reconnaissance mode. Jamele had his answers down pat. 'The Oxford', he went on, 'is Ralph Lauren, the jean jacket Levis, the belt Hermes, the pants also Ralph Lauren.' 'The shoes', Jamele stated emphatically, 'are Belgian Loafers.' He stressed that point again to make sure I didn't miss it. The Belgian part, he explained, is important. The sunglass frames, are Porsche Carerra, the hat, some vintage find he picked up on one of his many foraging expeditions. Everything he wears, he went on to tell me, is vintage. Jamele turned out to be an employee at a local vintage clothing store called 'Cultured Couture', owned, no less, by Erik Honesty, the very first street style subject I ever

FIGURE 4.5 Jamele, off 3rd St. Jamele, an employee of a local vintage clothing store, described his style to me as 'Fuck it! Ballsy' then went on to add 'Looks like an old person but is still young and hip.' He wears name-brand clothes, purchased second-hand, and retains the knowledge of what, or who, he is wearing, the way a curator retains the knowledge of her ceramics collection. For him, like many of my street-style subjects, it is not enough to wear a certain look. One must also know it. Photo by author.

shot for Urban Fieldnotes (see Chapter 3). Like Erik, Jamele seemed perfectly at ease in front of the camera, as if this happened to him everyday. It just might. My request to take his photo seemed utterly natural to him, as it did to many of my subjects, just a simple extension of digital culture into daily life.

It became clear early into this project that blogs were having some significant impact, if only among a select group of digitally savvy urban fashion-followers, on the way people dress and present themselves in public. Some of my subjects described dressing for the bloggers whenever they would go into New York City. Others complained – or is it bragged? – about being stopped by bloggers 'all the time'. They would put on a show of boredom at having their picture taken or otherwise demonstrate to me how it was 'no big deal'. One woman I stopped explained to me that she was, in fact, on her way to a street style photo shoot with a local photographer when I stopped her. 'So it'll have to be quick', she said. She was willing to stop, though, because she 'just loves street style blogs'.

And that attitude was more typical than the 'I'm so over-it' one I sometimes encountered. Many people I stopped were observably excited to be singled out, as if they had been waiting for this opportunity for years. They sometimes thanked me profusely afterwards or told me I had 'made [their] day'. I would often notice an increase in the referring traffic from Facebook and other social media websites to my blog when I posted those peoples' images online. They would do the work of promoting the image for me.

There are, however, more subtle – and arguably more pernicious – ways in which street style blogs have influenced how people dress, or at least, how they *think about* how they dress. Street style blogs have no doubt reinforced the brand-consciousness of their readers, their immediate recall of brand names, and their internal mapping of their outfits as pertaining to this or that category of fashion. Some of the people I stop on the streets tell me they 'have no idea' what they are wearing, the brands on their bodies holding about as much meaning to them as, say, the varieties of microorganisms populating their epidermis. But these individuals are relatively rare. Most everyone I stop can tell me at least some of what they are wearing, including such information as where they purchased the item and what brand label is attached to its collar. The fact of peoples' relative familiarity with the brands they were wearing seems to confirm a broad range of sociological studies that indicate brand awareness as a significant component of the process of socialization into American adulthood (see Holt 2004; Schor 2004). It also provides for some interesting observations about *how* people wear brands these days. Here are just a few of the things I have noticed.

(1) Fast-fashion brands, such an H&M, Zara, and Forever 21, are worn across Philadelphia's class, ethnic, and stylistic spectrum. They are so ubiquitous in the wardrobes of stylish Philadelphians as to be rendered a virtual non-issue,

FIGURE 4.6 Alyssa, 5th St, Philadelphia. Alyssa was the first person I stopped who specifically cited street-style blogs, and in particular Hel Looks, as a major source of her fashion inspiration. Her quirky, 'colourful' style is in conversation with blogs, placing Alyssa into a larger fashion context, and instilling her ordinary dress with the patina of internationalism. 'Does she always dress this colorfully?' I asked her friend, who was with her. 'You should see the rest of her wardrobe!' she told me. Photo by author.

a simple reality of anyone on any kind of non-millionaire budget. Miller and Woodward (2012) have argued that denim jeans may be the world's first 'post-semiotic' garment. They are worn by everyone, seen as utterly ordinary, and, thus, have little capacity to serve as markers of group distinction. People wear them because they want to think about things other than what they are wearing. Something similar can be said about fast-fashion brands like H&M and Zara. These may very well be on their way to becoming the world's first 'post-semiotic' brands. Although individual garments produced by fast fashion companies – a navy peacoat, for instance, or a pair of black skinny jeans – have some meaning for their wearers, the brand behind them has little meaning in itself. It is neither a source of pride nor a source of shame. 'It's just Zara.' The presence of fast-fashion items in the wardrobes of my subjects, then, tells us almost nothing about them. Even the brand-conscious people I stopped, those wearing notably upmarket or obscure designer labels, often supplemented such items with clothing from a fast fashion one.

Which leads us to my second observation: (2) Mixing and matching up-market and down-market brands is the norm for fashion-conscious people in Philadelphia. An item from here and an item from there; a second-hand jacket thrown over a brand new top; a luxury European designer label layered over a local independent streetwear brand: there is nothing unusual about any of this. For D'Angelo, it just makes sense. Up-market jeans make a bigger difference to him than his brand of bow tie. And a blazer is a blazer is a blazer, especially now that fast fashion labels have begun to employ the fitted cuts of the more up-market variety. Mixing and matching is not some covert mode of resistance. It is not a stance against brand hegemony. It is not even a tacit rejection of the logic of the market, a refusal to devote oneself to one product over another. It has taken on the status of simple common sense. 'I don't really think about it', said Katie. 'I just throw on whatever', said Nikki. 'I just find what I find', said Kelsey. In her case, that meant a 'navy style jacket from somewhere or other', a pair of Ray-Ban cat-eye sunglasses, and a scarf from H&M.

Tishia, in contrast to Kelsey, Nikki, and Katie, is decidedly more discerning about what she wears. When I stopped her walking past Sydenham Street, she was carrying an Alexander Wang bag in one hand, an American Apparel denim jacket in the other, wearing sunglasses by Miu Miu and shoes by BCBG. All of these are decidedly up-market brands. All of them are certifiably designer. And her dress? 'H&M'. She said it like it surprised even her. She just hadn't thought about it until that moment. H&M is a baseline brand, a blank canvas upon which to build a style. It is not a stylistically meaningful symbol of anything in and of itself.

(3) Some people put a lot more thought into the brands they wear than others. Some of the people I stopped could recite the brands they were wearing faster than they could name the members of their family. Others simply could not.

FIGURE 4.7 Kaila, Walnut St. Everything Kaila is wearing in this picture is from H&M. She does not, however, identify as an H&M kind of person. Indeed, it would be difficult to imagine precisely what that would mean. H&M is what is. It's 'just H&M'. Photo by author.

FIGURE 4.8 D'Angelo, off 12th St. D'Angelo in this picture is wearing shoes by Steve Madden, a bag by Fred Perry, jeans by Ring of Fire, and a blazer and bow tie from H&M. He describes his style as 'fashion on a budget', which in his case, means, lots of button-down shirts, lots of well-fitting jeans, and lots of H&M. Photo by author.

FIGURE 4.9 Taheira, off 17th Street. Taheira was wearing a 'thrifted shirt', a pair of Birkenstocks ('the cutest ugly shoes', she called them), and a skirt from H&M. 'I used to hate H&M', she told me. It was a matter of principle. She opposes fast fashion brands because they are fast fashion brands. But then she started to see a bunch of her friends wear clothes from H&M, 'cute' clothes, with really 'nice cuts', and she succumbed to its charms. Any reservations she once had about wearing H&M have since dissipated. Photo by author.

FIGURE 4.10 Tishia, Sydenham St. Tishia mixed and matched this outfit together out of both up-market and down-market brands. The dress is H&M. The shoes are BCBG. The sunglasses are Miu Miu. The denim jacket hanging from her right hand is from American Apparel, while the bag hanging from her left is Alexander Wang. What does it mean that she has assembled her outfit this way on top of H&M? Nothing. Photo by author.

FIGURE 4.11 Marie, Walnut St. Marie's outfit is like a visual record of her world travels. The 'adult blanket' she's wearing as a shawl she picked up 'from some little kid in Juarez, Mexico for like 15 bucks'. Her necklace is from Mexico as well. Her copper bracelet she got in Kenya; the 'leather, twisty one' from New York, the ring from a thrift store in Seattle. Photo by author.

FIGURE 4.12 Shakari, Walnut St. This is one of my most popular posts ever, viewed thousands of times. Shakari's outfit is pieced together from a combination of travel and personal connections. Her jacket is from a local 'DIY' vintage store called Rockers Closet. Her scarf is from Guatemala, her boots a present from her mom. Her pants, as if intentionally illustrating a theme from a few pages back, are from Zara. Photo by author.

'I have no idea what the lower half [of this outfit] is', said one of a number of 'Kelsey's I stopped in an alley off of 10th St. 'I'm not much of a brand person', said Jane, reclining against the wall at the corner of Walnut and 17th. 'Everything's thrifted', said Sooniyah, walking across Broad St, 'I only know the brand of the pants.' 'It was just a dress I found somewhere', said Christiana, sitting on some steps on 17th St.

Not everyone I stop, then, interprets the question of 'What are you wearing?' as a referendum on brands. Others take the opportunity to tell me the stories behind their clothes, particularly the human connections they represent. Danaya's brother had the scarf she was wearing made for him, then gave it to her as an act of sibling generosity. Shakari's boots came from her grandmother, her scarf from Guatemala. Her jacket she got from her favourite vintage clothing store in South Philly, a tiny place called Rockers' Closet. They purchase items in bulk from larger thrift stores, then 'upcycle' them into something edgier. Nikki's necklaces belonged to her mom. She gave them to her when she moved to Philly just a couple of weeks before. Nikki wore them like a souvenir from home. Sofia got her hat from a flea market in Nepal. A child of diplomats, she spent much of her childhood overseas. 'I call this an "adult blanket"', said Marie, of the poncho-like shawl she had thrown over her dress. 'I got it from some little kid in Juarez, Mexico for like fifteen bucks.' She'd had to bargain him down from around $50, she said. One of her copper bracelets she picked up on a trip to Kenya. One of her rings she got at a thrift store in Seattle.

Question two: How would you describe your style?

I had originally intended the question of 'What are you wearing?' to be open-ended, just vague enough to be interpreted in multiple ways. Like most anthropologists, I prefer not to unduly influence the shape or form of answers my interlocutors give to the questions I ask (Hollan and WellenKamp 1996). I like to leave my questions open to a range of possible interpretation so that my subjects can steer the question where *they* want it to go. But as it has turned out, the question of 'What are you wearing?' has yielded relatively few interpretations. The most common by far is the pre-award show red carpet solicitation of brands and designers. For most people, there is little else that 'What are you wearing?' could possibly mean. This, of course, is quite interesting in and of itself, and I have done little to dissuade my photographic subjects from such an interpretation, but it has frequently left me wanting more.

My second question, of 'How would you describe your style?' has had much more variable, and perhaps more telling, results. 'Preppy', Jackie told me almost reflexively, on her lunch break from a corporate job downtown. 'Artist', said Durrock, when I stopped him and his friend on South St. 'Grunge punk', said Melissa, taking a moment to reflect. 'Neo-soul', said Will, with an heir of confidence and conviction. 'Urban classic', said another Will, juxtaposing two common adjectives often thought of as contradictory. 'A mixture of urban, edgy, and preppy', stated Matt, pursuing a similar theme and begging the question of what precisely is meant by 'urban' (typically it was used as a synonym for African-American styles influenced by R&B and hip hop). One of my favourite answers was the one given by Jamele a few pages back: 'Looks like an old person but is still young and hip'. Another came from Mallory: 'all black, all the time'. Still another came from Chuck, sitting in the store window of Ubiq, a streetwear shop on Walnut St that turned out to be one of my favourite locations for finding street-style subjects. 'Boho hobo', he said, of his ragamuffin cool.

There were, however, three words that came up with more frequency than any other when I asked this question of how my subjects would define their style: 'eclectic', 'whatever', and 'comfortable'. Sometimes these words were used in combination, sometimes by themselves. 'Eclectic', said Lyani, in response to the question, then added 'comfortable' as if for good measure. 'Eclectic' said one of the Kelseys, then explained, 'anything I feel comfortable in'. 'Eclectic', echoed Dorothy, a thrift store connoisseur, explaining that she wears 'whatever', as long as 'it's cheap

FIGURE 4.13 Chuck, in the Ubiq Shop window on Walnut St. Chuck is wearing a pair of Air Jordan 3 Black Cement shoes, self-altered with White Out, Jeans by Righteous Rebel Denim & Apparel, a tank from H&M, a flannel from Old Navy, and a hat he found at a thrift store. Photo by author.

FIGURE 4.14 Lexi, in the Ubiq Shop window on Walnut St. Lexi is wearing a pair of Air Jordan Ones, jeans from the Gap, and a Hello Kitty T-shirt = Hello Kitty. Her style she described to me as 'Streetwear meets scene kid.' When I asked her which scene she was talking about, she told me she meant it in the 'old school sense…like emo'. She and I have a different understanding of 'old school'. Photo by author.

and different'. 'Whatever is comfortable', said Marley, for whom it appeared to be largely cut-off jeans and tank tops. But although frequently used together, each term has a separate meaning and should thus be considered individually.

'Eclectic' could be the prime descriptive term of street fashion since the 1980s. Kids today, if we believe a large body of literature in 'post-subcultural studies' (Weinzierl and Muggleton 2004), are reluctant to be pinned down to a particular 'subcultural' category or prefabricated youth culture identity (see Luvaas 2012; Muggleton 2000; Polhemus 1994). They shift allegiances, swap sensibilities. 'Reared on a constant diet of television programs and magazine articles about previous decades and Jurassic styletribes', (Polhemus 1994: 130) writes fashion anthropologist Ted Polhemus, this generation of European and US youth sample from stylistic affiliations the way connoisseurs might sample from a selection of fine wines. 'Instead of focusing on a particular styletribe of yesteryear, all of history's streetstyles, from Zooties to Beatniks, Hippies to Punks, are lined up as possible options as if they were cans of soup on supermarket shelves' (Polhemus 1994: 131). Polhemus observes a certain 'stylistic promiscuity which is breathtaking in its casualness. "Punks" one day, "Hippies" the next, they fleetingly leap across decades and ideological divides – converting the history of streetstyle into a vast

FIGURE 4.15 Jansen, in the Ubiq Shop window on Walnut St. This was the first set of photos I took in this window, of Jansen, in a Supreme t-shirt and pair of shiny spiked sneakers. Photo by author.

FIGURE 4.16 Phalla, Market St Bridge. I wouldn't know how to describe Phalla's style with any term other than 'eclectic'. In this photo she's wearing an oversize thrifted sweater, a scarf from the local boutique called Vagabond, a ski mask that she purchased 'from some surf shop in Brooklyn', which she is wearing here as a scarf, shoes by Jeffrey Campbell, a ring from her friend's jewellery company Rabid Fox, and a vintage Timberland backpack. Photo by author.

FIGURE 4.17 Demonté, off 16th St. Demonté had recently returned from a month-long meditation retreat in India when I stopped him. Most of his accessories in this outfit he picked up on that trip. His style he described to me as 'expressional', then explained that it varies substantially from day to day. Many of the subjects I stopped, like Demonté, stressed the fluidity of their style, its part-time-ness and malleability. In Demonté's case, his stylistic orientation mirrors his Buddhist spiritual-orientation, with its emphasis on flow and impermanence and its conception of self as an illusion. Photo by author.

themepark' (Polhemus 1994: 131). This is a tempting perspective to subscribe to. Indeed, the younger people I stopped on the streets, regardless of ethnic or class background, seemed to have an extensive subcultural vocabulary, peppering their self-descriptions with a healthy portion of 'mod', 'punk', 'indie', and 'goth' and demonstrating a willingness to cross between such subcultural boundaries that would have been practically unthinkable to me when I was in my teens or, for that matter, twenties.

René described her style to me as 'different everyday' but leaning towards 'goth', 'industrial', and 'vintage'; Britt as 'vintage-inspired punk rock eclectic'. Torre, after first describing his style to me as 'eclectic', then explained that 'most of the time [he's] in suits. The rest of the time [he's] a hippy'. Brianna told me that it's all about 'how [she] feel[s]'. Sometimes, she said, 'it's urban chic. Sometimes rocker grunge. But always a bit tomboyish'. Tevin told me that his style is 'different things on different days', and included among the styles he chooses from 'retro and hipster'. Sometimes he likes to 'go classic' in wingtips and button-ups. Other times he aims for more 'urban' in hightops and T-shirts. He doesn't 'like to be pinned down', he told me. 'Demonté, however, perhaps best summed up the emphasis on eclecticism when he told me that his style is 'expressional', meaning not only that it expresses something meaningful about him but that it reflects the subtle shifts in his moods. Like Demonté's Buddhist-inspired self-concept, his style is fluid. Sometimes he will wear a turban, he explained, other times a dashiki. Sometimes he is preppy, other times punk.

There are, however, reasons to be sceptical of Polhemus' description of the carefree, happy-go-lucky, highly individualized 'style surfing' (Polhemus 1996) of today's youth. I have found little evidence that young people in Philadelphia treat their styles with such playful abandon. Their styles are carefully groomed and cultivated, not picked up and dropped on a whim. Their outfits contain numerous items of personal significance and value. And I would often find myself shooting multiple individuals of a single peer group, whose stylistic commonalities were quite obvious, even while remaining eclectic.

Style, here, is not evidence of some unprecedented and emergent individualism, some breakdown in sociality of the sort disgruntled literary critics and sociologists have been bemoaning for decades (see, for example, Bauman 1998; Giddens 1991; Lasch 1979, 1994). Nor is it free-floating in empty space. We are not witnessing a loss of a master signifier (see Dean 2010) that used to lend significance to one style over another nor some 'waning of affect' (Jameson 1992), where all styles become magically equivalent, no one feeling a strong sense of connection with any of them. Literary criticism has gone decidedly overboard in making such a case. What I have found, talking with a range of Philadelphians about their style, seems to suggest the contrary. The outfits of the people I stop are riddled with personal significance. They contain a sampling of items found and given, that retain for them some trace of that association. But more importantly, they are riddled with

FIGURE 4.18 Brianna, Walnut St. Brianna is an employee at Urban Outfitters, and like the clothing company she works for, her style is a mash-up of subcultural influences. It's all about 'how I feel', she told me. Sometimes that means 'urban chic'. Other times it means 'rocker grunge'. But the consistent thread that runs throughout is her 'tomboyishness'. Photo by author.

FIGURE 4.19 Ajzha, off 17th St. Philly-based fashion designer Ajzha Khan 'never has fewer than two colors in her hair at any time' (from her Instagram page). She changes her look continually, sliding between points on a spectrum of styles that includes punk, hip hop, hippy, and high-fashion. Nonetheless, she is always immediately recognizable on the streets of Philly. She always looks like her. Photo by author.

FIGURE 4.20 Kelsey, on Sydenham St, described her style to me as 'eclectic' then added 'anything I feel comfortable in'. She exemplifies the sheer variety of looks a single individual can subscribe to on her daily 'outfit of the day' post on the social media site Instagram. For Kelsey, style is both costume and self-expression, a continual play with new looks and themes. Photo by author.

social significance. Items given as a present link their wearer with the person who gave it. Items that connote punk, hip hop, or mod symbolically link their wearer to those who originated the look. Styles mean *something*. And they connect people with something. They simply fail to correspond with a neat and tidy configuration of sociological categories. Traces of punk, hip hop, hippy, and hipster circulate and replicate, appear in the outfits of people across genders and ethnicities, classes, and sexualities. They fail to adhere steadfastly to one identity or type.

Culture and media scholar Dominic Pettman, drawing on the work of the radical social critic Giorgio Agamben, uses the term 'whatever being' to describe 'new modes of community and new modes of personality anticipated by the dissolution of inscriptions of identity through citizenship, ethnicity, and other modern markers of belonging' (cited in Dean 2010: 66). For Pettman, whatever being is the kind of being left over when you strip off all the old categories that used to define us. It is the 'bare life' (Agamben 1998) of individual expression.

'Whatever being', for both Pettman and Agamben, is 'an enactment of existence without qualities, or at least qualities so interchangeable and obvious that they erase all identity' (Pettman 2006: 9). It is state of being, in fact, that resists other peoples' efforts to place and to classify. It is what it is, *such as it is* (Agamben 1993), nothing more, nothing less. Anything specific you say about it tends to read as false, added on and out of place. 'Whatever' is an utterance that deflects communication, acknowledging that someone has spoken, while neither answering nor refusing to answer their question (Dean 2010: 67). 'Would you be comfortable defining yourself as punk?' asks the diligent researcher of style. 'Whatever', responds her subject. Whatever being, claims Agamben, is not anti-social. It is not individualistic or solipsistic. It engages in acts of communication. It speaks. It acknowledges. It reaches out. But as it does so, it remains steadfastly what it is: whatever. As such, whatever being bespeaks a thoroughly contemporary form of 'belonging' (see Agamben 1993; Maffesoli 1995), tuned in and turned on without dropping out. It is a state of connection and exchange, where one assumes the attributes of a type or a category without necessarily being 'of' that type or category. For whatever beings, the simple fact of belonging – the simple thrust of social connection – is what matters, not the group to which one belongs. What one wears, how one dresses, what styles one embodies connects them to here and to there. It makes them a part of, a participant in, an actor among. But it does not supply us, as observers of them, with a convenient shorthand for understanding who they are. Style of the sort I see regularly on the streets of Philadelphia is at once too expansive and too personal for that.

No wonder, then, that one of the most frequent words I hear on the streets of Philadelphia, when I ask my subjects about their style, is 'whatever'.

'I just throw on whatever', Nicole told me, as we chatted on the corner of Walnut and Broad in Center City, Philadelphia. 'Whatever I like', said Angela from just

FIGURE 4.21 Lady London, South St. What is this style again? I can't seem to place it, and Lady London provided few clues for how to interpret it. Photo by author.

FIGURE 4.22 Luna, Chancellor St. Everything Luna is wearing is thrifted, except the denim vest. He borrowed that from his mother. I have no idea how to describe Luna's style. Neither did he. Photo by author.

FIGURE 4.23 Stephanie, off 5th St. 'I just wake up and throw on whatever', Stephanie told me, when I asked about her style. In her case, that's generally 'shorts all year round', high-socks and tights. 'I guess I'm kinda grungy', she said, but the grunge here refers more to a general lack of concern – or at least a performance of the lack of concern – than a lack of soap. Photo by author.

across the street. 'Whatever I like', echoed Crystal from a few blocks over on Chestnut and 16th. 'I just wake up and throw on whatever', said Stephanie, posing in an alley off of 5th Street. 'Whatever' is a street-style conversation-stopper. It rebounds the question back to the asker. 'It's in your court now. Go ahead and make another move.' Deftly employed, it rejects the efforts of an interlocutor to inject meaning into the thought processes of the other, but even casually used, it implies that what the questioner is after is not really worth the effort. 'There is nothing to know here. Read whatever you want into it.' In some instances, 'whatever' makes the questioner look foolish for even asking the question. 'I've never really thought about it', I often hear from my subjects, or, 'I have no idea.' But what I hear beneath the sentiment is something else: 'Like I would give that any real thought! Like there is even any explanation to give.' I have come to interpret 'whatever' as both capacious – in that it could potentially include anything – and reductive – in that it says almost nothing, indeed, has nothing to say. But that doesn't mean it doesn't communicate. The fascinating thing about whatever being is that it never stops communicating, even – perhaps especially – when it has nothing to say (Dean 2010). Street style today is an impossibly dense text of undecipherable hieroglyphics. It is laden with symbols layered on top of symbols that refer to all sorts of things but *mean* essentially nothing. If the scholar of fashion interprets clothing as a system of meanings (see Barthes 1990), gradually compiling a virtual dictionary of sartorial significance, the styles on the streets are like a spill of water across the pages of that dictionary, blurring its words together, making its page stick. The subjects of street style thwart interpretation, render themselves illegible. For many of the subjects of my photographs, the quest for meaning itself is misplaced. Clothes are clothes. They look pretty and refer to stuff. So what? Whatever.

And yet, one only has to glance at the subjects of my photographs to know that, for them, not just any clothes will do. They have to mesh with a subject's self-concept. They have to look 'cool' on them and be read as 'cool' by others. And to do that, they have to look like they 'fit' that person, both as a body and an embodiment of style. The person wearing them has to look 'comfortable' in them.

'Comfortable' was one of the most common adjectives used in conjunction with 'whatever' by my street-style subjects, as in 'whatever is comfortable', or 'whatever, as long as it's comfortable'. My photographic subjects repeatedly mention comfort as a prime criterion for how they dress. Shakari, with the green dreads a few pages back, described her style to me for another shoot more than a year later as 'comfortable', then added 'schnazzy' as a descriptive qualifier. 'With an "h"?' I asked. 'With an "h"', she confirmed. Emily described her style as 'comfort meets unique'. One of the 'Kelsey's supplemented her description of her style as 'eclectic' with 'anything I feel comfortable in'. Here, in Kelsey's comment is the crux of comfort, 'Anything *I* feel comfortable in', for comfort is not a quality intrinsic to

FIGURE 4.24 Alex, a Philadelphia-based menswear blogger, feels most 'comfortable' in a jacket and tie. It is a look he has cultivated over the last several years, but now it fits him like a glove. He wears his retro Ivy League clothing to school, to work, and around town, and never complains about his tie being too tight or jacket stifling movement. Alex also exemplifies a common menswear trend I saw in Philly in the spring and summer of 2013, men wearing loafers, brogues, and other dress shoes without socks, an action taken ostensibly in the name of comfort, which, in fact, causes greater friction of the skin against leather, and compromises one's bodily comfort for the sake of a certain aestheticized casualness. Photo by author.

FIGURE 4.25 Katie, for a number of months, was my most popular post on Urban Fieldnotes. In part, I would attribute that popularity to the iconicity of the photo. It's a classic straight up of a girl exemplifying a common street style aesthetic. Add in a bicycle and it is elevated to a whole other level. But I would also attribute its popularity to the ease with which Katie wears her look. It looks natural on her, comfortable. She wears the look with nonchalance and ease, as if she threw it on that morning without thinking. And yet, a simple glance at her high maintenance hairstyle belies that interpretation. Katie's cool is composed out of a calculated indifference, one which the oversize military shirt, looking like a hand-me-down from dad, reinforces. Photo by author.

an item of clothing. It is a feeling attributed to an item of clothing by a particular individual, operating from a particular cultural vantage point.

Miller and Woodward (2012), in their work on denim, discuss at length the quality of 'comfortable' that their interlocutors frequently ascribe to jeans. It is an adjective, say Miller and Woodward, that people use habitually, almost without thought. Of course jeans are comfortable. That's why we wear them. But what does comfortable mean? Is it a description of how nice denim feels against one's skin, how well it conforms to the shape of one's body? Or is it description of how denim makes one feel as a social actor, 'comfortable in one's own skin', appropriate for the occasion, cool. There is nothing intrinsically comfortable about denim, Miller and Woodward contend. In earlier iterations, in fact, when jeans were made by selvage loom, they were often stiff and rigid, taking months to fully break in. If this is 'comfortable', then so are wool and polyester. And people often wear their jeans tight, constricting the movement of their legs and cinching in at the waist. Yet, even in such instances, people describe jeans as 'comfortable'. Comfortable here, clearly has more than one meaning. It means 'appropriate' but 'casual', the kind of thing you wear for work or leisure but not for stuffy corporate jobs that require 'uncomfortable' suits. But it also means representative of the kind of image that one wants to project, a style one can be 'comfortable' with and in, and this is the way I heard the word 'comfortable' used most frequently on the streets of Philadelphia. 'Comfortable' describes clothing that easily aligns with one's sense of self, that feels natural to wear, that doesn't take overcoming any great psychological obstacle to put on. Comfortable is clothing you don't think about. When you put it on, it feels right. 'Uncomfortable', on the other hand, is something that forces you out of your state of continuous being. It causes you to question what you are wearing, whether it 'fits' your body, your self-concept, or your way of being in the world. Like 'eclectic' and 'whatever', then, comfortable refers to someone being *such as they are*, without belabouring the point, without adding any social artifice. If 'cool' is a state of effortless self-possession, of stylistic autonomy that sticks steadfastly to who one is, it would follow that cool people would wear clothes they feel comfortable in.

Question three: What kinds of music are you listening to these days?

Cool is the quality of calculated indifference embodied by a stylized subject. It is a posture that resists easy definition, that presents its subject in such a way that she is both recognizable as cool and illegible as a text. Cool insists on being what it is without being swayed in some other direction or made to fit uncomfortably within a category. It is *such as it is*. Whatever. If it were too easily described, too easily pinned down and confined, it would be outside the boundaries of cool. It would be fashionable. It would be *trendy*. It would be *cliché*. My photographic subjects seemed to recognize this quality of cool intuitively, and I often got the impression that they listed multiple, contradictory adjectives for me when I asked questions of them about their style in part to throw me off the scent. Even if they had some internal category in mind for defining themselves, they weren't going to give it to me. That would be too precarious a manoeuvre. It would make them too easy a target. This strategy certainly seemed to apply to the issue of music as well. Few people were content to limit themselves to a single genre. If I were to believe the people I stopped on the streets, most people listen to 'everything'.

'Honestly, pretty much everything', Machy told me in response to my question of what he has been listening to lately. 'I like pop to rock to alternative to folk – whatever.' 'I'm kind of like all over the place', said Najé. 'Right now', admitted Shawn, 'I really haven't been listening to too much music. But on the regular I listen to a lot of different things. I like SZA. I like Chance the Rapper. I also like people like Paramour. It's like, I'm very eclectic when it comes to music. I like a lot.' Alex, on the other hand, was willing to make a gesture towards pinning down a particular genre but only a gesture. 'I guess maybe alternative-ish', she told me. The 'ish' speaks volumes.

The eclectic musical tastes proclaimed by my street style interlocutors is fairly consistent with observations made by social theorists and other documenters of public taste in recent decades. The 'postmodern condition' identified by theorists like Baudrillard (1994), Lyotard (1984), and Jameson (1992), and characterized by a super-abundance of signs all competing for public attention, has broken down barriers between high and low culture, flattened the hierarchy of cultural production, and made all generic styles essentially equivalent. Where once the aspiring elite demonstrated their superior social status through their adherence to rarefied musical forms, these days, in the age of instant downloads, they demonstrate it through the sheer eclecticism of their tastes (Holt 2000). We access music so easily today, through free and subscription–based music-streaming services like Spotify, Pandora, and Last.fm, that there is little reason to commit oneself to a genre, as I did with 'indie' and 'alternative' back in high school, little incentive to wear one's musical taste as a badge of identity. Better to just hit 'shuffle' on your iPod and move on (Powers 2014).

Nonetheless, not everyone I stopped had musical tastes that were so ecumenical. If street style is a documentation of exceptions, then it is also a documentation of exceptions to the exception. I have noticed two types of instances where people I stop list one, and only one genre of music. In the first instance, the person I stopped holds to a relatively 'conservative' subcultural tradition, such as punk rock, goth, or heavy metal (see Wallach 2008). These genres are not 'conservative' in the common use of the term. Indeed, they often

FIGURE 4.26 Najé, Walnut Street. I would be hard-pressed to predict Najé's musical taste from what she was wearing when I stopped her. Her outfit signals a range of subcultures from rock to beach bum. Unsurprisingly, then, when I asked her about her taste in music, she told me, 'I'm kind of all over the place'. Photo by author.

FIGURE 4.27 Shawn, 16th Street. Shawn claims to be very 'eclectic' when it comes to music, singling out hip hop artists like SZA and Chance the Rapper to juxtapose against 'alternative' rockers Paramour in his description. From his choice of ensemble, I am inclined to believe him. Shawn's outfit traverses the realms of hip hop and goth, while making a nod to couture labels like Commes des Garçons and Rick Owens. Photo by author.

FIGURE 4.28 Alex, Chestnut Street, claims to listen to 'alternative-ish' music. When I questioned her further, she mentioned punk bands like Merchandise and Gag, then threw in the early 1990s shoegazer band My Bloody Valentine as another (perhaps counter?) example. 'Ish' is as close as most people I stop will get to isolating a single genre of music as their preference. Photo by author.

FIGURE 4.29 Kas, Third Street, adheres to a punk rock look largely unchanged from when I was her age. Not surprisingly, she also professed to be a fan of punk music. Nonetheless, there were some small ways in which her look had been individualized and updated. For instance, Kas was wearing a pair of multi-coloured hightop Reebok sneakers when I stopped her, well outside the punk rock canon of Converse and Doctor Martens. Photo by author.

FIGURE 4.30 Alexis, Chestnut Street, has updated the punk look in a number of ways, with her imitation Doctor Martens untied in the style of hip hop and her hair only dyed at the ends. And yet she remains recognizably punk. Photo by author.

FIGURE 4.31 Craig, in a pair of locally made, selvedge Norman Porter jeans, a used Levis jacket, a beard, and a vintage fedora is almost textbook 'hipster' as defined in 2014. He could be in an indie samba band or DJ at an EDM club. And yet he describes his musical taste his curt exactitude: 'country'. Photo by author.

FIGURE 4.32 Aryelle, Walnut Street, admits she doesn't look like the typical metal fan. That's the whole point. She would prefer you didn't know what she listened to from what she is wearing. Not that she isn't proud to be a metal fan. She just prefers the shock value of telling you. Her preference for metal is proof that she isn't who you think she is. Photo by author.

FIGURE 4.33 Emily, Walnut Street, with some tongue in cheek, professed to listen to nothing but Top-40 mainstream pop. She smiled when she said it, as if the very idea delighted her. Photo by author.

appear quite radical to outsiders, referenced through torn up clothes, spikes, and extreme hairstyles. And yet they adhere to a relatively steadfast form, resisting the currents of change in musical and sartorial fashion, and remaining recognizable despite changes in the overall fashion system. Polhemus (1978), for this reason refers to punk and other such genres of dress that accompany a preference for particular, subcultural music forms as 'anti-fashion'. The philosopher Gilles Lipovetsky, in arguing that 'hypermodernity' leads us to attach less importance to a particular sound or style (Lipovetsky 2002) acknowledges that there are certain groups – whom Lipovetsky labels as 'fundamentalists' – unwilling to go with the tide. Punks and metalheads are the fundamentalists of music, sticking steadfastly to one variety or type in the face of mass diversification. Consequently, these groups were the most likely of the people I stopped to tell me they listened to only one thing. Usually I was not surprised. I recognized them as punk, goth, or metal from hundreds of feet away.

The other instance of my subjects claiming to listen to one, and only one type of music, might be best described as ironic self-classification. This is when a subject deliberately indicated a genre that appeared out of sync with their dominant sartorial style. 'Country', insisted Craig, in his all-denim look others would likely classify as 'hipster'. 'Top-40', said Emily, in a pair of Doctor Marten boots, a bright red skirt, altered denim jacket, tattoos, and other markers of an 'alt culture' sensibility. 'Metal', said Aryelle, whose projected persona was more mainstream contemporary. Here, preference for a single genre serves a similar function as out-and-out musical eclecticism: it refuses type. The surprising genre choice demonstrates that a person is more complicated than they may at first appear. It attests to the slipperiness of their self-identity. 'Don't pin me down', a subject pursuing this strategy insists. 'I am not what I seem.'

Capturing the Philadelphia style

This is the lesson for anthropologists that street style photographs drive home: pictures show us a lot about people, but they don't show us everything. They convey an over-abundance of information, a surplus of signs. At the same time, they are missing those imagined markers of identification that definitively categorize a person as a member of this or that group. They are *nominalist*, rather than *realist* (see Chapter 1), singular rather than general. Street style photography is a practice of documenting exceptions. It singles out individuals who already do not fit type. But when out on the streets, camera in hand, everyone starts to look like an exception. Through the practice of street style, convenient social categories used as a shorthand by social scientists begin to break down.

What then, if anything, can we learn about a city, like, say, Philadelphia from looking at street style photos taken there? Are there generalizations we can make, imprints of place we can identify? Is there a Philadelphia stylistic *habitus* in formation? Well, yes and no. Philadelphia, my photographic subjects often explained to me, is hugely varied. 'I think that everyone has like their own diverse style', one of my subjects told me during our street interview, ''cause it's, I guess, important to stand out.' 'There's kinda all these hands in the pot', said another, 'trying to stir things up a little bit. You never have one real trending fashion statement. It's really everybody does what they feel like.' 'There's no such thing as a Philly style', said a third. 'That's why I love this city. Everybody has like their own individual creativity, and they just make it happen.' The people I stop on the street stress the individuality of Philadelphia style, its failing to be exactly one thing or another, its being such as it is. And yet, there are certain words that come up repeatedly, when I discuss the subject of Philly style with my interviewees: 'comfortable', 'edgy', 'gritty', 'expressive', 'free'. 'I definitely think in general Philadelphia is a comfortable place', one interviewee told me. 'We're cheaper than New York. And that's what's so great about this place, that we have this freeness and comfortableness to just be ourselves.' Notice the way he uses New York as a measuring stick. New York, in my street interviews, came up continually, like a shadow Philadelphians would never be quite able to step out of. 'It's predictable', said another interviewee of Philadelphia style. 'It's more like urban type', said a third, wrestling for an appropriate adjective. One of my interviewees associated Philadelphia with classic American style, another with traditional menswear, another with scruffy hobo chic. Clearly, as a city of more than one and a half million people, with a diversity of ethnicities, religions, and languages spoken, Philadelphia is not easily characterized. Its street style embodies contradictions. And yet, these contradictions are configured in a way that it is distinct to there.

Street style photographs from Philadelphia, like street style photographs from Helsinki, Cape Town, or Beijing, are more a record of the singular modes of embodiment that occupy a place than a clear indication of some citywide zeitgeist. They reveal *something* about the mood, feeling, or attitude of the place, something palpable in the subjects depicted there, something that exemplifies what is emergent, dominant, and residual (Williams 1977) in its shared culture, but they do just as much to complicate and complexify that picture. They remind us, that is, to remain humble in what we assert about others, the patterns and structures we fit them into. Sometimes we just have to observe them for ourselves. Sometimes our words fail to do justice to the lived richness and complexity of a place. Sometimes we just have to see its style for ourselves and come to our own conclusions.

FIGURE 4.34 Zack, 3rd St, Philadelphia. Photo by author.

FIGURE 4.35 Marcus, Walnut St, Philadelphia. Photo by author.

FIGURE 4.36 Alyssa, off 17th St, Philadelphia. Photo by author.

FIGURE 4.37 Aaron, Walnut St, Philadelphia. Photo by author.

FIGURE 4.38 Amy, Rittenhouse Square, Philadelphia. Photo by author.

FIGURE 4.39 Wanda, Sansom St, Philadelphia. Photo by author.

FIGURE 4.40 Swabreen, an alley in Old City, Philadelphia. Photo by author.

FIGURE 4.41 Designer Sophi Reaptress, Chestnut Street, Philadelphia. Photo by author.

FIGURE 4.42 Skillit, South St, Philadelphia. Photo by author.

FIGURE 4.43 Uyen, South St, Philadelphia. Photo by author.

FIGURE 4.44 Bernard and Larry, American St, Philadelphia. Photo by author.

FIGURE 4.45 Richie, Sydenham St, Philadelphia. Photo by author.

FIGURE 4.46 Olivia, Walnut St, Philadelphia. Photo by author.

FIGURE 4.47 Michael, Chestnut St, Philadelphia. Photo by author.

FIGURE 4.48 Marcus, Broad St, Philadelphia. Photo by author.

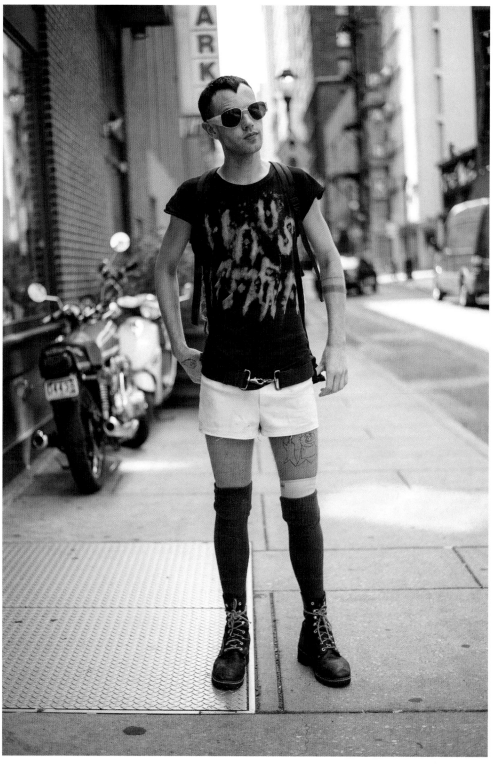

FIGURE 4.49 Yurek, Sansom St, Philadelphia. Photo by author.

FIGURE 4.50 Paul, Broad St, Philadelphia. Photo by author.

FIGURE 4.51 Katie, Sansom St, Philadelphia. Photo by author.

FIGURE 4.52 Lukas, Chestnut St, Philadelphia. Photo by author.

FIGURE 4.53 Harry, Walnut St, Philadelphia. Photo by author.

FIGURE 4.54 Eric, Chestnut St, Philadelphia. Photo by author.

FIGURE 4.55 DJ, Walnut St, Philadelphia. Photo by author.

FIGURE 4.56 Barry Jackson, Sansom St, Philadelphia. Photo by author.

FIGURE 4.57 Brae, Sydenham St, Philadelphia. Photo by author.

FIGURE 4.58 Lyn, 17th St, Philadelphia. Photo by author.

5 THE BUSINESS OF BLOGGING: FREE LABOUR, FREELANCING, AND FREE STUFF

Everyone's a marketer now

We want to make you into a rock star!

That was what the Chief Strategy Officer for a New York-based department store told me – without any hint of irony – as we chatted, four months before their local launch, in the private pavilion of a hotel rooftop lounge in Philadelphia. It was mid-afternoon in early summer, over two years into my street style project, and this was the first time I had met face-to-face with brand representatives from the fashion industry. It wouldn't be the last. There was a round conference table in the centre of the sunlit drafty room, a buffet spread of fruit, cookies, and coffee placed against a wall of windows to my right. A vaguely Tuscan theme of sandy taupes and decorative pillows tied together the décor, and a calculated mood of quiet indulgence offset the seriousness of the task at hand. The Chief Strategy Officer too was dressed casually, in an all-black streetwear look that belied his prominent position. He had a faint Italian accent, a habit of mixing youth slang with marketing jargon, and an 'a ha!' style of vocal delivery that made every sentence he uttered sound like a revelation. He seemed to embody, almost down to a T, the character of a record company executive in some rock 'n' roll screwball comedy, that smooth-talking Artist & Repertoire guy, who meets the wannabe starlet protagonist in a dingy Hollywood club and promises to make all of her dreams come true.

The Chief Strategy Officer roamed restlessly around the room, moving from his chair at the head of the table to a sofa behind me and back again, while the five of us – two other members of the department store's marketing team, a consultant from their local PR firm, the officer, and myself – were 'brainstorming collaborations' between my blog and their company. How could we 'synergize' my blog's 'vision' with theirs, we wondered? How could we 'create value' for both my readers and their potential customers, and, well, maybe just maybe convert a few of the former into the latter at the same time? How might Urban Fieldnotes benefit from the 'vast digital resources' already at the department store's disposal? And how might the department store benefit from its association with Urban Fieldnotes? As we talked, the officer grew more and more animated. He riffed on my comments, created flushed out versions of whatever suggestion I might make. 'I'm just thinking out loud here', he would say, as if protecting himself from accusations of impropriety, had he gone just a little too far. My improvised suggestion of featuring different looks from different neighbourhoods in Philadelphia morphed into a countdown to the store's opening, one look for every day leading up to it. My mention of a possible future project on fashion's role in Philadelphia's urban renewal became a glossy, promotional coffee table book financed, at least in part, by them. There was talk of 'guerilla marketing' and collaborations with street artists, posters of my images scattered through prominent neighbourhoods of the city. Most of these were 'just ideas', as the Chief Strategy Officer frequently repeated, but clearly the marketing team had a few plans in place coming in to this meeting. I, along with six or seven other bloggers – 'the crème de la crème of stylish bloggers in Philadelphia', as their PR firm's email to me read – would be 'taking over' their social media accounts at a set juncture prior to the opening. We would promote each other's content, and this content, in turn, would promote the imminent arrival of the department store. My website's content would be featured on their website. And my images, taken on the streets of Philadelphia, would be blown up and broadcast on a seventy-foot LED display on the outside of the historic building that would be their new store's home. They would bring their in-house photo crew out to Philly to shoot a two-minute documentary about me, based on my persona – an anthropologist of fashion, a professor of style, they would let me dictate the narrative – and they would show this film on their website and intermittently on the LED screen as well. My URL would be writ large for all to see. My image would be imprinted onto the minds' of their customers. If I wasn't a big deal in Philly already, they promised, no problem. They would just make me one.

Now in those rock 'n' roll comedies – 'Wayne's World', 'Rock of Ages', 'Josie and the Pussycats', 'Almost Famous' – that record company A&R character, of course, always turns out to be the villain, undermining the goals of the wannabe starlet protagonist and stripping her of agency, even as he makes her into the rock star he promised her she would be. Capitalism, as personified by the A&R guy, will always ruin rock 'n' roll. It can't help it. It's in its nature. In those films, you can almost hear the gears moving behind the mask, the slow creak of the scorpion's tail retracting into place. But here I was in the midst of the marketing machine, the scorpions' den, primed and ready for some serious manipulation, and all I could hear was the sound of my coffee being poured and the tapping of painted fingernails on laptop keys. Was I being naïve? Was I missing the subtle chess moves through which they were making me into their pawn? Was I was a fool for thinking this might be an interesting angle to take with my street style project, entering into a situation I couldn't fully understand? Or was that situation really as clear-cut and straightforward as it seemed to be? They would make me into a 'rock star', and I, in turn, would shoot images of stylish local people, tagged with the name of their store.

The truth is, I felt comfortable with this group, relaxed. My defences were down, my knee-jerk Marxist antipathy towards corporations nowhere to be found. Clearly the department store team had gone to great lengths to create that effect. Our room was resort-like, the tone of our conversation decidedly low key, and the dress code cool and casual. I could see all that. But my sense of ease went beyond it. I understood what the team was trying to do with the opening and could relate to it, even respect it. I used similar language when talking with other bloggers about expanding my readership. I too 'strategized' about 'partnerships' and 'collaborations', bringing more 'value' to my 'brand'. Moreover, I was in a similar age range to the team, had a similar fashion sensibility, made use of the same pop cultural reference points. These were my peers, both in age and interest. And we shared a common project: marketing.

Marketing today is not just about invasive Facebook posts targeted to your Google search habits. It is not just about spam clogging your inbox. It is not just about overblown billboards and blaring Superbowl ads. It is also, more and more frequently, about 'collaboration' – multiple parties promoting each other across multiple platforms and media. Its ethos is democratic, its methods fundamentally social.

There are some decidedly positive things about this trend in marketing. Marketing is no longer a top-down proposition, men in flannel suits designing targeted messages from their penthouse offices on Madison Avenue. And it is no longer about simply feeding the coffers of an established publishing sector. In the fashion industry today, it is equally important to recognize 'influencers' from outside the industry's perceived boundaries and direct their 'influence' towards one's own interests. The Japanese fast fashion brand UNIQLO, for instance, recently gave away $50 gift cards to well-known Instagrammers, including myself, for 'hashtagging' their product at various events in Philadelphia. In the fashion industry today, marketing is as much about blogs and social media as it is about magazines. Branding budgets are broad enough to incorporate the ambitious 'amateur'.

This is a much more inclusive model of marketing than past models. It distributes the wealth more broadly. It casts a wider net. But it also comes at a cost. We are all, in a sense, marketers now, with the rights and obligations that entails. 'Everyone' claim Bakshy et al. in a 2011 study on Twitter, 'is an influencer' (Bakshy et al. 2011). Consequently, that fine line between friends, networks, and cross-promoters is getting murkier all the time. We advertise our achievements to our families. We solicit them for our Kickstarter campaigns. We draw from our social networks in ways that were once confined to the Amway fringe. That's just how it's done these days. And sitting in that plush Mediterranean lounge that day in early summer, meeting with the department store's marketing team, I understood that. We were here to promote each other. The department store wanted me to promote them on my blog, and they would promote my blog through their social media. A simple exchange. What could be more transparent than that? What could be more prosaic?

Were these marketers overselling their case, exaggerating what they could do for me? Were they selling me a beautiful – and slightly ridiculous – dream? Of course. That's what marketers do. They can't help it. It's in their nature. But I was selling them a dream too: Urban Fieldnotes as just the right mix of street authenticity and fashion sophistication and Philly as the new, grittier home of style – like New York before Giuliani.

By the time of my meeting with that New York-based department store I had already taken on a blogger's vocabulary and a blogger's preoccupations. I thought, more often and more deeply than I am comfortable admitting, in pageviews, followers, and 'likes'. I had accepted the basic tenet, for better or for worse, that exposure is currency and branding is value. I had begun, in fact, to see myself as a brand, complete with certain signature characteristics. I cultivated a look. I policed my content for continuity. I sought out ways to expand my blog's readership and reach. I could see, that is, what the department store had to offer me: a larger potential audience base, a symbolic merging of their brand and my own. I even understood the marketing lingo its representatives were throwing my way: 'presence', 'value', 'synergy', 'content'. They expected me to. This was not a talent agency, plucking a starlet out of obscurity. This was a meeting between marketers, one set for a company, the other for a blog.

This chapter chronicles the business practices of street style bloggers today through my own experiences and encounters with other bloggers and brands. I depict a fraught digital terrain, where the dividing lines between professional and amateur, insider and outsider, friend and cross-promoter are getting hazier all the time (Chia 2012; Hearn 2008; Ross 2013; Terranova 2004, 2013). Even the most amateur of bloggers have learned to think of themselves as brands (Banet-Weiser and Sturken 2010; Gershon 2011). Even the most 'hobbyist' of street style photographers runs their hobby as a business. Whether you read this trend as a diabolical plot – the encroachment of neoliberal capitalism into nearly every facet of our personal lives (Hearn 2008; Rose 2006) – or as an encouraging sign that more and more people are finding ways to turn what they love into what they do for a living (Dawson and Tran 2013; Ziv 2011) – there can be little doubt that blogging is increasingly an entrepreneurial activity, a form of what media theorist Brooke Duffy has referred to as 'aspirational labor' (Duffy 2014). Street style blogging overlaps and intersects with a range of commercial interests, some obvious, some less so. The savvy blogger can see where these overlaps and intersections occur, and she learns to navigate them according to her own set of ethics and rules. But even the least savvy blogger is forced to contend with them. In blogging, self-expression and brand promotion are one and the same thing. Hobbies and businesses are part of the same continuum of practice. We are all marketers now. It is time to come to grips with what that means.

Blogging in a brand culture

My meeting with that department store was a meeting between marketers, two business-like entities with promotional interests at stake. What we were discussing was a variety of opportunities for 'co-branding' (Blackett and Boad 2000), the cross-fertilization of affective traits between separate branded units. Urban

Fieldnotes would exchange a little bit of brand DNA with the department store. The department store would exchange a bit with Urban Fieldnotes. We would both walk away promotionally enhanced. This is brand virology. Too bad Deleuze and Guattari didn't live long enough to complain about it.

We could spend the rest of this book talking about what a 'brand' is and means and the consequences of our culture becoming increasingly centred around brands, but so much has been written on that subject already, it hardly seems an effective use of the space here. A good place to look for additional background is Celia Lury's book *Brands: The Logos of the Global Economy* (Lury 2004). In it, Lury defines a brand as a 'set of relations between products in time' (Lury 2004: 2). A brand is an *interface* or *assemblage* (Entwistle and Slater 2013) between an object and its attendant associations, meanings, and attributes. It changes over time, evolves as it moves across borders, and as different actors, situated in different ways, invest it with new associations, meanings, and attributes. It is, in other words, not really a thing at all, but a process. Nonetheless, in common parlance, we talk about brands as if they were things – things that can be touched and manipulated, things that can be described in tangible, verifiable terms. We talk as if a brand were the indisputable possession of an individual or a company, something they own and control. We have gotten used to doing this because the logic of brands and branding has become second nature for people in developed and developing nations alike. Brand culture is *our* culture (Banet-Weiser 2012), a pervasive way of thinking and being which infects nearly every aspect of our personal and social lives. Anything can be a brand. *Anyone* can be a brand. And when everything and everyone is a potential brand, every utterance is a potential marketing pitch for that brand. Every Facebook post is a potential advertisement, every phone call a solicitation. In brand culture, there is no space beyond commodification. There is no outside capitalism, no pure, utopian terrain still resonant with the vitality of the 'authentic'. There is only effective marketing and less effective marketing.

The only way to understand the brand culture of today is to understand the distinct moment in the evolution of capitalism we are currently living through. Social theorists have proposed a number of terms for this moment – 'late capitalism' (Jameson 1992); 'post-modernity' (Harvey 1989); 'hyper-modernity' (Lipovetsky 2005); 'communicational capitalism' (Dean 2010) – but they agree on most of its basic features. We live in an age when capitalism is the only game in town. All other economic systems have receded into the background, losing relevance if not outright disappearing. The flow of capital connects the most and least developed of societies, and we measure their development according to the degree of their incorporation into the global capitalist system. It is no longer necessary, that is, for the capitalist class to impose its ideology on everyone else through overt colonial apparatuses. Nearly every society on earth has already adopted capital as its dominant driving force. Capitalism has already remade the world in its image.

It has established a singular global 'Empire' (Hardt and Negri 2001) ruled by a simple, repetitive logic: profit or perish.

This is not to say that capitalism is a monolithic entity, uniform in every part. One of the most significant contributions that anthropologists have made to the study of global capitalism is our attention to local varieties and the way they intersect and overlap with state, hierarchy, tradition, and religion, among other elements, to form complex 'assemblages' (Deleuze and Guattari 1987; Hardt and Negri 2001; Ong 2006) that evolve over time and take on new features as they move from place to place. My capitalism is not necessarily your capitalism. There are, instead, many capitalisms, with their own local flavours and characters. Each, however, upholds capital as a central preoccupation.

The most dominant form of capitalism operating today is undoubtedly what theorists refer to as 'neoliberalism' (Gershon 2011; Harvey 2005; Marwick 2013; Ong 2006; Ortner 2013; Rudnyckyj 2009). Neoliberalism describes both an ideology and a mode of capitalist practice that emphasizes the deregulation of markets and the privatization of public assets. Like capitalism more generally, it is diverse and varied in its implementation (Ong 2006). But neoliberalism remains recognizable in its various incarnations. The driving idea behind neoliberalism, as articulated by conservative politicians, free market economists, and academic critics alike, is that if government simply got out of the way, the market would regulate itself. Capitalism, according to the tenets of neoliberalism, is a self-regulating feedback loop, like an ecosystem or an organism. As such, in order to work effectively, it needs to be given free reign to regulate itself. Barriers to trade must be minimized, regulations eliminated.

Anthropologists have been vocal critics of neoliberalism for some decades now, and they have pointed out a number of significant negative ramifications that have relevance for us here. For one, neoliberalism tends to consolidate wealth among a smaller and smaller class of people (Graeber 2011; Harvey 2005). Without social safety nets and various checks and balances in place, neoliberal capitalism furthers inequality, serving the interests of those with the power to influence the market and government regulators. It also tends to create hierarchies of labour, where the western world, now free to outsource manufacture to the developing world, concentrates on more 'immaterial' or 'affective' forms of labour (Hardt and Negri 2001; Lazzarato 1996): marketing, design, research, the development and promotion of brands. Neoliberalism creates, that is, a globalized class system that maps onto previous colonial relationships. In the global fashion industry, the example most relevant to street style blogs, this has meant that design and marketing has become even more firmly entrenched in the 'fashion world cities' (Gilbert 2006) of New York, London, Paris, and Milan, while the physical labour of manufacture is carried out in Bangladesh, Indonesia, China, and elsewhere in the developing world. And within those centres of 'immaterial labour', consumption has increasingly replaced production as the principal economic activity. The west used to produce products. Now, says Lazzarato (1996), it produces consumers of those products. All of society has become a sort of cultural factory, producing desire, channelling emotion, serving the ends of capital (Hardt and Negri 2001; Lazzarato 1996; Terranova 2013).

At the same time, the deregulation of industry and the privatization of social welfare brought about by neoliberalism has left labourers in general in a more precarious position than they experienced in decades past, including those 'cultural labourers' that do the work of marketing and design intrinsic to brand culture. Neoliberalism has created a global 'precariat' (Ross 2009) of freelancers and part-time employees with little job security and little expectation of attaining one in the future. Under neoliberalism, the labour movement is in decline and the social safety net has been ripped to pieces (Klein 2007). We are all left dangling by a thread.

But neoliberalism proposes a working 'solution' even as it creates new problems. We are to become, espouse the prophets of capital, entrepreneurs ourselves, forging our own opportunities, carving our own paths. Under neoliberalism, each of us is expected to become our own individualized and specialized entrepreneurial venture. We have little choice but to run our lives as if they were businesses (Gershon 2011), and as such, we begin to think of ourselves as if we were brands (Banet-Weiser 2012). All logic becomes economic logic, subject to the same calculative rationale.

Becoming a blogger, I would learn pretty immediately when embarking on this project, is like Brand Culture 101. You learn what kinds of content attract readers. You learn what kinds of content leave them cold. You learn to use the word 'content' as if it were a pithy synopsis of your online thoughts and images, as if everything were reducible to something that can be posted online. You learn what titles, tags, and metatags result in maximum search engine optimization (SEO), which key terms circulate and reproduce, and which ones stand idle and impotent. You learn what kinds of photos of what kinds of people attract attention, and which just linger there online, twiddling their digital thumbs. It is hard – perhaps impossible – to completely ignore this data once you have encountered it, and it is hard – if not impossible – to not let it influence your blogging decisions in some way. Do my readers seem to like those posts of photographers posing outside runway shows? Well, I do have a few more I could put up ... Are they tired of seeing my Fashion Week pics already? Time to hit the streets of Philly again. If there was a moment in blogger history, where blogging was simply a form of 'self-expression', no thought given to the marketability of that expression, that moment has passed. In its place is a moment of active self-promotion, where every post is a potential career opportunity, if only you can leverage it right.

I do not mean to suggest that bloggers are a bunch of cynical manipulators, putting on false fronts, feigning interests for the sake of drawing in readers. Or at least, I do not mean to suggest they are any more cynical or manipulative than the rest of us. And I don't think we should discredit the work they do simply because they have financial interests at stake. So, after all, do writers. So do filmmakers. So do scholars, competing in an increasingly impacted academic job market. No artist wants to have to keep their day job forever. No one wants to sacrifice their personal passion for the sake of profit. As Astra Taylor (2014) claims in her recent takedown of pumped-up internet optimism, the exaltation of amateurism characteristic of so much of the writing on internet culture does working creative people a disservice. Digital enthusiasts like Clay Shirky (2009) equate amateurism with intrinsic motivation. Amateurs do what they do for the *love* of it. They are not tainted by commercial interests. They aren't selling anything, and certainly aren't 'selling out' in the old school punk rock meaning of the term. That's all well and good. But where does this leave professional musicians and playwrights? Where does this leave painters with gallery representation, aspiring designers, or anyone who strives to earn a living from what they enjoy doing? Though the 'distinction between love and money seems self-evident and uncomplicated' (Taylor 2014: 48) it is, in fact, deceptive and counterproductive. 'What sounds like idealism,' writes Taylor, 'upon further reflection, reveals itself to be the opposite' (Taylor 2014: 48). This conceptual distinction between professionalism and amateurism casts professionals in the light of suspicion. It makes them into capitalist conspirators.

I have something else in mind here. My intention in this chapter, and in this book more generally, is to reveal the logic and motivations behind the business of blogging, without casting aspersions on bloggers or judging them from the comfortable remove of my academic position. If there is one thing my experiment in auto-ethnographic street style blogging has driven home for me more than anything else, it is that the comfortable distance of scholarly critique is a luxury and a privilege, and it is not necessarily one we academics have earned. It perpetuates a stark divide between researcher and researched that casts the latter in a position of relative weakness. We interpret *for* our subjects. We assert *ourselves* as experts and *them* as that which we are experts on. All too often, we assume a patronizing tone towards the people we study (Ingold 2013; McCracken 2005) thinking 'we know best', and carrying on the vulgar Marxist tradition of projecting 'false consciousness' onto anyone who doesn't share our anti-consumerist worldview.

In becoming a blogger, I have gained a new vantage point, one no doubt steeped in the logic of brand culture. But I have lost one as well. No longer can I critique from the sidelines or claim any sort of moral superiority. I have done what my interlocutors do. I have acted – and continue to act – as they do, and though my intentions may have served more than one purpose – for the sake of research and for the sake of the blog – they have still followed a similar sensibility and rationality. I too want more pageviews and exposure. I too want people to 'like' me and the kind of 'content' I produce. I have had to accept the logic of self-marketing to make this happen. Was this a sacrifice? I can't say for sure. But I think it is problematic when academics criticize the prevalence of brand culture in our everyday lives for its perceived shallowness or superficiality, when they talk as if there were some sort of pure, authentic reality against which to measure it. Such a perspective fails to understand brand culture, let alone the constructed nature of 'reality'.

As I left my meeting with the New York-based department store that day in the early summer of 2014, the representative from their Philadelphia PR firm pulled me aside. 'We'll be in touch in the next few weeks', she told me. 'This is just the beginning of the conversation.' 'I am excited about this', she went on. 'I really I like your blog, because it's not just style. It's got substance behind it'. That 'substance', of course, is precisely what the department store hoped would rub off on them through our exercise in co-branding. The department store wanted its brand injected with something weightier than 'just style', something more resonant with meaning. The advent of brand culture, whatever we may think of it, does not represent the emptying of culture of all its meaningful content. It is not the famous waning of affect predicted by Jameson (1992). On the contrary, as Banet-Weiser (2012) explains, brand culture is about saturating the material world with meaning. It is about the hyper-production of affect. And it is for this precise reason, I would argue, that bloggers' role as documenters of sartorial meaning and marketers of self and brand are not in conflict. They are intertwined. One goal cannot be separated from the other.

Collaborations and partnerships

There are two words that are commonly used to describe arrangements between bloggers and brands like that between me and the department store. These words are 'collaboration' and 'partnership'. Both terms imply an equal footing between the two parties that often disguises the actual power differentials operating between them. In 'collaborations' like my own with the department store, for instance, one side had all the money and name recognition. One side had an army of lawyers, executives, and marketers to buttress it. One side wrote the contract for our agreement, and one side had the means to enforce it. The other side, that is, me, had only the digital mouthpiece of his blog. The terms 'partnership' and 'collaboration' are meant, no doubt, to downplay the inherent inequity of the relationship. They minimize the perception of exploitation. They treat the blogger as an empowered agent, calling the shots as much as the other party. This is, of course, not always the case. As Van Dijck argues, 'partnerships' are, in many instances, a 'new variant of the takeover (2013: 37).

FIGURE 5.1 An image from my collaboration with Dahsar, a Philadelphia streetwear brand. Photo by author.

FIGURE 5.2 From my collaboration with Philadelphia streetwear brand Dahsar. Photo by author.

It is important to mention, however, that the inherent inequity in such relationships is not always in the company's favour. Sometimes it is the blogger with the upper hand. During the course of this project, I occasionally collaborated with local Philadelphia bloggers and brands with substantially less reach than my own. There is still a marginal gain in SEO ranking and web traffic that can result from such a partnership. There is still a marginal gain in association. But more typically such partnerships cost the blogger, both in pageviews and prestige. Their readers may simply not care about the brand in question. Feature too many such brands, and it can have long-term consequences for the size of a blogger's audience. Nonetheless, bloggers do, quite often, promote brands and other bloggers that they 'like' or 'believe in', even if those parties have little to offer them in return. Their transactions, in these cases, are more 'gift' than financial exchange (see Tsing 2013). The promoted party may return the favour eventually, but its reciprocity is indefinitely delayed. Bloggers assume the role of a fashion curator in these cases, introducing their readers to fashion personalities and products they had not previously been aware of. Sometimes these arrangements can enhance the prestige of a blogger by showing the forwardness of their thinking. Other times they take on the feeling of charity work. A blogger helps out a brand. The brand gains from the association. The blogger takes the hit for the team. It is widely understood in the fashion blogosphere that the only way to climb is to be helped up by others, and consequently an ethos of charitable collaboration is pervasive. As Tsing (2013) has argued, the capitalist economy continues to depend, in fact has always depended on such gift-like acts to operate effectively. This situation is no exception. Bloggers help out others in a similar position as they themselves were helped before. They create ties with local businesses, brands, and bloggers. They become mutually entangled. Blogger marketing, that is, is not simply a financial transaction. It often takes on the weight of social obligation. Marketers market each other. Bloggers blog each other. In the social media era, this is how brands are built, one branding collaboration at a time.

Most collaborations between blogs and brands, or bloggers and other bloggers, are unpaid. A brand may contact the blogger with a request to collaborate or, conversely, the blogger may contact the brand, recognizing a cross-promotional opportunity. In these cases, payment takes the form of exposure. Marketing is paid with more marketing. Often times these arrangements also come with token gifts, generally from the brand to the blogger. Dahsar, for instance, a Philadelphia streetwear brand, gave me several hats in exchange for my shooting their clothes and posting some of those images on my site. Aphillyated Apparel gave me a couple of their T-shirts. When Goorin Brothers opened their Philadelphia hat shop in October of 2014, they contacted me several months in advance. 'I've been doing a bit of research to capture Philadelphia's fashion scene to get an idea of how we may be received as soon as we open our new location in Rittenhouse Square', wrote their district manager. 'I found your street style blog, was really impressed, and felt compelled to reach out.' They then invited me to their 'soft opening' to

FIGURE 5.3 An image from my shoot for Aphillyated Apparel, a Philadelphia streetwear brand. Photo by author.

FIGURE 5.4 Another image from my collaboration with Aphillyated. I am still debating whether this collaboration helped or hurt the Urban Fieldnotes brand. On the one hand Aphillyated is a bigger brand than my own. On the other hand, they have a decidedly less 'urban' or 'street' aesthetic. These are the kinds of issues a blogger must weigh before entering into a collaboration. Photo by author.

FIGURE 5.5 Ky Cao of the Philadelphia streetwear/menswear shop Ps and Qs. I did a street style shoot with their crew in October of 2014 at the request of a mutual friend. 'This helps you both out', he told me. Cross-promotion easily takes on the rhetoric of mutual empowerment. Photo by author.

FIGURE 5.6 Eric, Co-owner of Armour, a menswear shop in Philadelphia. They invited me, and a variety of other local bloggers, to an event at their shop. Cross-promotion was the order of the day. Photo by author.

FIGURE 5.7 When my good friend Shana Draugelis relaunched her popular 'mommy fashion' blog Ain't No Mom Jeans as The Mom Edit, she and I collaborated on a photo shoot. I shot pictures of her and her family that she used for her blog, linking them back to Urban Fieldnotes, and I featured her images on my blog, linking back to The Mom Edit. Ostensibly, the arrangement benefitted us both. But in this case, I was more the beneficiary than benefactor. Shana's posts drove thousands of readers to my blog. My blog drove a few dozen to hers. Photo by author.

meet their CEO and receive a complementary hat a few months later. A couple of weeks after that, I received an email from one of their marketing team members to set up a phone conversation with their CEO. He asked me to shoot a series of street style shots of pedestrians on Walnut Street, Philadelphia's main shopping thoroughfare, wearing their hats. I would stop people who I thought looked cool, one of their staff members would outfit them with a hat, and we would shoot it just like any of my other images, as if those pedestrians just happened to stroll past the shop wearing Goorin Bros products. The images would then appear in a gallery in their shop for their grand opening. They would also be used in their marketing materials. Once again, this gig was unpaid. But, their CEO assured me, they would be using various local media channels to promote their opening, and that, in turn, would promote me and my blog. My pictures, by the way, remain on exhibit in their Walnut Street shop as of this publication.

Bloggers, that is, are most frequently paid in exposure. Or they are paid in parties. By my third year of blogging, I had made it onto the email lists of the top PR firms in Philadelphia. I was invited to store openings and 'meet and greets' nearly every week. I was invited to interview CEOs of some rather big companies and designers behind emerging labels. I received free entrance and 'VIP passes' to runway shows and presentations, even some in New York, Milan, and Paris. I got free food and drinks, swag bags, and gift cards. The expectation, of course, in inviting me to these events, is that I would cover them on my blog, providing free publicity for the company that held them. Sometimes I did. Sometimes I didn't. The companies were willing to take their chances. Even when I chose not to post on the event, it was a cheap marketing move for them.

Not all collaborations between bloggers and brands are conducted in the currency of social capital, however. Some are in fact paid in good old-fashioned cash, particularly as a blogger rises in prominence. When her readership reaches a level desirable to a brand, that brand is often willing to pay for her readers' attention in the same way they would a magazine or a newspaper. In this case, collaboration is a euphemism for a simple financial transaction. A company pays a blogger a negotiated fee to feature content from that company on their blog. In it simplest form, this may be a banner ad on the sidebar, top, or bottom of a blog page which links to the company's website. A blogger will be paid a set amount every time a visitor clicks on that link and then makes a purchase on the website. Most bloggers are perfectly happy to feature such ads, especially when the company is a good fit with the blog's image. Even largely hobbyist bloggers, like Dana Landon of Seattle's It's My Darlin', have entertained the idea of allowing ads on their sites, just so long as they are companies whose products they 'like' or 'believe in'. But several bloggers told me that they make very little money from these ads. It is enough, said one, relatively prominent blogger, to go out to eat a couple times a month, but not enough to live off of. My own American Apparel ad, which I ran for around a year and a half, yielded me a total payout of $280, not bad for doing essentially nothing,

FIGURE 5.8 Claire, one of the subjects I shot for my collaboration with Goorin Bros hats. Goorin Bros supplied the hat. She supplied the outfit. I took the photos, treating them as if they were just ordinary street style pics, caught on the streets of Philly.

but also not nearly enough to tempt me to quit my professor job. The primary motivation for posting ads for brands like American Apparel, then, is that it shows that brands like American Apparel are interested in your blog. The ad itself carries cachet. Other bloggers, like Liisa Jokinen of Hel Looks, told me they have chosen to feature no ads at all so as to preserve the perceived integrity or 'clean design' of their blogs. But don't start thinking this is an anti-commercial motivation. These bloggers tend to think of their blogs as online portfolios for their work, a way to get sponsors, advertisers, and brands interested in working with them in some other capacity. Their collaborations simply take place outside the space of their blogs.

Collaborations may also come in the form of 'sponsored content' in which a blogger agrees to feature already created content on their blog that an advertiser supplies to the blogger (Ziv 2011: 143). It may be a story about their product or an 'infomatic' that casts them in a positive light. Featuring such content is potentially risky, though, as it can compromise the original voice of the blogger or muddle the vision of the blog. Ziv (2011), a blogger, author, and founder of the blogger marketing network Style Coalition, advises against featuring too much sponsored content on one's blog and to do so selectively. Readers will forgive some, she says, but not too much. You always have to keep your blog's 'authentic' brand in mind. I, for one, have never featured sponsored content on Urban Fieldnotes, and it is a relatively unusual thing for a street style blogger to do. Nonetheless, it happens.

A somewhat safer and less controversial bet is 'advertorial content'. This is content created by the blogger that features a product by the company on the blogger's own site. Scott Schuman's 'The Art of the Trench' features, done in collaboration with the UK luxury brand Burberry, are an example of this, as are Yvan Rodic's short 'I love my city' videos for Esprit. Advertorial content is written in the blogger's own voice and is crafted with their brand's theme in mind. Sometimes a blogger is paid for these. Other times they simply receive a 'gifted' item from the company with the expectation that they will review or feature it. This was the case for the Members Only jacket I received from that company. I featured it in a self-portrait post in which I discussed the terms under which I agreed to do the feature. I said some fairly unflattering things about the brand in my efforts at full disclosure, though Members Only seemed happy enough with the results, linking to the post and liking it on Instagram. And I got a free jacket in the exchange.

Advertorial content is meant to reflect the blogger's own point of view about the product in question. It enables a blogger to both advertise and maintain their sense of personal integrity and autonomy. According to the US Federal Trade Commission laws, bloggers are required to disclose when an item featured on their blogs was gifted or paid for. Most bloggers are quite clear about it on their blogs. Many see it as an important ethical issue. Gunnar Hämmerle of StyleClicker described his feelings on the subject to me like this: 'I think it's okay as long as they [posts] are marked as 'sponsored content.' I don't like sponsored content that, as a reader, I cannot identify as sponsored content. Actually, that is not legal. But I think it's quite common. I think it's no problem if it's sponsored, so long as it is content readers are interested in, and that has been my experience. I also have sponsored posts, and these posts get many 'like's on Facebook. So it's not that readers do not like sponsored content. It's just that they don't like to be fooled. And they want to have content that is valuable in a way. Sponsored content should also be good content.'

A variation on sponsored content is 'paid reviews', where a blogger writes a review for a product on the company's dime. This last form of content is probably the riskiest for a blogger, as it casts doubt on the legitimacy and autonomy of her point of view. If her opinion can be bought, after all, then what good is it? How could we trust such a person's blog to provide an alternative to the overly commercial sphere of fashion publishing? If paid reviews are not done right, that is, they damage a blogger's brand. Notice, once again, that the concern here is not with 'selling out' or some equally abstract notion about a blog's conceptual purity. This is not about taking a stand against commercialization. It is, on the contrary, about protecting the perception of one's brand.

Most collaborations between bloggers and brands, however, are unpaid and ungifted. In these instances, as previously mentioned, a blogger labours for something more abstract: exposure. In the case of the collaboration with the department store, only one blogger of the eight bloggers who ultimately participated in the marketing campaign was paid in cash. The rest of us were paid in cachet. Our blogs would theoretically become better known, get more clickthroughs and pageviews. Our SEO would go up, with more backlinks out there that refer to the blog. Our number of social media followers would multiply. And in the process, we would gain credibility in the larger fashion world and the street style blogosphere alike, 'cultural' and 'social capital' (Bourdieu 1984) that afford us entrance to even more runway shows, parties and events. In some cases, if a blogger is smart and strategic, they might succeed in converting this social and cultural capital into 'real' paid business opportunities like ad campaigns and sponsorships.

So, is this free labour (Terranova 2013) for the fashion industry, a cheap way for them to get their products out there and circulating around the web, without having to pay old-fashioned marketing agencies to do this work for them? You bet it is. And is it exploitative? Well that's a trickier question. Both parties, after all, gain something from the arrangement. Both get to promote their mutual interests. Both get to build their brands. For if there is one thing a blogger values above all, it is their brand, that intangible, almost metaphysical assemblage of signs and meanings that make their blog a viable commodity in the first place. According to the logic of brand culture, these sorts of brand-building exercises are valuable. Indeed, they are critical, and a blogger would be foolish not to undertake them in any circumstance. But do both parties benefit equally from the exchange? That depends. Often times, in my case, my expenditure of time and labour was

FIGURE 5.9 Assisted self-portrait for my 'advertorial content' feature for Members Only. Here is a small portion of what I wrote about Members Only on my blog: 'So, do I like Members Only jackets? I guess I have to confess that I do. I kind of wish I didn't. They are rife with the symbolism of tacky 1980s self-indulgence. They make me think of Rob Lowe cocaine parties in the Hollywood Hills. But I do like them, in that my own sense of identity is wrapped up in them in some small way. In fact, I've liked them for a long time, ever since they were popular the first time around, when I was like 9 years old. They were some other world that fascinated me, even if I wasn't sure I wanted to live there. I have never, however, owned a Members Only jacket until now. I could never quite commit to it. I was afraid it would make me look like a douche bag. I'll let you be the judge of whether I was right about that. So, should you go out and buy one? I really don't care. My links to Members Only's website are not affiliated links. I do not stand to benefit from you buying anything from them. My agreement with Members Only was only to feature them. I've done that. I have no further obligation to them'. Photo by author (with help from Jessica Curtaz).

substantially greater than that of my 'partner', and just as often, the amount of exposure my partner gained from working with me was greater than my own. In other instances, however, as in my partnership with the department store, I may have gained some followers and pageviews in the process. It's hard to know. The gain may primarily have been due to posting a number of images a number of days in a row. And at least I got a $500 gift card to spend in their stores. I was never broadcast on a seventy-foot LED screen. I was never made the subject of a documentary. And my rock star status is still, sadly, in question. Was it worth, then, the amount of time and energy I put into the campaign? I can't say for sure. But I was happy for the anecdote the experience supplied for this book. What I can say is that within the world of blogging partnerships, most bloggers find them worthwhile, at least on occasion, but they also complain about many of them failing to have lived up to their expectations. Bloggers, thus, do cost/benefit analysis on each potential partnership that arises, and they determine what they would need to receive in return to make them worthwhile. As a general rule, the higher a blogger rises in profile, the more frequently they expect cash in exchange for their efforts. Social capital is lovely and all, but it only goes so far.

Freelancing, or, cobbling together a career in photography

Few street style bloggers make enough off their partnerships to cover the expenses of their hobby, let alone make it into a career. Street style bloggers intent on pushing the practice beyond avocation have to pursue other means of making money. The most common method – aside from the near ubiquitous 'day job' – is freelancing for commercial fashion websites and magazines. Tommy Ton of Jak & Jil contributes to *Style.com*, YoungJun Koo of I'm Koo to *New York Magazine's The Cut*, Diego Zuko of The Outsider Blog to *Harper's Bazaar*, Phil Oh of Street Peeper to *Vogue.com*, Michael Dumler of On Abbott Kinney to *NYLON*, Adam Katz Sinding of Le 21ème to a long string of clients including *W Magazine*, Popsugar, and *Elle*. This is only a small list. Most street style bloggers, if they stick with the game long enough, do at least occasional freelance work.

As for myself, I eventually would shoot images for *Racked Philadelphia*, *Racked National*, *Kenton Magazine*, and *Refinery 29*, all well-known fashion and lifestyle websites that do frequent street style features. I got the gig for *Racked* through my friend Driely S., their staff photographer – and a street style blogger besides – whom I got to know through shooting at Mercedes-Benz New York Fashion Week. Most freelance gigs seem to happen this way.

A photographer recommends their friend to one of their current clients for a specific project; that client then contacts that friend; and that friend then forwards

FIGURE 5.10 Image taken for one of my shoots for Racked.com. Photo by author. Originally published on Racked.com.

FIGURE 5.11 Image taken for one of my shoots for Racked.com. Photo by author. Originally published on Racked.com.

them a portfolio of street style images. They discuss terms, the photographer signs a contract and W-2 form, and street style photography ensues. If all goes well, the client then contacts that photographer for future gigs. Occasionally, the photographer, now on the radar of the client, may also contact the client with pitches for specific projects. Sometimes the client bites, other times not. And so the game goes. In street style, like every over creative occupation, who you know matters, and as such, most street style photographers interested in transitioning into professional photography ultimately decide to attend events where other street style photographers are present. These include fashion weeks, 'tweed rides', the New York Governor's Ball, Blogger meetups, and conferences. Some bloggers also choose to frequent neighbourhoods with more than their share of street style bloggers. In New York, SoHo is that neighbourhood. Shooting there, I would occasionally see packs of street style photographers lounging together on the steps like a trenchcoat-clad hit squad. Other bloggers would accuse these street style gangs of being elitist cliques. They pull each other up. They get each other gigs. And they keep largely to themselves. I never had trouble with them. They were mainly friendly towards me. But in any case, they demonstrate a continuing social fact of the street style blogosphere: knowing people offline still matters. Where you blog counts. A blogger's public activities may happen largely online, but her professional connections continue to be forged in physical space.

My contracts with *Racked* and *Refinery 29* prohibit me from publicizing their exact terms, but suffice it to say, most street style photography gigs do not pay well. Magazines tend to pay $25 to $100 per image, sometimes varying their price based on the size of the photos used.

Photographers are then sometimes placed in the uncomfortable position of having to argue with the publications after the fact about the actual sizes of the images. Also, if a photographer is contacted to shoot images for a publication and the publication then chooses not to feature them after all, the photographer can end up with nothing for her efforts. Online magazines and websites may pay either by the image or by the 'gallery'. In this case, a single image might yield $50, where a gallery of fifty images yields only $100. Some magazines and websites also pay by the day or by the shoot, though this seems to be a relatively less common practice. Even top-tier street style photographers receive rates roughly similar to this, though they tend to be paid by the image, rather than the gallery. They also tend to have more of their images featured on more occasions. Hence, their take-home is substantially larger than other, lesser-known street style photographers. Tommy Ton is rumoured to get $100 an image for ten images per day from Style.com for his coverage of the four major fashion weeks (also known as 'Fashion Month'). That would yield around $32,000 per Fashion Month, twice a year, thus producing a total yield of $64,000 per year. Not bad for a photographer. Add in the income he brings from advertising revenue and commercial campaigns, and his

FIGURE 5.12 Image taken for my 'Mall Style' shoot for *Refinery 29*. Photo by author. Originally published on Refinery29.com.

total income is likely well over a $100,000 per year. Scott Schuman is rumoured to make substantially more, with a total annual income of well over a million dollars. I cannot verify either of these amounts. Nonetheless, Scott Schuman, and Tommy Ton are at the top of their game. Most street style bloggers, selling their images as freelancers, make substantially less.

My own limited experience with freelance street style photography was eye-opening, to say the least. While I was happy to get a little bit of extra income for a project I was doing anyway, it drove home the point that it would take a great deal of cobbling together to make anything that even approached my (then) assistant professor salary. After a day of shooting some fifty individuals at an outdoor summer concert for approximately six hours, then going home and editing those photos for an additional four hours, I would find myself making well below minimum wage. Friends of mine who shoot at New York Fashion Week for paying clients often have it substantially worse. One contact told me he made a grand total of $1,000 for the eight days of New York Fashion Week. He would shoot approximately 2,500 photos per day, working from around 9am to 6pm, then return home to edit from around 8pm to 4am, get a couple of hours of sleep, then get up the next morning and do it all over again. That is an eighteen-hour workday at $125 per day, yielding an hourly rate of $6.94. By the end of each New York Fashion Week, the photographers would be exhausted. But New York Fashion Week, happening twice a year, only accounts for sixteen days annually. The rest of the year is spent finding other avenues to make ends meet.

FIGURE 5.13 Picture taken at the Dîner en Blanc party for *Racked Philadelphia*. Photo by author. Originally published on Philadelphia.racked.com.

Of course, money is not the only reason street style photographers accept freelance gigs. They help photographers build their portfolios, their resumes, and their client lists. They also put them into contact with other potential clients. Photographers I know will carry a stack of business cards with them when they shoot an event. As the people they feature in their shots tend to work in creative industries, these same people sometimes contact them for other photographic work, including model portfolios, headshots, and promotional events. I have had a number of such offers over the course of the last three years. I have yet to take anyone up on them, though. Also, since many clients allow photographers to maintain copyright over their images and use them for other commercial purposes after a designated period of time (often sixty days), photographers sometimes find themselves able to sell those images, either to the people they shoot or the company they work for. Finally, shooting for websites and online magazines can lead to a substantial spike in a blogger's traffic, particularly if that website or magazine links directly to their blog via their author credit or biography. When *Refinery 29* posted the 'Mall Stalking' street style shoot I did for them in September of 2014, my blog had a one-day spike of around three thousand visitors. It is hard to know, however, if this spike yielded much in the way of return visits. It can be a rather depressing reality to face when one's pageviews return to their normal range after a several-day upsurge. It leaves you wanting more, seeking out new clients and new opportunities for cross-promotion. Freelancing is a quick fix kinda job with long dry spells in between, and photographers, attempting to cobble together a living, find themselves in the same position as thousands of other freelance creative labourers, part of a new urban 'precariat' (Ross 2009) work force, who have sacrificed financial stability for the staggered rewards of 'doing what they love' (see Hesmondhalgh and Baker 2011).

The problem with the whole professional vs. amateur thing

I get asked a lot when I am out on the streets of Philadelphia whether I am a 'professional' or an 'amateur' photographer. People have different reasons for asking. For some, it seems to be little more than a mild curiosity, something to say to that guy standing next to you on the corner, so that he doesn't seem like quite so much of a stranger. For others, there is clearly a promotional interest at stake. Working photographers give me their business cards and their Instagram handles. Musicians, managers, and magazine editors size me up for future jobs. In any case, I am never entirely sure how to answer the question. Neither 'professional' nor 'amateur' seems quite right to describe what I am. I am not a professional photographer by my own reckoning. Although I have taken a few photography classes, I am not formally trained, nor I do make my living from photography, barring the couple of hundred dollars I have brought in from ad revenue and the sporadic income I have made from shooting street style for *Racked* and *Refinery 29*.

However, as a professional anthropologist, working on a research project that requires me to take pictures and who then publishes his pictures in journal articles and books, some of which I get paid (a nominal amount) to do, my picture-taking hardly seems to qualify as 'amateur' either. I am not just doing this for the love of photography – though that motivation certainly entered in to my desire to do this project in the first place. Instead, I find myself wishing there were some third category to respond to the question with. Street style blogging occupies something of a neither/nor space, or in many cases a both/and space in regards to the professional/amateur question. It complicates any neat binary division between the two categories.

Many bloggers began their blogs as purely 'amateur' pursuits, with no intention, or even thought, they claim, of monetizing them. Hämmerle of Style Clicker, Landon of It's My Darlin', and Jokinen of Hel Looks fall into this category. Nonetheless, their blogs have yielded professional opportunities for them along the way. For some, like Hämmerle and Jokinen, blogging has defined their careers, opened up doors for them, and assigned them a place within their local fashion industries. For others, like Landon, it has remained a side interest. And yet even in the case of Hämmerle and Jokinen, both continue to see blogging as a 'hobby', existing apart from the professional opportunities their blogs have opened up. Other bloggers began their blogs as side projects for their work in fashion. Schuman falls into this category, as does Oberholzer and a broad number of personal style bloggers. Some, especially those with more formal training in photography, began their blogs as online portfolios advertising their work as freelance photographers. YoungJun Koo of I'm Koo (koo.im), Wataru 'Bob' Shimosato of An Unknown Quantity (anunknownquantity.com), and Diego Zuko of The Outsider blog (theoutsider.us) fit into this category. And yet, for many of them, the blog became an avenue towards professionalization *after* its launch. They were not professionals prior to their blogs. Nor does their primary source of revenue come from their blogs directly.

But even in the cases of Schuman and Rodic, their status as professional photographers is far from certain. Neither has professional training. Neither did any kind of professional photographic work prior to their blogs. Although both now frequently do ad campaigns and various other kinds of brand collaborations in order to make a living, they are hired primarily to do the kind of photographic work that they already do on their blogs, which is to say, street style straight ups. Rodic, for years, played down the quality of his own images, using point-and-shoot cameras, professing to know little about fashion and even less about photography. He began his blog as a series of snapshots at art shows and parties. The casualness of his images has always been part of their appeal. His 'amateurishness', in other words, has been key to his professional success. Schuman, on the other hand, began as something of an amateur photographer from within the fashion industry. His knowledge of its people and products gave him a leg up on other street style photographers, but his images always existed in contrast with the kinds of work being done by professional photographers in the industry. He did not do studio work. He did not shoot editorials. He shot 'real people' in unstaged public settings. His work was meant to capture something of the impromptu lives of insiders that professionals could not – or at least did not. His photographs' apparent lack of slick photographic tricks, their use of natural light over studio lighting, and their un-posed casualness was precisely what made them interesting. Once again, it was the *amateur* quality of his work – its seemingly noncommercial, unpolished, 'unprofessional' quality – on which he forged his brand. And yet, he most definitely has forged a brand, a *professional* brand, from which he makes, by all accounts, a healthy annual income.

For street style bloggers, the professional/amateur divide is hazy in the best of cases. Consequently, even the bloggers I have interviewed for this project are uncertain of how to answer the misleadingly simple question of 'are you a professional photographer?' Adam Katz Sinding of Le 21ème put it this way: 'You know, my girlfriend is constantly correcting me when someone's like 'Oh, are you a photographer?' 'Are you a professional photographer?' is a question you get all the time. Which to me is kind of a funny question, because you're walking around with a $10,000 piece of equipment around your neck. You're either a surgeon or you're a professional photographer. One or the other. Number one, you have to be able to get the money for the camera. So I always will say, 'You know, kinda.' And she'll be like, 'Yes. Yes, he is. Shut up. Quit being so modest' or whatever. It's very difficult, again, for me to label myself as something. I feel like I'll leave that to other people. I really just don't know.'

This is not false modesty on Sinding's part. Shooting street style was a side gig for him while he worked full-time as a concierge at the W Hotel. He didn't make any money doing it for years, not until he started selling his images to magazines and allowing advertisers to place banners on his blog. But then, for several years after, he kept his day job. He just did not make enough money shooting for it to pay the bills – his SoHo apartment or his expensive taste in clothes. It was only once Sinding had crossed the threshold of 150,000 plus pageviews per month and had already established a substantial name for himself in the fashion industry that he decided to quit his day job and do street style photography full time. By then, he told me, his job was getting in the way of his making money.

It seems relatively clear that Sinding is a 'professional photographer' now, at least in the conventional use of the term. He is paid for his photographs. He shoots full-time. But when exactly did he cross over the line from amateur to professional? Was it when he first started collecting a paltry income from advertisers several years back? Was it when he sold his first image to a magazine? Was it when he traded up his camera to the hefty (both in weight and price tag) Nikon D4 he was using as of 2014? There is, I would propose, no clear dividing line between the two positions, no clear moment of transition. The digital economy has rendered such a moment obsolete.

I am, of course, not the first person to recognize this. The literature on the digital economy is rife with terms designed to describe the fuzziness of the current state of creative labour. 'Prosumerism' (Kotler 1986). 'Produsage' (Bruns 2008). 'Playbor' (Küchlich 2005). 'Weisure' (Misch 2011). 'Blurk' (Misch 2011). 'Lark' (Misch 2011). These are just a few of the pithy – and perhaps a bit too cute – neologisms employed by scholars, journalists, and critics to describe modes of production similar to that of street style bloggers, somewhere outside of the old-fashioned designation of professional vs. amateur. In the digital age, these writers argue, cultural production is increasingly crowd-sourced to a volunteer labour pool, willing to put in hours of work in exchange for the simple prestige of their accomplishments (Terranova 2004) and the slim promise of future financial reward (Duffy 2014; Ross 2013). Street style bloggers are one sort of volunteer, prestige-incentivized, 'aspirational labourer' (Duffy 2014) among many. They give away their content for free, at least at first, hoping to build their names, and if the opportunity should arise, they use their name recognition to turn a profit.

Blogging, then, is *both* a labour and a leisure activity. It is a hobby, no doubt, but a *serious hobby*, carried out with a fastidious attentiveness to detail, quality, professionalism, and brand identity. Blogs have often gotten a bad rap in the press and earlier scholarly accounts as a scrappy, careless medium, the digital equivalent of zines, in which hobbyists of all sorts throw some stuff haphazardly online and then move on. This may have been the state of the blogosphere once. It may even describe a significant portion of the blogs out there today. But it describes very few street style blogs. These days, street style blogs launch as sleek, professional-quality ventures from the start. They may not be professional per se, but they sure *look* professional. And in the world of street style blogging, looking like something and *being* something are just not that far apart.

Serious hobbies

In using the term *serious hobby* to describe the act of street style blogging I am referencing the concept of 'serious games', a term first coined by the anthropologist Clifford Geertz in his famous essay, 'Deep Play: Notes on the Balinese Cockfight' (Geertz 1977). It was later theorized and further developed by one of Geertz's students, a distinguished anthropologist and theorist in her own right, and my dissertation adviser at UCLA, Sherry B. Ortner. Geertz used the term to describe the real social stakes involved in seemingly trivial activities like cock fights. A game is 'serious' to the extent that it reflects, reinforces, or restages the larger social dramas of the group engaging in it – its power struggles, its inequities, its quests for identity and recognition. Ortner takes the concept a step further, using 'serious games' as 'a model of practice that embodies agency but does not begin with, or pivot upon, the agent, actor, or individual' (Ortner 1996: 12). 'The ideas of "the game"', she writes 'is meant to capture simultaneously the following dimensions: that social life is culturally organized and constructed, in terms of defining categories of actors, rules and goals of the games, and so forth; that social life is precisely social, consisting of webs of relationships and interaction between multiple, shiftingly interrelated subject positions, none of which can be extracted as autonomous 'agents'; and yet at the same time there is 'agency,' that is, actors play with skill, intention, wit, knowledge, intelligence. The idea that the game is 'serious' is meant to add into the equation the idea that power and inequality pervade the games of life in multiple ways, and that, while there may be playfulness and pleasure in the process, the stakes of these games are very often high.'

The players of serious games are seldom the inventors of those games. They enter a playing field established well before their own time. They play by rules that are not of their making for goals determined by other people in advance. In their act of playing them out, however, those rules and goals are simultaneously made, remade, and reinforced. They shift in subtle ways. They take on new connotations. They become something else. Serious games are *serious*, then, in that they have real social consequences. They can remake the playing field, or, as is far more likely in practice, stack the odds of the game in favour of the previous victors.

Ortner suggests other possible substitutions for the term 'game' in her model, recognizing the limitations of the term to describe the myriad social dynamics in which an agent might find herself. 'Project' is one suggestion, 'drama' another. 'Story' and 'narrative' are additional alternatives. She admits to using each to describe many of the same processes in her work. Each term, on its own, feels inadequate, a gross oversimplification of something far more complex. It is in this same spirit of the inability of written language to capture the fluid, inchoate experience of actual embodied practice that I propose the term *serious hobby* here. We could substitute any number of other terms to achieve roughly the same effect. 'Project', in particular is *apropos*, in that it has been used by such thinkers as Simone de Beauvoir and Jean-Paul Sartre to describe 'the intentionalized vision of purpose, of making or constructing the self and the world' (Ortner 1996: 13). Street style blogging, as we have already seen, is inseparable from the making of the self and of the world. The pictures bloggers take are meant to reveal as much about themselves as those they photograph. Their blogs – particularly those devoted to specific cities or types of people – play an active role not only in depicting place, but in reinventing it. There is no question that blogging is a 'project' of great importance to those who take part in it. But I use 'hobby' here because it is a term that often comes up among bloggers themselves as a conceptual counterpart to its most likely alternative: 'job' or 'profession'. Blogging, for most street style bloggers, is a *hobby*, in that it yields little – if any – financial reward. It is done, most bloggers tell me, for 'its own sake' – the enjoyment of taking pictures, the satisfaction of building a relationship with one's readership, the sense of accomplishment and engagement it provides. But it is also *serious* in that reflects, reinforces, and re-stages a set of social dramas larger than the bloggers themselves. The most conspicuous of these social dramas transpire in that ever-evolving mammoth I shorthand here simply as 'the fashion industry'. But it is also possible to see 'brand culture' more generally as a kind of social drama bloggers take part in. It is a pervasive logic they inherit and work within as denizens of the digital world – a world structured by the marketing and profit-making interests of innumerable corporations.

Bloggers, particularly those shooting at Fashion Week (see the next chapter), have assumed a subject position in relationship to the fashion industry that is simultaneously outside its ordinary strictures and yet acting according to its very same set of rules. They practice their blogging according to standards and conventions that are not of their own making. They present themselves as brands. They engage, that is, with the industry on the industry's own terms, using concepts like 'branding', 'exposure', 'synergy', and 'collaboration', even while engaging in a set of practices they define as 'just a hobby'. This is not a capitulation on the bloggers' part. It does not mean compromising who they are or adopting *someone else's* values. These are *their* values. This is *their* language. Raised in a day and age when mass consumer capitalism is the only game in town, they have made their home in the only territory available to them: brand culture. And they tend to have few regrets about doing so.

Amy Creyer, the blogger behind Chicago Street Style (chicagostreetstyle.com), summed up this position much more succinctly than I have in the following blog entry, posted on 25 February 2014: 'I've been freelancing in the digital space for nearly four years', she writes, announcing her role in the forms of 'precarious labour' so often described by sociologists. 'It's hard to believe my blog is that old. As a newcomer to Chicago and a grad student with spare time over the summer of 2010, I started my blog to celebrate fashion while getting to know the Windy City. Within months it became a full-time job of its own. When I realized that I could be creative for a living it was an epiphany. A career as a creative had always seemed out of reach for me, like a dream. When companies began reaching out to me for social media projects, I realized I could leverage my blog into a professional career in advertising to make my dream come true. After all, being a professional fashion blogger, as glamorous as it is, was always just for fun. I never saw it as an end unto itself. Plus, full-time street style photography is a tough way to make a living. So I became a copywriter.'

'I'm extraordinarily lucky I was able to build a career in advertising based on the wonderful work I've done with all of my corporate partners. This year, I skipped New York Fashion Week to work on several agency projects as a freelancer. Thankfully, my decision paid off with a permanent job offer at Draftfcb a couple weeks ago. I'm excited to finally have an agency to call home, on a team I love, for a creative director who's passionate about creating good digital work. It's all the more thrilling to be part of an ongoing creative renaissance.'

'My blog has come full circle from a hobby to a job and back to a hobby once again. I wasn't trained in advertising, and I didn't go to portfolio school. All I did was create a blog and throw myself passionately into creating work. My photographs and blog posts got better over time. It took me almost four years to get to the point where a global ad agency would hire me full-time.'

Notice the celebratory tone to the post. Notice how she treats advertising as a mode of empowerment. Notice how she conceptually conflates her hobby with her career, both done out of 'love' and 'passion', both circulating in and out of different categorical markers. Of course she does. Thinking like a marketer enabled her to 'pursue her passions' as a career choice. Adopting the logic of a business in pursuing her hobby enabled her to easily transition into a career she finds 'satisfying'. Her hobby as a blogger was *serious* indeed. It changed her life. And it helped lay a career blueprint for others to follow.

But not all bloggers start their blogs simply to 'celebrate fashion'. Others approach them as potential career-advancing opportunities right from the start, even if they begin as apparent 'hobbies'. That was certainly the case with Guerre.

Brand new guerre

I caught up with Brooklyn-based street style photographer Karl-Edwin Guerre at a 'Cyber-Saturday' event at a small menswear boutique in Philadelphia called Armour in late spring of 2014. We had briefly met a few times before at Mercedes-Benz New York Fashion Week, where he shoots each September and February. I had shot a couple of images of him for my blog, and I had shot beside him outside a number of runway events. I wasn't sure if he would remember me, but he acted as if he did, and I appreciated the gesture. Guerre (pronounced like 'gear' in English rather than 'war' in French) had been invited by the creative director of the shop to mull about, chat with guests, and do complementary 'style consultations' with interested would-be customers. Several other Philadelphia-based fashion bloggers, myself included, were on the guest list, though I was the only one who showed up. Prosecco and cookies were on offer in the back.

Street style, Guerre told me, while we hung out – somewhat awkwardly – around the table in the centre of the shop, is 'not something you just do'. At least not for him. It's something you use to get somewhere else. While it may, for an earlier generation of bloggers, have been 'just a hobby', it is impossible to enter into the field these days without being aware of the potential career opportunities it may bring your way. You shoot street style for a while, you build your brand, then when a better paying gig comes along, you grab it. Guerre himself is moving away from shooting street style as best he can. He still does some, he says, just to keep his foot in the door and his blog in public view. It is what he is best known for, after all. His blog, Guerreisms.com, is one of the higher profile street style blogs in New York. It was featured on *Esquire Magazine*'s list of the top-ten street style blogs just a week or two before this event, and it has been featured on similar lists in *Complex Magazine*, Style.com Arabia, and *GQ Japan*, among other places. But Guerre sees his primary work these days as consulting – whether for PR firms interested in more effectively utilizing social media, or with menswear lines, hoping to improve their image. Guerre's dapper, fedora-cocked-to-the-side look has made him something of a menswear icon. He regularly shows up on other peoples' blogs, from Citizen Couture to Mitograph, and his visibility has been key to his success.

Guerre is now working on establishing an online men's fashion television network. He has been shooting video footage of stylish men buttoning their suits, straightening their bow ties, and walking in slow motion down the narrow streets of Milan. These days such videos are hot. They are practically a genre. 'Menswear porn', we might call it. But the videos have yet to pay the bills, so Guerre concentrates on social media consulting instead.

Most companies, says Guerre, have no real sense of how to use social media. They blast out spam. They post too much easily discardable crap. They alienate a large portion of the very readers they hope to attract. That's where Guerre comes in. Having a blog for a number of years now has been an exercise in market experimentation, figuring out what works to draw in readers and what doesn't. Like other street style bloggers, he has crafted himself into something of a social media marketing expert. As of the writing of this chapter, he had 10,000 followers on Instagram, a humbler 4,026 on Twitter. His blog was getting around 20,000 unique visits per month, pretty good by street style standards (though, admittedly, nowhere near The Sartorialist's unmatched 1.8 million).

As for street style, Guerre shoots mostly at Fashion Week and other high profile fashion events these days, Pitti Uomo in Florence perhaps the most significant of them. The annual menswear showcase has become a key destination for many street style bloggers. As with other major fashion events, there are almost as many photographers there as people to shoot, hoping to get 'clean shots' of Sam Lambert, Angelo Flaccavento, Nick Wooster, and other current style stars of the menswear scene whose personal style is intimately intertwined with their personal brand. Pitti Uomo is stocked with stylish men the way manmade lakes are stocked with fish.

Guerre doesn't comb the streets of Brooklyn or Manhattan anymore. It's just not worth his time, he says. It used to take him two to three hours minimum to find a shot. That is a lot of pavement to walk. When he started shooting street style in 2008, he told me, his feet were a size 8. Now they are a size 9. It is a better use of his time and energy to stick with the big menswear events. Nonetheless, walking

FIGURE 5.14 Karl-Edwin Guerre, shooting outside Pier 59, New York. Photo by author.

the streets of New York gave Guerre his start in street style. It is where he honed his craft. It is where he cultivated his aesthetic and developed his signature style of shooting, mostly detail-heavy bust shots captured in landscape mode. And he developed a number of tricks to keep his street style expeditions from taking up too much of his time while out on the streets.

Guerre would hit the same parts of town repeatedly: Williamsburg, SoHo, the Meat Packing District, places practically guaranteed to put you face to face with the hip and the chic. And when there were not that many cool people out walking the streets, Guerre would venture into stylish boutiques to find his subjects, places like Armour. Boutiques keep cool people on hand like they are wardrobe staples. Their employees become part of their brand image, an extension of their marketing. Guerre spent a good deal of time pulling shopkeepers and retail workers out onto the sidewalk to get his street style shots back in the day. It is not just easier than combing the streets, he says, it is also more pragmatic. Shooting retail workers helps establish relationships with their companies. It sets up possible future collaborations. And collaborations are always on a successful blogger's mind. Guerre didn't write the rules of the street style game, but he knows how to play it, and he is willing to play it, as long as necessary, in order to get where he wants to go.

The street style hustle

Reuben 'Big Rube' Harley has been playing the same game for several years now. A larger than life Philadelphia personality, he seems to know everyone. People shout his name out car windows. He is on the invite list of the biggest parties and events in town. Well over six feet tall with a hefty build and a proclivity towards unbuttoned buttoned-down shirts paired with dainty, pattern-print neck scarves, he can be spotted nearly any day of the week, weaving his bicycle through the streets of Center City, a Canon EOS 5D, Mark II permanently affixed to his shoulder. Occasionally he will stop his bike, ask some lady in a mini-skirt to pose for him or lean against an alley wall, or he will shoot off rapid-fire candids of passing pedestrians. 'Nice style!' he often shouts as his subjects pass out of view. They smile and keep on walking, granting Big Rube a degree of license that less of a smooth-talking salesman couldn't possibly get away with.

Big Rube is the photographer behind 'Street Gazing' (www.streetgazing.com), a Philadelphia-based street style blog, and the only continuously running one in the city besides my own. We run in similar circles. I bump into him at events, always seem to find him lingering somewhere in the big tent at New York Fashion Week, on the few occasions when I have entered it. When I met with the marketing representatives of that New York-based department store in June of 2014, he was just completing his own meeting with them.

Big Rube also does a regular Sunday column in *The Philadelphia Daily News* with the same title as his blog. He grows vegetables and sells them at the Rittenhouse Farmer's Market, does occasional stints as a 'guest chef' at various Philly restaurants, shoots the sporadic feature for companies like American Apparel and Hush Puppies, and works various Philly fashion and entertainment events with the smooth come-ons and gift for gab for which he is perhaps best known. He is also, it may not surprise you to learn, a first-class 'hustler'.

A high-school drop out turned Vice-President of Marketing for Philly-based vintage sportswear label Mitchell & Ness, Big Rube got into street style photography a few years back when he 'recognized a gap' in the Philadelphia market and decided that he was just the person to fill it. Street style was already a big thing in New York at the time. Self-trained photographers like Scott Schuman, Yvan Rodic, and Tommy Ton were doing well for themselves, attracting major sponsorship deals and becoming minor celebrities. Big Rube had always loved fashion, a trait he made good use of at Mitchell & Ness, and he had a long-time admiration for Cartier-Bresson and classic Parisian street photography, even if he didn't know much about shooting it. So he taught himself the basics of shutter speed and aperture, 'learned on the go' as he put it, and thereby thrust himself into the street style game.

In his words: '[My shooting street style] goes back to my childhood, and me just being a hustler. Everything that I've done, I've done on the highest level, from selling ice, to going around to barbershops and hair salons all over Philly in my pickup truck and selling food, to stepping into Mitchell & Ness in 2000 and making that a worldwide phenomenon. So I figured, if I've got a camera I'm going to be the best photographer there is. And seeing that void out here in the market, where it was just wide open in Philly, I said, 'Hey, the *Daily News* doesn't have no lifestyle thing going on,' and I just asserted myself. Being brash is my forte. I ask for what I want.'

'So' I asked, following up, in our formal interview in the summer of 2012 at a Center City pizza shop, where he gets meals on the house 'is street style blogging a form of hustling?'

'Oh yeah', responded Harley. 'No doubt about it. I look at it as like a business. You know, I'm gonna take it there. Then I did my research on guys like Tommy Ton and Scott Schuman, and I was like, ok, this is going to fill that gap in the Philly market. Because I had no formal training or education, I relied on working my mouth. Soon, I had exhibitions going on, businesses approaching me. I started doing headshots. Up the street at 500 Degrees [a hamburger restaurant] they have a wall mural of my photography of people eating burgers, and that just grew out of the street style stuff I was doing. I mean, a good image is a good image, no matter what it is. You get that great lighting, you capture that subject in a certain way, and people are going to respond to it.'

Harley was a fashion marketer for going on a decade. He knows how to work angles, how to follow up on leads. He has appeared frequently on local television

FIGURE 5.15 Reuben 'Big Rube' Harley, cruising the streets of Philadelphia. Photo by author.

discussing style and has made himself into a Philadelphia fashion personality. As he sees it, shooting street style photography was the natural next step, and an easy transition besides. It is all, in Harley's mind, the same thing: marketing. Now he is working on transforming his website into something bigger and grander, with plenty of collaborative, co-branding opportunities for local and national companies.

When I asked Big Rube Harley what advice he would give to aspiring street style bloggers, looking to get into the game, this is what he told me: 'If anything, don't take no for an answer. If someone says "no," you're talking to the wrong person. I don't have any formal training or anything like that, but I have an innate nature not to be mediocre, not to be regular. Everything I do, I do at the highest level. I kicked down that door. I've spoken at colleges and prisons, juvenile centers, schools, and people are surprised by my story, and it's like, ok, he had all the odds against him, but he didn't let that take him in a direction that most people do in life. If you put your boundary up against me, that's your problem. It ain't mine. Just kick it down. Keep your mouth talking. Somebody's gonna listen. Somebody's gonna open that door for you. But you can't play Double Dutch with it, you know, ring and run. Either you in, you in, or you out, you out. I want in.'

The new generation

It is hard to imagine the first generation of street style bloggers – Liisa Jokinen, Alkistis Tsitouri, even Yvan Rodic or Scott Schuman – talking about street style blogging in these terms. For them, street style was – and is – a project of personal passion, a curatorial activity, off the radar of the fashion industry, and outside of its purview. And yet they laid the groundwork for the next generation of street style bloggers and gave them a game plan to use, a new *serious hobby* to adopt as their own. They found their way into the fashion industry, gradually transitioning their blogs from 'amateur' labours of love to projects of professional development. Each gradually shifted from a dot Blogspot to a dotcom platform, hiring designers to streamline and upgrade their blogs or using their own expertise to give it as 'clean' and 'professional' a look as possible. Each learned to make the most of collaborations and partnerships, how to feature sponsored content and advertisement on their own terms, without alienating their audience or compromising their own brand. They learned, that is, to be effective marketers. They learned to leverage the *serious hobby* of street style blogging. By the time Guerre or Harley entered into the street style game, it was already a marketer's game, entrenched in the logic of brand culture. And it was, as we shall see in the next chapter, an increasingly crowded game, with more and more players, and higher and higher stakes. Bloggers may not have made up the rules of the game, but they were sure eager to play it. The next chapter explores the consequences.

6 SCENE FROM THE SIDEWALK: SHOOTING STREET STYLE AT NEW YORK FASHION WEEK

The spectacle of fashion week

In a now infamous *New York Times T Magazine* editorial entitled 'The Circus of Fashion', veteran fashion journalist Suzy Menkes reminiscences about the relative austerity that used to define her industry. 'We were once described as "black crows", she writes, ' – us fashion folk gathered outside an abandoned, crumbling downtown building in a uniform of Comme des Garçons or Yohji Yamamoto. "Whose funeral is it?" passers-by would whisper with a mix of hushed caring and ghoulish inquiry, as we lined up for the hip, underground presentations back in the 1990s' (Menkes 2013). The events of Mercedes-Benz New York Fashion Week, the American fashion industry's premier showcase of the coming season's collections, were staid and serious affairs, at least as Menkes tells it, more experimental theatre than Broadway musical, more Mozart's *Requiem* than Vivaldi's *Spring*. They were exclusive, closed-door events with a strict invite list of buyers, editors, and journalists. Either you were firmly installed in the industry, sitting quietly in a darkened room as models strut past, or you were stuck somewhere else, imagining what it might be like to do so. Boy how things have changed! Someone let the fashion riffraff in, and no one told them about the all-black dress code.

'Today', laments Menkes, 'the people outside fashion shows are more like peacocks than crows. They pose and preen, in their multipatterned dresses, spidery legs balanced on club-sandwich platform shoes, or in thigh-high boots under sculptured coats blooming with flat flowers' (Menkes 2013). The scene outside shows at Fashion Week, whether in New York, London, Milan, or Paris, has become a 'circus', where style icons like Anna Della Russo, Michelle Harper, and Miroslava Duma back up traffic in their brand-loaned couture, while street style photographers encircle them from all sides (see Figure 6.1). 'Stand a little to the left, Mira!' calls out one of the photographers. 'Three-quarters profile', orders another. 'Eyes over here' says a third. 'You can hardly get up the steps at Lincoln Center, in New York, or walk along the Tuileries Garden path in Paris because of all the photographers snapping at the poseurs', writes Menkes.

And just who are these poseurs? Who are these preening peacocks in their too-high shoes and flashy coats? Who is it that has distracted the fashion crowd away from the stuff that 'really matters': the season's trends in colours, the structural innovations of the new line of Thom Browne coats? Menkes has no trouble identifying the culprits. It is 'the celebrity circus of people who are famous for being famous'. 'They are known', she explains, 'mainly by their Facebook pages, their blogs and the fact that the street photographer Scott Schuman has immortalized them on his Sartorialist Web site. This photographer of 'real people' has spawned legions of imitators, just as the editors who dress for attention are now challenged by bloggers who dress for attention'. Ah, the bloggers! We should

FIGURE 6.1 Miroslava Duma posing for street style photographers at London Fashion Week. Photo by Adam Katz Sinding.

have known it was them all along. It is those insta-famous interlopers, hell-bent on wrestling Fashion Week away from the black-clad business folk who are to blame, those wannabe-Scott Schumans loitering on the sidewalk, and those would-be Anna Della Russos strutting past them. Everything was so much simpler before the bloggers showed up.

Menkes' article, perhaps not surprisingly, faced a staunch backlash from the fashion blogosphere when it came out in February 2013, just as the Fall/Winter 2013 collections were making their runway debut. 'Reducing an entire generation of sprouting professionals (the bloggers) to the perpetual black (well, actually neon) sheep of fashion just doesn't seem very open minded', wrote Leandra Medine on her popular blog, The Man Repeller (www.manrepeller.com). Besides, wrote Jennine Jacob, founder of Independent Fashion Bloggers, on her own blog, The Coveted (the-coveted.com), 'The history of peacocking at Fashion Shows goes back a few years (as does the complaining)', and 'a lot of the people peacocking (Michelle Harper, I'm looking at you) are not bloggers'.

It is not so much that bloggers disagreed with Menkes. That, in a sense, is what really got their blood boiling. 'There was a deluge of factual evidence', wrote Medine, 'that I couldn't argue'. Fashion Week *has* become a circus, and the bloggers – bedecked in their borrowed Balmain and Balenciaga – have a good deal to do with that. Yvan Rodic of Face Hunter has compared shooting at Fashion Week these days to shooting animals in a cage. 'It became kind of a red carpet

FIGURE 6.2 Blogger Maja Wyh strolling through the corridors of Lincoln Center, her personal photographer in tow (www.majawyh.com). Photo by author

FIGURE 6.3 Street style photographers/bloggers chasing a model through the streets of New York. But is she running away from them, or providing a memorable photo op? At Fashion Week it is sometimes hard to tell the difference. Photo by Driely S.

situation', he explained to me, as we ducked into Chelsea Market for a brief respite from the madness. 'There's no style involved.' 'It's just not fun anymore', complained Phil Oh of Street Peeper, when we first met at the Independent Fashion Bloggers conference in February of 2013. He compared shooting at Fashion Week to trench warfare.

Bloggers, that is, had already come to more or less the same conclusion as Menkes. They too think that Fashion Week is a circus. They too think that the street style hype machine is spinning out of control. They too wonder whether the blogger revolution ushered in a fashion democracy or just a new variety of industry oligarchy. They did not, however, so much like the tone of what Menkes had to say, nor did they appreciate the way she singled them out for special scorn.

Menkes' article treated bloggers as if they were hapless, clueless newcomers to an industry that was doing just fine without them. Her article condescended to bloggers, and it failed to recognize the increasingly important marketing function they have taken on within the industry. In addition, her article assigned to bloggers more than their fair share of blame for what Fashion Week has become. Who, after all, hired all of those street style bloggers as freelance photographers in the first place, paying them for their *serious hobbies* (see last chapter), and insisting they point their lenses at editors, models, and other rising style starlets? That, of course, would be the magazine editors, Menkes' peers within the industry. And who equipped all those personal style bloggers, editors, and sundry socialites with free clothes to borrow or keep, thereby introducing product placement to the sidewalks of Fashion Week? That would be the Public Relations firms for major fashion labels, operating with the full endorsement of those labels. In other words, the street style phenomenon of Fashion Week was produced by a range of actors, both within and outside of the industry. It was not the sole – or even the primary – creation of bloggers. Yet Menkes made bloggers into a scapegoat for the spectacle of Fashion Week, acting as if they were somehow uniquely responsible for a self-promotional subculture that has long been endemic to fashion – some might even argue is the whole point of fashion.

This chapter presents a messier and more complicated picture of Mercedes-Benz New York Fashion Week than that depicted in Menkes' editorial. It is not, I argue here, a case of outsiders – that is, bloggers – storming the gates of Fashion Week and supplanting the all-black flag drooping from its pole with a garish, multi-coloured one. The bloggers, rather, were invited in. And those who weren't invited were cleared space on the sidewalks out front. Bloggers, whether they are paid by the industry or not, are part of the larger network of actors promoting that industry, publicizing its products, and driving its trends. It no longer makes sense to talk about bloggers as if they were somehow *outside* the industry. The industry is broad and expansive enough to include them.

FIGURE 6.4 Posing outside the Jason Wu show at New York Fashion Week. Photo by author

FIGURE 6.5 A personal style blogger posing for street style bloggers/photographers outside the Ralph Lauren show at New York Fashion Week, Spring/Summer 2014. Photo by author.

FIGURE 6.6 Alone in a crowd of photographers. The same blogger posing at Ralph Lauren. Photo by author.

But that doesn't mean Menkes is wrong about Fashion Week. It is not my intention to contradict her conclusions here. Fashion Week is, as Menkes points out, an absurd spectacle full of inflated egos, larger-than-life personalities, and oversize handbags, where a whole range of actors – including editors, PR agents, and, yes, street style bloggers – work to promote themselves, their brands, their products, and one another. It is, in other words, what the fashion industry has always been, only more so. What I do instead in this chapter is add another perspective into the conversation, that of the street style bloggers shooting from the sidewalks. The complaints of the editors and journalists have been recounted well enough already. Drawing from my own experience of shooting street style at Mercedes-Benz New York Fashion Week alongside dozens of other bloggers and photographers over five seasons between 2013 and 2015, I describe the scene on the sidewalks of Fashion Week more as a spontaneously choreographed dance than a circus, a gruelling, multi-act, eight-day ballet, filled with countless solos and slow pirouettes. But this is not about battling metaphors. Whether Fashion Week is best described as a circus or a dance, it clearly requires coordination. Those photographers shooting out front of the runway events have developed their own etiquette and protocol, their own networks of friends and collaborators, their own junket rules and disciplinary procedures, their own emergent structurations of practice. This chapter describes those emergent structurations from the ground-level blur of the sidewalks.

The scene outside Lincoln Center

Mercedes-Benz New York Fashion Week is the first of four major Fashion Weeks advertising the forthcoming collections of various fashion designers and brands. It is followed – in immediate chronological order – by London Fashion Week, Milan Fashion Week, and Paris Fashion Week. The four together are often referred to as 'Fashion Month', and they represent the four biggest events marking the professional calendars of those designers, buyers, editors, and journalists who work in the international fashion industry. Street style photographers often refer to the four weeks together as 'the complete circuit', and measure the seriousness of their involvement with street style photography by how many of the weeks they shoot. The higher profile the photographer, the more likely they are to shoot the complete circuit, and the more likely they are to complain about doing so. Mercedes-Benz New York Fashion Week (hereafter referred to simply as 'Fashion Week') always begins and ends officially on a Thursday, after which editors, buyers, and journalists cram their things into a suitcase and rush across the Atlantic to London. It starts off relatively slowly, with a smidgeon of offerings popping up on the Wednesday beforehand, and builds towards a Ralph Lauren/Calvin Klein/Marc Jacobs finale. There are two Fashion Weeks held in New York every year, each revealing the collections of New York-based fashion labels six months before they will be hitting the stores. This, ostensibly, is the whole function of Fashion Week, to generate buzz around one's products well in advance of their release and to facilitate their purchase by various stores and distributors. This is also why Fall/Winter Fashion Week happens in the mid-Winter of the previous year (typically February) and Spring/Summer Fashion Week happens in the late summer (typically September). Fashion purchasing operates on a six-month cycle. Fall/Winter 2014, then, refers to the Fashion Week taking place in February of 2014; Spring/Summer 2015 refers to the Fashion Week taking place in September of 2014.

Between 2010 and 2015, Fashion Week events ostensibly centred around Lincoln Center, an Upper-West-Side performing arts complex, where a large, laboriously decorated tent housed several venues – The Theatre, The Pavilion, and The Salon – along with a lounge area and a café, and a twenty-seven-foot screen broadcasting various Twitter and Instagram feeds. Lincoln Center, however, hardly contained the bulk of the events of Fashion Week. Many of the shows, including the most obscure and the most exclusive, happened 'off site', in a variety of locations throughout Manhattan. As a general rule, the bigger the designer the further away from Lincoln Center their show. What better way to demonstrate your influence within the industry than the ability to make the industry come to you? For his Fall/Winter 2014 show, designer Alexander Wang demonstrated his influence by making his show attendees travel all the way to the Brooklyn shipyards on a Saturday night. Editors and journalists had to be ferried over from Manhattan. By all accounts, the show was a success. But those accounts had less to say about the clothes shown than the circumstances of their showing.

There is no shortage of displays of authority, influence, and exclusivity at Fashion Week. High-end labels abound. Elusive editors emerge from brand-loaned town cars. Security guards stand poised before the entrances of events, checking the credentials of those who enter. The location of the most sought-after shows is often listed only as 'TBD' (to be determined) or 'TBA' (to be announced) on the various schedules published on industry websites. It has become a measure of one's status in the industry to have a schedule in one's possession that reveals the actual locations of those shows. Such schedules are called 'editors' schedules', and they are distributed to a select few. Photographers often have to consult their editors ahead of time to find out where TBD shows will take place. When that fails, they consult each other.

Some of this Fashion Week posturing I had an inkling of coming into this project. It is no secret, after all, that the fashion industry trades in exclusivity. Some of it, however, was still veiled in mystery for me, and some of it remains veiled. Which is why I felt so intimated and uncertain the first time I set foot in the courtyard of Lincoln Center on Thursday 7 February 2013, the beginning of Fashion Week Fall/Winter 2013. As a street style blogger and researcher of street style blogs, who had been shooting on the streets of Philadelphia for nearly a year by that point, it felt like my debutante coming out party, and I had all the nerves one might expect to go along with that. I didn't sleep well the night before and woke up at 4:45 in the morning raring to go.

It is hard to remember now exactly what I was imagining shooting at Fashion Week would be like back then. I think I was picturing something of an occult society of elite bloggers, moving through foggy city backstreets in Burberry raincoats. I think I was picturing secret handshakes and back alley deals, giant security guards barring access to everyone but Scott Schuman and Tommy Ton. I was prepared to comb the grounds for hours prior to finding a good place to shoot. I was prepared to feed false names and publishing info to guys with earpieces and security badges. What I was not quite prepared for was how easy it all was. You just walk up to Lincoln Center with a camera and join the dozens of other photographers hanging out in the courtyard. I had no idea.

The scene outside Lincoln Center that first day was like the scene outside any major performing arts centre: a concrete courtyard with a fountain in the middle, imposing stately buildings with lots of space in between. Only, instead of pigeons, lingering on the concrete, waiting for passers-by to throw them some breadcrumbs, the Lincoln Center courtyard was animated by small clusters of photographers, waiting for well-heeled fashionistas to stroll by. From a distance, in fact, they could easily be mistaken for pigeons (see Figure 6.7). They moseyed here and there, occasionally took flight when someone 'of note' entered into view. Lesser-known fashion show attendees would be wandering lackadaisically towards the entrance

FIGURE 6.7 The 'pigeons' of Lincoln Center. Photo by author.

to the tent, stopping for photographs when someone asked, loitering around the fountain when no one did. Other people present seemed to be there for the express purpose of being photographed, and yet they didn't want to be seen by others as being there for that. They had put on their best, bright pink fur coats and black patent leather boots, and then leaned against pillars, feigning indifference to the photographers' gaze (see Figure 6.8). Many carried cameras of their own, either to snap street style shots of other people, or to provide a cover story for their being there at all. As the clock was about to strike the hour, more prestigious guests would begin to arrive: editors, name-brand bloggers, buyers. The photographers would spring into action.

Nearly all of the big-time street style photographers I had been following up to that point were there that first morning: Scott Schuman (The Sartorialist), Garance Doré (garancedore.fr), Tommy Ton (Jak and Jil), Phil Oh (Street Peeper), Adam Katz Sinding (Le-21ème), YoungJun Koo (I'm Koo), Vanessa Jackman (vanessajackman.blogspot.com), and Tamu McPherson (All the Pretty Birds) among them. Yvan Rodic of Face Hunter showed up the following day. There were also plenty of freelancers for the major style magazines and newspapers. In addition, there were a couple of dozen newbie bloggers, armed with cheap Canon Rebel digital cameras and bright, furry accessories. There was often little distinguishing the photographers from the photographed at Lincoln Center, which is why, during slow periods, photographers would

FIGURE 6.8 Linda Tol posing for me and a couple of other photographers in a staged scene meant to appear as the kind of candid shot taken by a street photographer. Photo by author.

often turn on each other, stacking their street style shots with images of other street style photographers.

And yet, the scene outside Lincoln Center was also strangely calm, long periods of quiet punctuated by occasional flurries of activity. Photographers stood around in small groups or moved from group to group, chatting with one another, sharing information about upcoming shows. As they did so, their eyes continually darted from one end of the courtyard to the next to see who was coming their way. Whereas from a distance, they looked like nothing so much as pigeons around a fountain, up close, they looked more like the guests of a cocktail party at an academic conference, where one's conversation partner continually looks over their shoulder to see who else – as in some other, more important scholar – is there. But at Lincoln Center, where the courtyard spans almost the length of a city block, it can be very difficult to tell who is there, or more importantly, who is arriving and departing. So, the photographers pay attention primarily to one another. When the crowds of photographers move, they move. Often the movement seems organic, fluid even, a formation of birds (to beat a dead metaphor), switching course in mid-flight. The action is pre-cognitive, almost automatic. A known entity, say, an Eva Chen or a Taylor Tomasi-Hill, would emerge onto the concrete field of Lincoln Center, and the flock would congeal around them.

FIGURE 6.9 Photographers springing into action outside Lincoln Center. Photo by author.

Those few *somebodies* among all the stylish someones

It seemed abundantly evident to me, that first day of shooting at Fashion Week, that the intuitive tool I had developed on the streets of Philadelphia for identifying my photographic subjects (see Chapter 3) had little immediate use amidst the crowds of photographers outside Lincoln Center. Style radar comes into play there, no doubt, but it often does so *after the fact*. Otherwise, one's style radar would be overwhelmed. Fashion Week is so riddled with style radar signals, they cross and tangle, weave into a kind of dense tapestry of seeing and being seen. There are so many signals sent out into the ether that it is hard to get any reading at all. And so photographers, working within a crowd of photographers, depend on something else: movement. They see movement. They react to it. They shoot whom the crowd shoots. And then, when sorting through their files on Adobe Lightroom at home later, they decide if it was worthwhile to have done so. In my own case, I would delete hundreds of photos without a moment's hesitation on the bus ride home to Philadelphia each night. Most had little to do with the look and feel I had been developing on my blog up to that point. Most were of bland fashion-followers that held little interest to me. I would, eventually, learn how to make use of my style radar at Fashion Week, but it took separating myself from the crowds of photographers, walking down the block from venues to, say, the corner of 22nd and 10th, next to the Comme Des Garçons store, to get shots no one else was getting. This, by the way, is also what many well-known street style photographers – like Scott Schuman, Eddie Newton, and Yvan Rodic – were doing.

It also bears pointing out that at Fashion Week the calculus of what constitutes a worthwhile street style photo is different than it is on the streets of Philadelphia. It is not just about whether someone is 'cool' or not or has something distinctive or interesting about them. It is not just about that incalculable aura of affect that surrounds them, their raw Weberian charisma. It isn't even about the clothes they are wearing, although that certainly enters into it. It is largely about whether someone has already been designated as *somebody* or not. People who are *somebody* get pageviews for one's blog. When you 'tag' them on Instagram you get new followers and more likes. Google searches turn up more results for them, and those results link back to your blog. Magazines take more notice of you. Brands begin to contact you. Doors open up. People, especially magazines, will pay for images of *somebody*.

So, if breaking into the big time is your game – and if you are shooting at Fashion Week chances are that it is – then you need to be paying attention to those *somebodies*. The allure of capturing a *somebody* is so strong, in fact, it is often hard to tell it from the sensation of style radar. It has the same intuitive tug, the same mysterious, magnetic draw towards a person. And yet it is their digitally mediated aura that attracts you, their brand superimposed on real life, not the direct pull of some affective trait that oozes out of them.

But to feel such a pull towards a *somebody*, to be overwhelmed by their presence in physical space, you have to know who that *somebody* is in the first place. You need to be able to identify them. Of course, it helps if you know what a person's function is within the fashion industry, whether they wield power or not, whether they have been converted into an icon by the industry's cultural production factories. Such powerbrokers wield a particularly strong influence on those photographers who hope to someday work with that person in some capacity. This is where allure begins to transform into intimidation. The motivations for shooting become muddled, complex. But how do you know if someone is *somebody* or not? And who gets to decide that anyway?

The first question has a relatively simple answer. Street style bloggers/ photographers know someone is *somebody* either because other street style bloggers/photographers are shooting them or because they know who that person is from reading fashion magazines or other street style blogs. Barring this, they know that a person is *somebody* because other photographers have told them so. Photographers often ask each other who a person is when they are out of hearing range. Names pass through the crowd in a game of photographer telephone. And the names don't always survive the journey intact. I hear occasional stories of

FIGURE 6.10 Blogger Ella Catliff of La Petite Anglaise on 10th and 22nd, somebody I photographed after moving away from the crowd outside the Kate Spade show. Photo by author.

certain name-brand photographers refusing to share such information, saying something along the lines of 'it's your job to know! I'm not gonna tell you', but I have never experienced this sort of proprietary name-keeping myself. For the most part, photographers actively share their information about people and titles, especially once you have established some sort of rapport with them.

Photographers also know that someone is *somebody* if they have a clearly defined place in the fashion industry. Models in the shows of a premium brand, for instance, are *somebody* as a default setting, even if the photographers cannot identify precisely which *somebody* they are. Buyers for department stores and rich heiresses with a taste for couture are *somebody*. Designers are *somebody*. Fashion journalists like Suzy Menkes, Angelo Flaccavento, and Lynn Yaeger, on the other hand, are *somebodies* of a sort, but they occupy a different order of *somebodies*. They seldom get much attention from the photographers, except a few who 'geek out' in their presence. I did, on occasion. Editors for major magazines are the biggest *somebodies* of all. Of course they are. They have stacked the decks that way. They are the ones paying the photographers' bills. Some editors will even text their house photographers ahead of time to make sure they get a shot of them entering the show. Editors negotiate for weeks ahead of time with various fashion labels to secure their clothes for the events, and then pretend to be put-off when people stop them for photos. Anna Wintour, the editor-in-chief of *Vogue Magazine*, and one of the most powerful figures in fashion worldwide, is the biggest *somebody* of them all. But she doesn't stop for photos. Getting good shots of her, then, is like landing the biggest fish of the day. Bloggers often compare their images of Wintour on the LCD screens on their cameras as a kind of competitive sport. 'Here's Anna escaping into a town car.' 'Here is Anna striding past the crowds at Jason Wu, her icy gaze staring right through me.'

As for personal style bloggers, they have to earn their status as *somebodies*, and it takes time. It is not a given that they will be photographed, and photographers often dismiss the most dressed up and readily available bloggers, lingering near the entrance, as 'trying too hard'. But it is usually clear when a personal style blogger has become *somebody*. The photographers begin to know their names. They surround them when they walk the sidewalks. Chiara Ferragni, Susanna Lau, Rumi Neely, Aimee Song, Shea Marie, Nicole Warne, Kristina Bazan. These are some of the most sought out among them.

Experienced street style bloggers memorize the names, occupations, and faces of all the *somebodies* they can, in order to make sure that they (A) photograph them, (B) correctly label them on their blog, and (C) 'tag' them on Instagram, Facebook, and Twitter, once they have posted their pictures. My first time at Fashion Week, I was rather blown away by the sheer number of names the street style bloggers/photographers had memorized. They knew the names of obscure models, editors for third-tier magazines, Russian socialites, and Brazilian fashion bloggers. Murmurs would go through the crowd, 'Ulyana Sergeenko, third cab down. Chriselle Lim, across the street. Helena Bordon, just exiting the show'.

Many of these figures were called by a single name: Anna (Wintour), Michelle (Harper), Eva (Chen), Chiara (Ferragni). Other times, we would all simply snap away on the off chance that the person in question was *somebody* without our knowing it. We could then interrogate other photographers near us to determine precisely which *somebody* they were. Sometimes photographers will ask their subject directly who they are, especially if they are shooting for a publication that requires names. But this is a relatively uncommon thing to do, first, because many bloggers/photographers are shy and prefer to let someone else do the asking; second, because it potentially reveals that a blogger/photographer does not already know – hence, potentially placing the blogger/photographer in a 'one-down' position in other peoples' eyes; and third, because if the other bloggers/photographers around also do not know who a person is, then by definition, they are not *somebody*. As for myself, I never intentionally set out to remember the names of the people I shoot at Fashion Week, and yet by my second or third one – after posting so many of their pictures on my blog and spotting their faces on numerous other blogs – I was able to call out dozens of their names myself. By my third Fashion Week, the industry had begun to conceptually shrink. It felt like a small network of friends, a social club I was more and more familiar with, and yet one I was only tangentially a part of. I knew their names. They did not know mine.

The answer to the second question – of who gets to decide if someone is *somebody* – is a bit more complicated. The short answer is that street style photographers/bloggers decide. This is, perhaps, the most significant power they wield in the fashion industry today. The more frequently someone is featured on street style blogs or in the street style sections of fashion websites, newspapers, and magazines, the more of a street style *somebody* they become. When they have reached some critical mass of representation, wherein publications are willing to pay money for their images and other bloggers compete to get the best shots of them, they get the additional label of being a 'street style star', perhaps even a 'style icon'. Street style stars then use this 'cultural capital' (Bourdieu 1984) to gain real advantages in the industry. Russian socialite turned fashion buyer Ulyana Sergeenko, for instance, used her status as a street style star to begin her own couture line. Nickelson Wooster used his to land a (temporary) gig as director of menswear for JC Penney. Michelle Harper continues to use hers for whatever vague entrepreneurial activity she does in the industry. But becoming a street style star can take years to achieve. Becoming *somebody* can happen much more rapidly. Over the course of several fashion weeks, I got to watch a number of these *somebodies* emerge out of the crowd of fashion show attendees – Danielle Bernstein, Linda Tol, Nasiba Adilova, Irene Kim. They all crossed that threshold of frequent representation on street style blogs that enable this cheap phenomenological trick. Once they were pedestrians wandering through Lincoln Center; now they are *somebody*, a sought-after subject of the photographer's lens.

There is more than one way to become *somebody* in the eyes of a street style photographer/blogger. It might be that you become known for your especially sharp fashion sense or especially ostentatious attire. Anna Della Russo became *somebody* this way. So did the Beckerman sisters, Caillianne and Samantha. It might be that you become friends with the people snapping the photos, chatting them up between shows, offering them rides in your cab. It might be that you give generous portions of your time to the photographers before stepping into a show – but not so much that they get bored of you. It might be that you re-blog, re-gram, and re-post the street style bloggers' images of you to such an expansive list of followers that it ups your profile – and theirs – in one swift move. It might even be that you run up and down the street, spinning and twirling, climbing onto stray tractors and ladders, and otherwise making a spectacle of yourself, as did model and television personality Irene Kim over the course of 2013 and 2014. Kim rose from street style obscurity to street style stardom in as short a period of time as I have personally witnessed. By Spring/Summer 2015 photographers were already beginning to tire of her. In any case, there is no getting around the fact that without the attention of the street style photographers/bloggers, one cannot be a street style *somebody*.

Of course, individual photographers/bloggers do not make the decision of which someones become *somebodies* alone. They make it *collectively*, as an emergent structuration of their practice. *Somebodies* crystallize into being, the way a blood clot forms in an artery. Activity becomes centred around them. They become *a thing*, not because one blogger decided they were, but because bloggers as a group did. And bloggers make this designation with the 'help' of editors. As more and more street style bloggers sell their work to *Vogue, Elle, Marie Claire, W,* and other publications, they must continually negotiate their interests with the interests of their publication. Style radar adapts accordingly.

Of course, it helps if one of the bloggers photographing a someone is Scott Schuman, Phil Oh, or Tommy Ton. Their power to create *somebodies* is unmatched in the street style blogosphere. When featured on one of their blogs (or in the images they sell to *GQ, Vogue,* or Style.com, respectively), obscure fashion journalists, menswear tailors, and brand managers can become style stars seemingly overnight. But even they cannot do it alone. Their selection of subjects has to resonate beyond their own blog. They have to be picked up by other blogs, re-blogged, liked, and commented upon. They have to generate buzz. Street style bloggers/photographers cannot always predict who will be dubbed *somebody* next, nor can they determine whether other bloggers/photographers will follow their lead. They make this determination in continual negotiation with one another, along with editors, brands, and readers, whose pageviews translate into visual status. In addition, they make this designation in negotiation with those someones themselves.

FIGURE 6.11 Preetma Singh, formerly fashion editor for the Wall Street Journal, now Fashion Editor for NYLON, has effectively utilized her status as a street style star to climb ranks within the industry. Photo by author.

FIGURE 6.12 Model and Korean television personality Irene Kim emerged as a street style somebody at NYFW F/W 2014. It was something of a phenomenon, orchestrated, to no small extent by Kim herself. She posed on a tractor in the middle of 11th Ave, ran back and forth down the bike line of 8th Ave, and danced on ice, as in the picture above, on Wooster St. The photographers ate it up. Fall/Winter 2014 was Kim's season. Photo by author.

Paparazzi vs. street style photographers

It is worth pointing out at this juncture that street style stars are not the same as your regular, everyday 'celebrities'. There are celebrities at Fashion Week, but they belong to a different class of *somebody*. They operate in a different 'field of cultural production' (Bourdieu 1993) to use Bourdieu's term. My very first day at Fashion Week, for instance, I caught sight of the actresses Sarah Jessica Parker, Drew Barrymore, and Christina Ricci. I would later spot Joe Jonas, A$AP Rocky, Nicki Minaj, Rihanna, Will.I.Am, Paris Hilton, and various other stars – major and minor – of film, television, and music. These are *celebrities*. They are written about in the tabloid press. They are gossiped about on television. They are not, by and large, directly involved in the fashion industry. They do, however, often attend shows at Fashion Week – perhaps to shop for red carpet looks, flaunt their connections with designers, or be captured by photographers and television crews looking chic in fashionable company. The street style photographers usually do not bother to photograph these celebrities. They cater to the wrong crowd. They draw the wrong readerships. But the *paparazzi* do photograph them, and when a Sarah Jessica Parker emerges from the crowd, the fluid movements of photographers are supplanted with a more frenzied rush. These often stocky, puffy-parka-clad men (they are almost uniformly men) push their way through the crowd and form a blockade before and after a celebrity. They lunge at them, snap away with all the nuance of a machine-gun. They seldom seem to care who they knock out of their way as they do it. On a couple of occasions, I was one of the people they knocked out of the way. After shooting a few hours, or days, at Fashion Week, it is easy to start thinking of street style bloggers as artsy, better-dressed paparazzi. They compete for images. They chase the occasional model or editor down the street. They obsess with whether someone is *somebody* or not. When I asked blogger Phil Oh what the difference is between paparazzi and street style photographers, he just laughed and told me he wasn't sure himself. But then the real paparazzi show up. And the difference is like night and day.

There are several marked differences between paparazzi at Fashion Week and street style photographers/bloggers at Fashion Week that warrant pointing out. First, they are interested in shooting different people. Paparazzi shoot celebrities of interest to the readers of *OK Magazine*, *The National Enquirer*, and *TMZ*. Street style photographers shoot fashion people – editors, buyers, models, and bloggers, and other 'cool kids' with a distinct look – of interest to the readers of *Vogue*, *Nylon*, and *W*. They are not above market concerns by any measure. On the contrary, the decision to photograph *somebodies* in the first place is rooted in market concerns. But they cater to a different market than the paparazzi. There are, however, a few points of overlap: musicians Kanye West, Rihanna, Nicki Minaj, and Rita Ora, for instance, make regular appearances on street style blogs, as they do in the tabloid press. When Rihanna showed up at the Alexander Wang show at Pier 94 during Fashion Week Spring/Summer 2015, she was instantly engulfed by the crowd of photographers – both street style and paparazzi. I couldn't get anywhere near her and didn't bother to try. Bloggers put up their Instagram pics within hours, taking advantage of the boost in followers they knew such an image would generate. But when Paris and Nicky Hilton sauntered slowly down 15th Street my second season of Fashion Week, they received a muted response at best from the street style photographers/bloggers that lined the sidewalk. The two seemed stunned by the lack of attention. They slowed their pace even further to be captured by whichever of the photographers actually cared. Few did. My own images of them felt oddly like pity shots. I never posted them on my blog. Outside the old post office on 33rd Street, pop star Joe Jonas was almost totally ignored when he walked by. The street style photographers/bloggers were looking straight through him towards Susanna Lau and Chiara Ferragni, two well-known fashion bloggers who are, nonetheless, positively obscure relative to Jonas.

Another difference between paparazzi and street style photographers centres around the photographic conventions they employ. Paparazzi shoot snapshots, often hoping to catch celebrities in compromising, or at least attention-getting positions. They get paid by their editors by the image – the more salacious the better – and so they snap off as many of them as they can, hoping that they turn out, rather than look good per se. They often shoot in automatic mode, or in fairly basic camera settings, with a reasonably deep depth of field so that the subject, and the context in which she was shot, are all in focus. They do not care much, that is, about aesthetics. What they do care about is that the subject in question is recognizable, and that they have as many serial images of them as possible (Jerslev and Mortensen 2014).

Street style photographers, on the other hand, are preoccupied by aesthetics. They want good shots of street style stars, flattering shots, commercially viable shots. They are often willing to sacrifice recognizability for mystique, frequently cutting off the heads of their subjects to capture a stylized frame or a particularly interesting detail on an outfit. After all, they can always just label the image with its subject's name later. Then they get both the composition they wanted *and* the name recognition. Bloggers seek to enhance the visual appeal of the people they shoot, and they want to instil their images with their own artistic signature. Their work should be recognizable as *their* work. That is why Vanessa Jackman uses the same Lightroom preset on all of her photos, bringing out the white tones, desaturating the colours, and enhancing the grain. That is why Adam Katz Sinding shoots with his aperture wide-open on his crystal clear 85mm lens. That is also why street style photographers place a premium on shooting their images manually, with careful attention to depth-of-field, white-balance, proper exposure, and composition. They want to be able to claim full authorship over their photos, to emphasize their own agency.

Like paparazzi, street style photographers often do get paid by the image – that is, if they sell their images to magazines or websites – but they get paid only for images selected and used by editors, and those images have to adhere to a strict set of aesthetic standards, employing a look and feel compatible with the types of editorial and other photographic materials used by the magazine. Sometimes, this means they have to compromise their own aesthetic taste. Shooting for *Harpers Bazaar*, Diego Zuko (outsider.us) has to get full-length straight-ups to showcase the clothes worn. Shooting for *Racked*, Driely S. has to emphasize the subject of her photos over the context in which they were shot. As she frequently complained to me, her (and later my) editors have little appreciation of the kinds of critical juxtapositions evident in street photography. They are not interested in irony. They do not care about composition. They want sharp, flattering images that showcase the clothes worn. Nonetheless, street style photographers have learned to work within these parameters to instil their own signature in their work, whether that is through a preference for a greater or lesser depth of field or the film-inspired presets they employ.

Even, however, if street style photographers/bloggers do not sell their images, they value their aesthetic quality. Those aesthetics are perceived to reflect back directly upon them. They measure their worth as a photographer. They testify to their taste and sophistication. Plus, successful street style bloggers often tag the subjects of their images on Facebook, Twitter, and Instagram in hopes that the subject herself will re-blog that image, 'like' it, or otherwise make her followers aware of it. This then potentially increases the number of pageviews and followers a blogger has. But none of that will happen if the subject does not like the image taken of her. In other words, not just any picture will do. The relationship between street style bloggers and would-be style stars is symbiotic. They enhance each other's brands, increase each other's traffic, promote each other's careers. Aesthetics are a key part of this exchange.

Third, paparazzi and street style photographers occupy different physical space at Fashion Week. Paparazzi typically shoot at the back entrance of a show, where celebrities enter and exit. Street style photographers shoot near the front entrance, where everybody else enters and exits. The people street style photographers shoot, after all, need to be photographed. Their jobs in the industry depend on their enunciated brand image. Editors are hired based on their reputations, and reputations are increasingly built on street style websites. It is telling, then, that the editors attending the shows, no matter how pronouncedly they perform their lack of desire to be photographed, still come and go through the front entrance. Anna Wintour, we are on to you.

Finally, paparazzi and street style photographers differ in their self-presentation. It will probably come as no surprise that street style photographers tend to take their personal appearance more seriously than the paparazzi do. Paparazzi are often distinguishable for their distinct lack of distinctiveness.

They disappear into the crowd. They fail to register in one's peripheral vision. They intentionally do not attract notice. It is to their advantage not to, but it does not gain them fans among other photographers at Fashion Week. I would sometimes be blindsided by paparazzi. 'Where did they even come from?' I wondered, and overheard others asking. They didn't appear to have been there before. Street style photographers/bloggers like YoungJun Koo (koo.im), Jessie Bush (wethepeople.com), and Wataru 'Bob' Shimosato (anunknownquantity. com), on the other hand, have highly developed personal styles. You can recognize them from far across the courtyard at Lincoln Center. They are hard to miss. And as such, they regularly appear on other peoples' street style blogs. Some, like Dapper Lou (dapperlou.com) or Karl-Edwin Guerre (guerrisms. com), are known for their jaunty hats and tailored jackets. Others, like Julien Boudet (bleumode.com) and Nabile Quenum (jaiperdumaveste) are known for their long, drapey, gender-neutral coats and shirts. Boudet wears a signature dangling cross earing from one ear and, in the winter, a rather sinister black mask that covers the lower half of his face. He has, in other words, an immediately recognizable visual brand. The look of his images is continuous with his own personal style.

There is one specific look that has become most closely identified with the male street style photographers who shoot at Fashion Week, a look, in fact, that is rather eerily compatible with the description of the 'fashion people' Suzy Menkes used to begin her article on what Fashion Week has become. We might call this look – in homage to Menkes – 'the crow'. Blogger/photographer Angel David Verde (angelspov.com) perhaps summed it up most succinctly on his Instagram page when he posted the ironic mock question: 'Can anyone help me I.D. that one street style blogger who wears all black, has a beard and shoots a lot during NYFW?' The joke, of course, is that there is no shortage of people who fit that description: Michael Dumler (onabbotkinney.com), Diego Zuko (theoutsider. us), Adam Katz Sinding, even, to a certain extent, myself. The look is high-end and minimalist: basic black in trim, tailored cuts, drop-crotch sweats or tight-black jeans, high-top black sneakers or boots. In New York, the street style photographers adhere to an edgy 'downtown' look similar to the kinds of people they might shoot in SoHo or Chelsea. It is a fashion look, no doubt, but a look out of sync with the bright-coloured *somebodies* of Fashion Week. This is the look of a self-conscious *outsider*, someone who has embraced their peripheral status as a key aspect of their identity. And this is the look of those mournful fashion folk, Menkes' described as lingering outside shows in the 1990s.

If I were to distil the difference between bloggers and paparazzi down to one key element, it is this: bloggers invest a great deal of themselves in their photographic work. It is meant to be a representation of *them* as much as a representation of the people they shoot. They have a brand to develop, and a photographic brand depends upon a recognizable signature. They do not want their images to be the work of an anonymous person behind the lens. They want photo credit. They want links back to their blogs. They want recognition for the work they do. Otherwise, what's the point?

The etiquette of shooting street style at fashion week

'Every season', Adam Katz Sinding told me of Fashion Week, in keeping with the general sentiment, 'is more [of a mad house]. And then all these magazines are hiring us [bloggers] and other people to go out there and shoot for them. Which means now there's a lot more money involved, and more people are wanting to get into [street style blogging]. I've only been shooting fashion week for four seasons now, and when I started there were maybe 15 to 20 photographers out there. Now there are probably 40, maybe 50. And it sucks, because you lose a lot of fantastic shots. The big thing the magazines want is brand information, so as soon as some photographer's done, they just go walk up to the subject that everyone's taking photos of, start talking to them and getting their brand information, which really destroys a lot of opportunity. Some of my best shots of men's week I lost because of other photographers walking into the shot. I understand [, though]. If it's show-goers [walking into the shot], I don't mind that. It's just part of the reality [of fashion week]. But [when] the other photographers [do it], it's a little bit upsetting, because it's all kind of self-centered. The whole thing about blogging is it's all about me, and my vision, and my perspective, so [those bloggers] don't care that they ruin other peoples' shots. They just want to make sure that they get their own product'.

Shooting street style at Fashion Week, in other words, is much more difficult than it used to be, and if photographers are to be successful at it, they have to be able to trust that other photographers will let them do what they are there to do. Sinding's description, though in many ways representative of my own experience, is lacking one key piece of information: that those bloggers who 'walk into shots' are also violating a key rule of photographer etiquette, and as such, they are often reprimanded – at times loudly – by the crowd of other photographers for doing so.

The street style bloggers/photographers I shoot beside at Fashion Week are now good friends of mine. We talk during downtimes between the 'entrance' and 'exits' of shows, share information about upcoming shows, eat meals together, get drinks together, share taxis together, complain about other photographers together, and take a number of precautions to keep on each others' good sides. In a sense, we have little choice. Otherwise, none of us would have much hope of getting the shots we need. But this also speaks to the general convivial atmosphere of the scene. The mood at Fashion Week is largely friendly and relaxed. And most photographers take pains to be considerate of the other photographers around them.

Since framing and composition are so critical to the work street style photographers/bloggers do, and each places a premium on instilling their photos with their own unique artistic signature, their own 'vision' and 'perspective' as Sinding put it, they have, out of necessity, developed their own system of etiquette to enable each to get the shots they need while shooting among a crowd of other photographers attempting to do the same. Not that everyone follows this system. If they did, they wouldn't have needed to develop it in the first place. Nonetheless, the majority of bloggers/photographers I have talked to seem to agree about what the basic rules are. In the words of street style blogger Simbarashe Cha of lordashbury. com: 'There are what I would call the junket rules, [that is], rules that apply to every professional photographer who's working alongside other photographers, things like, you carve out your space. You mind your space. You don't intrude on other people's space. You don't obstruct or remove a shooting lane for other people. Pushing and shoving, that happens in France. It doesn't really happen in New York so much. Even in London they're pretty polite mostly. And for the new photographers who are on the scene, being respectful to the people who clearly know what they're doing goes a long way.'

Distilled to their most basic essence, the 'junket rules' boil down to this: don't 'walk into' or 'jump on' someone else's shot. If someone has already set up a shot, their viewfinder held up to their eye, their posture set to hit the shutter button, that is *their* shot. You do not walk in front of them. You do not bump them. You do not talk to them. You do not do anything that will diminish their ability to get the image they are after. And what's more, under ideal circumstances, you should not attempt to get the same image yourself. To do so compromises the originality of both your photo and the other photographers'. This is particularly the case when a photographer has stopped a subject and asked them to pose. Once a photographer has done this, this subject is *their* subject until the point at which they thank the subject and allow them to move on. Once a subject has been thanked, they are once again fair game.

Some photographers will go to great lengths to enforce this rule. Stories abound of fights breaking out over violations, though I have never witnessed this myself. Sinding and Cha both claim it happens more frequently in Paris, and that the New York scene is relatively more civil. I did, however, once see a certain prominent street style photographer yell at a group of other photographers gathered around him for jumping in to his attempt to get an exclusive shot of Irene Kim running up and down the bike lane of 8th Avenue. The blogger berated the crowd belligerently amidst various shaking heads and grumbles. The widespread feeling was that said blogger had gone too far. 'Real cool', I heard someone mutter. 'Real classy', said another. The shot may very well have belonged to the photographer in question. Or it may not have. The trouble is that in practice, it is often quite difficult to tell to whom a shot belongs. And if it is good enough of a shot, photographers are often willing to temporarily breech photographer etiquette to get it. Best to stand your ground, take your shot, and let others do the same.

The second most basic rule of street style photography/blogging etiquette, then, is 'keep your cool'. Get worked up and yell at the other photographers, and you are going to win enemies. Win enemies, and you are going to find it a lot more difficult to do your job. As Cha put it: 'There's one consequence [of breaking the rules of etiquette] that's not always apparent, and that is: if the photographers don't like you, they won't talk to you. And sometimes the only way that you can get information or be in the position to succeed is by communicating with the other photographers, and being friends with the other photographers, because at the end of the day, there's competition, but right equal to that there's altruism. You know, it's very common that you'll see, [for example], Adam [Katz Sinding] and [YoungJun] Koo shooting next to each other. Adam will get his shot. Then he'll get up and move so Koo can get his shot. And if they don't like you, maybe they're not that courteous. If they don't like you, maybe they won't tell you that there's this show that's going on at this secret location. You don't want to be, even in business, that one person that no one likes. And if other people know that everyone else hates you, then maybe they're going to hate you too.'

But it is not as if the most successful street style photographers/bloggers don't also occasionally – or even frequently – jump on each other's shots. It is not as if people stick steadfastly to these rules in all circumstances. As with most rules, there are rules for breaking the rules.

The main rule for breaking the rule of not jumping on someone else's shot is that if you do jump on someone else's shot, stay put. Lock yourself into place. Stay away from the frame of their lens, and give the person who set up the shot space to do what they need to do. Once you have assumed a position, keep your movement to a minimum. Shooting at Fashion Week, I have often had the experience of stopping to set up a shot, getting engrossed in taking it, then attempting to step back or otherwise move to get a better frame, only to find that I am locked into place by a crowd of other photographers, all attempting to get the same shot. Once the viewfinder is up to your eye, people will assume that you are in the position you need to be. They will try not to get in your way, but they will do what they need to do in order to get their own shot.

A third, but related rule of street style photography etiquette, is that once you have taken your own shot, get out of the way so that other people can do the same. Do not horde a subject. And if you have stopped them to take their picture, or jumped in on someone's else's stopping of them, a fourth rule is to thank your subject, by name, if you know it, before moving out of the way. Treat them, in other words, like a human being. Perhaps even tell them that they look great or to enjoy the show. Act, that is, like something other than a blown-out stereotype of a paparazzo.

FIGURE 6.13 Bloggers on 8th Avenue in New York, frozen in place to as not to jump on each other's shot. Photo by author.

Note, however, that not all street style photographers stop their subjects to pose. Some, including Sinding, but also YoungJun Koo, Tyler Joe, Michael Dumler, Tommy Ton, H.B. Nam, and others, prefer to take candid shots of their subjects, sometimes standing outside the line of other bloggers and using telephoto lenses, sometimes crouched down low and running backwards in front of them to get dramatic shots of their subjects walking. Still, it is always good form to thank them for the shot afterwards, and most of the top street style bloggers/photographers do, taking care to cultivate a relationship with their subjects over time. It is not uncommon to see bloggers/photographers who have been shooting Fashion Week for a while hug their subjects after their shots, or even, on occasion, share a cab ride with them to the next show.

The ideal relationship between street style photographers/bloggers and their subjects – like street style photographers with one another – is casual and friendly. Many bloggers attend the same parties as their subjects. Many follow each other on Facebook and Instagram. Some have even dated. If there was a conceptual or social divide between the fashion industry and the fashion blogosphere, that divide has dissipated. They are all part of the industry now, striving for a place within the fashion hierarchy. The most successful street style bloggers are able to use their relationship with their subjects to their advantage. They are often able to get subjects to stop for them when they refuse to stop for anyone else. They even sometimes ask the subject to come with them to another location to get a better shot away from the crowd of photographers. In the first situation, bloggers seldom hesitate to jump on the shot, albeit following the rules mentioned above. They recognize the advantage that blogger has over them and tend to see it as a means of levelling the playing field. In the second, however, to do so would be seen as gauche, and I have never seen anyone attempt it. In either case, however, it is clear that being a successful blogger entails blurring the line between subject and friend. Work life and leisure life maintain no clear separation, just as the dividing line between 'insider' and 'outsider' has gotten harder and harder to see.

Outside/Inside

What these common relationships between the subjects of and photographers behind street style photography demonstrates is that any clearly demarcated line between *inside* the fashion industry and *outside* the fashion industry is a convenient fiction at best. The industry is a porous and expansive thing. It is not a walled-off monolith, an insulated mass of black huddled in the corner of a downtown Manhattan loft, even if fashion journalists maintain nostalgic visions of it as such. The fashion industry does not have, and has never had, clearly defined boundaries. Fashion bleeds into marketing and manufacture, textiles, music, publishing, and film. It needs these other industries. They sustain it, feed it, expand it. It cannot survive on its own. Menkes' editorial seemed to suggest that bloggers forced their way into the industry. But that couldn't be further from the truth. The industry, of course, in the wake of declining sales of print publications, saw the potential of blogs for marketing their own products and invited the bloggers in.

Perhaps in the early days of street style blogs, the street style bloggers at Fashion Week had something of the character of a roving pack of carnies setting up their sideshows outside the runway. They were adjacent to the industry, *outsiders* in both the figurative and literal sense. Bloggers had no formal training in photography or ties to the industry, and yet they managed to capture the attention of millions of fashion readers with their simply composed images, presenting an apparent alternative to the industry's own, more predictable representations. They photographed people who had once been ignored by the cameras, respected tailors and obscure designers, stylists for the shows, journalists for fashion publications, and the occasional editors they found appealing. They showed, that is, an unauthorized view of Fashion Week. Such a state of affairs could not stand.

After shooting for just a year and a half, Gunnar Hämmerle of the long-running blog StyleClicker was contacted by Condé Nast, the titan of fashion publishing. They wanted him to produce images for their European digital division. This was shortly after Scott Schuman had begun to shoot for their Style.com. Bloggers were all the rage. 'I was quite lucky', said Hämmerle, of the opportunities this brought him. 'I supplied them with pictures for *GQ* and *Glamour* and *Vogue*. That made it possible for me to travel so much. I had a fixed stipend every month and could go to different cities, and through that it became a job in a way.' That job soon developed into a career. 'I would be contacted by PR agencies asking to do projects for their clients. It was a bit of a mixture of everything. Sometimes it was exhibitions or it was photo shoots. All different kinds of things. And that was very good, because I didn't have to acquire clients. They just came through the blog.' His career, as Hämmerle tells it, took on a life of its own, snowballing into more and more commercial opportunities, and launching him from 'amateur' obscurity into 'professional' fashion photography. Hämmerle has been grateful for what this has provided him. But, he says, it comes at a price.

'I think the fashion industry took the right steps to gain control over the fashion bloggers', he told me. 'When it all started it was something that was of out of the control of the industry, and I think now they are back in control. That's why I think that it's not so free anymore, and it's not so authentic as it was in the beginning.' These days magazines tell the bloggers what they want in advance. They require images of specific people in specific places wearing specific clothes. Oddballs and quirky individualists have taken a backseat to Russian heiresses and elusive editors. The sidewalks of Fashion Week are as 'on the street' as most street style blogs get these days.

'When I began the blog', Yael Sloma, an Israeli journalist and the long-time street style blogger behind Tel Aviv's The Streets Walker told me in our Skype conversation in November of 2012, 'I thought that it would give another point of view about fashion, a more relaxed and more reasonable one, in my opinion, and a more positive one. And in the end, I don't feel that it happened, not in the way I hoped it would.' 'Street fashion', she explained, 'is now just a part of magazines and the industry'. 'There are good aspects of it', she went on. 'I won't say there aren't. But it is completely inside of it now. We don't have the outside point of view anymore. It is just part of the old capitalistic world.'

Sloma's prose, disillusioned and cynical, could have been written by a scholar of the Birmingham School of Cultural Studies back in the late 1970s. She espouses an almost textbook neo-Marxist conception of cultural appropriation. Something organic and authentic rises up out of a groundswell of proletarian revolt, and the capitalists, hungry for novelty, gobble it up. 'We have no chance to rebel anymore', said Sloma, 'since any rebellion will be so sexy that someone will just appropriate it'.

I relate to both Sloma and Hämmerle's positions. They make a certain amount of intuitive sense, especially for someone, like myself, trained in the same schools of critical theory as Sloma. But these positions present too simple a case. The Fashion Industry did not generate some master plan to pull street style into its embrace. It simply saw something as potentially profitable and then attempted to profit from it. Street style bloggers, furthermore, were not unwitting victims. They were quite eager accomplices. Love or hate what Fashion Week has become, it is the product of multiple players, a co-production of bloggers, editors, journalists, marketers, and would-be street style stars. This is not a case of cooptation, but of *cooperation*. And the result is not so much that bloggers have been pulled inside the industry as that the very notion of inside or outside the industry has been called into question. Where does the circus of Fashion Week begin and end? Who are its actors and players? Who are its viewers and audiences? At Fashion Week, these roles are all mixed up. They are in a constant state of flux, as the slow dance of street style transpires out on the proverbial sidewalk.

Street style is dead. Long live street style!

In the weeks leading up to New York Fashion Week Spring/Summer 2015, a spate of newspaper articles and blog posts forecast the end of street style photography as we know it. 'Photographers have grown weary of the "peacocks" posing outside fashion shows', wrote Morwenna Ferrier in *The Guardian* on 12 August 2014. Two days later, *Refinery29*, one of the most prominent fashion and lifestyle websites, wondered whether the break up of street style power couple Scott Schuman and Garance Doré, announced on The Sartorialist blog the same day as Ferrier's piece appeared in print, was a harbinger of street style dissolutions yet to come. Editors had gotten bored of street style, the chattering classes concurred. Readers were losing interest. And bloggers were thinking out loud that they might skip the sidewalks this season altogether. They had better things to do. The buzz throughout the fashion blogosphere was that Fashion Week street style would soon be a thing of the past. The columnists covering the subject for *Dazed Digital*, *New York Magazine's The Cut*, *Business of Fashion*, and other fashion-related websites for their part seemed barely able to contain their Schadenfreude. Street style was finally dead! The new tyrant king of Fashion Week had been deposed.

I was prepared, then, to be standing alone on the sidewalks in September of 2014 for Fashion Week's Spring/Summer 2015 collection. I wasn't sure if I was happy or sad about that. Fashion Week had always left me exhausted and cynical, disgusted by what street style had become. Yet it also somehow always managed to leave me hungry for more. I liked shooting Fashion Week. I liked the rush and the frenzy, the thousands of pictures I accumulated, and I liked complaining about Fashion Week with other bloggers/photographers even more. It gave us a common object of contemplation and disdain. The first day of Fashion Week had become like the first day back at school. There were lots of hugs and handshakes, promises to get together for drinks later. The photographers on the sidewalk had become my friends, and I was going to miss them.

But I had no need to worry. The end of Fashion Week street style had not yet come to pass. The sidewalks of Fashion Week Spring/Summer 2015 were just as crowded with photographers as they ever had been. The peacocks were out in full force. The editors donned as luxurious of duds as they ever had. Signs of street style's continuing dominion loomed large. Despite the mounting gripes of industry insiders, street style did not seem to be going anywhere. It was too entrenched, too critical to the promotional needs of the industry.

This does not mean, however, that nothing had changed outside the shows at Fashion Week, though what had changed was not immediately visible to me. It took some time to see it. Where two years beforehand, street style bloggers had made up a significant – and conspicuous – portion of those shooting the sidewalks of Fashion Week, by September of 2014, photographers for commercial websites and magazines had overtaken them. Blogging was simply playing less and less of a role in the street style documentation of Fashion Week. Street style fans turned instead to mainstream fashion websites and various photographers' Instagram feeds to satisfy their Fashion Week fix.

Not that the actual people shooting on the sidewalks had changed. Sinding was still out there, as were Dumler, Quenum, Koo, Guerre, Jackman, McPherson, Rodic, and the rest. It was largely the same cast of characters I had come to know well over the previous three seasons. However, fewer of the photographers out there were now shooting primarily for their own blogs. Many of them had graduated to more commercial gigs. Some were doing ad campaigns, others selling their images to magazines. And as they made this transition, they seemed to gradually let their blogs go. Michael Dumler (On Abbot Kinney) and H.B. Nam (StreetFSN) hardly ever posted on their blogs anymore. Months sometimes passed with no activity. Tommy Ton and YoungJun Koo had both let their blogs expire. On the first day of that season, rumours abounded that Ton had retired. His long-running blog, Jak & Jil, showed a grim 'This webpage is not available' when clicked on in Google Chrome. And then we all started seeing Ton, lingering in doorways, loitering in the intersection behind the crowd of photographers as usual. He hadn't retired, not as a photographer anyway. He just wasn't blogging anymore.

By Spring/Summer 2015, blogs were old news. The kids weren't bothering with them anymore, heading straight to micro-blogging platforms like Instagram and Twitter instead. And when the street style photographers behind blogs reached a certain level of blogging success, they would move on to greener pastures – magazines, commercial websites, ad campaigns. This didn't change the look, feel, or flurry of activity happening on the sidewalks of Fashion Week all that much, but it did cast the sidewalk circus in a somewhat different light.

If the sidewalks outside Fashion Week were once fashion's great hope for a new 'public sphere' (Habermas 2001), a democratic arena where a plebiscite of bloggers gathered to add their voices to the cacophony of commentators that make up the industry, they were now, quite unequivocally, something else altogether: a further extension of the runways, another site of marketing to compete with the pages of magazines. The concrete spaces of the sidewalk had become an important site of fashion's immaterial labour, the work of instilling it with affect and personality. This, increasingly, is where fashion marketing is done. This is where editors, buyers, and for that matter street style bloggers go to socialize and self-promote. Street style bloggers had professionalized, and in the process they were transforming themselves into something more conventional and recognizable, something the industry has a much easier time figuring out what to do with. They were becoming commercial fashion photographers. They had no doubt gained something in doing so: respectability, exposure, income. But they had lost something as well: an easy claim to autonomy and authenticity, an 'outsider' perspective that challenged industry insularity. At Fashion Week, there were no outsiders any more. The industry had already absorbed the sidewalks.

CONCLUSION:
STRAIGHT UP, REDUX

In stark black and white

In October 2012, after six years of posting his photographs online, Gunnar Hämmerle, the veteran street style blogger behind the Munich-based StyleClicker. net, made a decision. He he'd had enough of Fashion Week self-promotion, of style stars in brand name dresses lingering outside runway shows. He he'd had enough of the grind and the buzz of the street style hype machine, the competition among photographers over the same image, the regurgitation of the same clean, high fashion aesthetic. It was time for a change. So he closed his blog for renovation. 'You may have noticed', he wrote to his readers on the blog post that announced the temporary closure, 'that during the last year, I have been posting not so often as I used to. The first reason was my little daughter Lilja who is now almost one year old. But the second reason was a serious lack of motivation. I simply had the feeling that I was somehow through with street style blogging the way I was doing it. It has become an industry, there are more street style blogs than you can count and all are doing basically the same thing. Joy has gone! At least for me'.

When he re-launched the blog a month later, the difference was striking. The banner ads had been removed. There were no more affiliate links, no more sponsored posts. In place of the boldly coloured full-body images for which he had been known, there were black-and-white portraits, bust shots of individuals, mostly from Munich, whom Hämmerle had encountered at various events around town (see figures C.1 to C.3). If you wanted to see the full-body image of them, you had to click on their portrait and link through to another page.

'When I started the blog', Hämmerle told me over Skype, just after I had returned from my first Fashion Week and he was about to depart for Paris for his first in a couple of years, 'I was mainly interested in the people I was photographing', club kids in public parks, DJs in bomber jackets, burlesque dancers in vintage coats, a compendium of Munich's quirkier characters. 'I did not come from fashion. Fashion was simply the running thread of the blog, a theme that I figured many people would be interested in, and it was a way of narrowing down my focus when choosing people to shoot. Plus, it was a good excuse to shoot people I did not know in the street. So that was good. But it was not so much that I was deeply into fashion when I started. It was through the blog that I had the opportunity to step into that world. But I saw myself with one foot in the fashion world and the other out. I was an insider, but I was also an outsider at the same time.'

Hämmerle enjoyed the perspective such a position afforded. It granted him a sense of autonomy and carved out a space for critical distance. There was no expectation that he would shoot particular kinds of people in a particular kind of way. There was no pressure to conform to industry standards. And Hämmerle didn't. His commitments lay elsewhere. He saw himself as carrying on a tradition

FIGURE C.1 A portrait from Gunnar Hämmerle's revamped version of StyleClicker. Photo by Gunnar Hämmerle.

begun by the Parisian street photographers of the early twentieth century, a project of social documentation, not aggrandizement. It was a hobby for him, but a *serious* one, and Hämmerle was committed to it like an aficionado or an enthusiast.

Hämmerle's images focused on the singular and the idiosyncratic, those stylistic elements that separate one person from another, and which could not be reduced to a particular social category or type. He trained his lens on the ruptures in the smooth space of trend dissemination, the fashion exceptions. And he was able to maintain this emphasis for several years. Indeed, there was never a point where he had to give it up entirely. Yet he too began to feel pressure to cover the 'main events' of the fashion industry, the fashion weeks and the big shows, the places where the world's fashion elite gather to strut their stuff. 'The competition', he said, 'is quite thick now. I don't want to talk about "the good old times", but I think that back then those blogs that really became big all had a unique way of looking at the whole topic. And they were of high quality. Otherwise they wouldn't have been successful. I think that maybe many people these days just start street style blogs without caring so much about the quality of their pictures or the quality of who they pick. They just want to be a part of the hype'. The Fashion Weeks have become saturated with bloggers, all vying for photographs of the same pre-certified style stars. 'And it's a bit strange, for example in Paris at the runway shows. Now there are more photographers than people to shoot. It's almost like paparazzo. Or like a war almost. And it's not so much fun for me anymore.'

Hämmerle gradually transitioned from a street style blogger into a 'professional' fashion photographer, from a participant-observer, hovering on the periphery of the fashion world, to a plain old participant, entrenched on the inside. He put up more and more ads on his blog, featured more and more sponsored content. He shot editorial and advertorial for a variety of clients, and as time went on, he found that he no longer needed the blog as a primary source of income. That was good. He was happy about that. It afforded him certain advantages. For one thing, it enabled him to use the online real estate that was once his virtual portfolio for something he found more interesting and fulfilling. If he didn't need his blog to serve as his professional calling card anymore, he could make it into something else: 'an old school' street style blog, full of straight-up portraits of 'regular' people in Munich.

And Hämmerle was not the only street style photographer re-thinking his art and practice in the wake of street style's incorporation into the fashion industry. Others, like Mary Scherpe of Stil in Berlin (stilinberlin.de) and Søren Jepsen of The Locals (thelocals.dk), have expanded their blogs into virtual lifestyle portals, emphasizing travel and the arts over street style alone. Garance Doré continues to shrink the portion of her blog devoted to street style. Tommy Ton and YoungJun Koo have let their blogs go as they do their street style work for other clients instead. Yael Sloma, the journalist turned photographer who started The Streets

FIGURE C.2 Photo by Gunnar Hämmerle.

FIGURE C.3 Photo by Gunnar Hämmerle.

Walker, decided to give up street style photography altogether. She does fine art installations now. By 2013, a certain brand of street style malaise had set in. Many first-generation street style bloggers felt it was time to move on.

Back to the roots?

In the late summer of 2014, in the build up towards Mercedes-Benz Fashion Week Spring/Summer 2015, I was contacted by three separate publications to give my comments on the so-called 'return to the real' in street style photography. I, of course, was never convinced 'the real' had gone away. Its spectre still haunted the most polished of off-runway photographs. Images of Miroslava Duma on the steps of the post office on 8th Avenue where Prabal Gurung was to hold his show depended on the real for their very appeal to readers. 'This happened', they claim, 'and Mira was here. Don't you wish you had been too? And wouldn't you look great in this dress?' Nonetheless, the journalists who contacted me had something else in mind. The premise of their articles was simple: readers have grown bored with fashion week street style photos and are seeking out something else instead.

Featured in the articles were a variety of blogs devoted, once again, to 'real people' in 'real places', going about their 'regular lives'. David Luraschi, for instance, a French-American fashion photographer who has taken to shooting his subjects from behind while in motion, is mentioned as part of a 'new breed' of street style – or 'peep style', as *The Guardian*'s Morwenna Ferrier calls it (Ferrier 2014). Disenchanted with the industry hype, Luraschi hopes to invest his work with something, well, not industry hype. 'I work within the fashion world', he told Ferrier, 'and I understand that street style is embedded within it. But to me, style is something else – it might be a color, or it might be an attitude or a dialogue. I have nothing against it [street style], but there's something about someone posing that removes the naturalness' (Ferrier 2014). So, Luraschi photographs 'everyday people' without their knowledge – candid shots of women in unflattering dresses, boys in sagging pants, middle-aged men in loud print shirts that don't quite fit right around their shoulders, all ambling away from the camera like refugees from a fashion warzone. There are no faces in these shots, no identifying features. The precondition for their 'regular'ness, it seems, is their anonymity.

London-based photographer Alex Sturrock, in contrast, focuses on faces and gestures in his work, avoiding giving the clothes too much prominence within the frame. 'When I do street portraiture, someone's face is probably the most important thing and clothes can even be a real distraction', he said to Ferrier, distancing himself from the market objectives that have come to define street style. Sturrock's shots include elderly women pushing walkers down the sidewalk, leopard-print-clad ladies with matching leopard-print clad babies, groups of young men reclining on bleachers in ill-fitting sweat suits. 'Scrappy/devoid of ornament' reads the tagline of his Instagram gallery (@alexsturrock), and it could be the motto for this 'new breed' of street style photographers. They have brought the 'street' of 'street photography' – at its most mundane and pedestrian – back into the mix, and along with it, they have resurrected its promise of revelatory capture. The ordinary becomes the staging ground for the sublime. But in Sturrock's and Luraschi's work, that revelation seems to consist of a single reiterated thought: people, they dress so badly these days (Hill 2005). In the rush to distance themselves from the glitz and glamour of contemporary street style photography, 'realist' street style photographers like them emphasize the frumpy and the banal, and in doing so, seem to reinforce an impression the fashion industry has already had for decades, that most people have no real sense of style. There's just nothing you can do with them. If the work of Yael Sloma or Alkistis Tsitouri was meant to inspire 'ordinary' folks to do fashion 'on their own terms', this new work in realist street style photography implores them to not even bother. You're just gonna get it wrong anyway. Move on with your lives. This resurgence of street style realism, then, is couched in a fashion world cynicism that to me is even more damning than the product-placement mentality of fashion week imagery. It resurrects a conceptual barrier between fashion world insiders and everyone else, one that is even thicker and more impenetrable than what was in place before. These photographers still use *style radar* to identify their subjects, but they use it to find those people to avoid.

Other rising stars in the 'realist' street style blogosphere endorse a much more hopeful, if occasionally saccharine, message. They strive to be as inclusive as possible in their selection of subjects, turning their *style radar* off altogether and focusing instead on the 'human interest' element. Brandon Stanton, the former bond trader behind Humans of New York, is the best-known example of this emergent genre. His website features singular shots of a wide range of New York residents depicted, in situ, in the standard straight-up format of classic street style portraiture. His range of subjects is diverse, omnivorous. Overweight asthmatic working-class African Americans are welcome, tiny Latino toddlers with teary eyes and puffy coats *de rigueur*. Beneath each image is an extended, sometimes funny, sometimes inspiring, often strikingly intimate extended quote from the subject, taken from a longer interview Stanton conducts with each. We are seemingly let in to these subjects' lives, or at least the portion of their lives Stanton chooses to show us about them – their recent breast cancer scare, their ailing father, their stint in Afghanistan. We feel we *know* these subjects, relate to them. We imagine their lives to capture something universal about the human experience. Here 'the street' represents base-level social reality, the human condition exposed.

Stanton envisions the Humans of New York website as a kind of a humanistic reworking of the number-crunching project of government census takers, a testimony to the collective experience of being human today in all its myriad forms. This, apparently, is something his audience was hungry for. As of the writing of this conclusion, Stanton had already featured sympathetic portraits of some 6,000 New Yorkers. His Facebook page had 11 million likes, well above the population of New York City I might add, and his Instagram feed was viewed by thousands within seconds of each posting. Stanton describes himself as the most widely viewed photographer in the world, and this may, in fact, be true. He has been featured in numerous newspapers and magazines. His book, also titled *Humans of New York*, was a *New York Times Bestseller*. And he has spawned legions of imitators from Humans of Tehran to People of Boston. Humans of New York is a certifiable phenomenon.

And yet, I can't help but find something off-putting about it. Perhaps it is its syrupy sentimentality. Perhaps it is Stanton's overblown ambition. Or perhaps it is the uncritical way Humans of New York engages with the 'regular' and the 'real', as if they were observable characteristics of the natural world around us, rather than value judgements made by photographers. Humans of New York and its numerous imitators resurrect the early anthropological project of establishing a visual record of human diversity in the highly conventionalized style of social realist portraiture. His 'visual census' reads to me like an antiquated museum display. Here is a middle-aged black man with his family. They are just like you and me. Here is an elderly white woman on a subway platform. Don't you feel empathy for her, pushing a walker around like that? Here is a Chinese shop owner outside his store. See, he really is a nice guy. August Sander would have recognized a kinship between what he was doing in early twentieth-century Germany and what Stanton is doing today. Stanton's chosen title, 'Humans of New York', is an almost direct update of Sander's 'People of the Twentieth Century.' Both projects are wide-ranging and ambitious. Both projects catalogue the scope of possibilities for contemporary social types. Only Stanton invests his work with a treacly feel-good message Sander would have steadfastly avoided.

I do not mean to criticize Stanton, Sturrock, Luraschi, or other 'realist' street style photographers too harshly. I sympathize with their objectives, and I appreciate many of their images. I too find myself longing for an earlier moment in street style portraiture when photographers focused their lenses on subjects well outside the bounds of fashion industry representation. Every time I return to Philadelphia after Mercedes-Benz New York Fashion Week, I take to the streets with a vengeance, eager to put 'the street' back into my own street style photos. I cherish the grit and the edginess of Philly's streets. I look for the vaguely subcultural, the undeniably urban. And yet, I realize that there is nothing more intrinsically 'street' about my images in Philadelphia than my images at Fashion Week. Both take place on the concrete corridors of 'real' metropolitan areas. Both capture images of 'real' people doing things that people 'really do'. It just so happens that for one set that means attending runway shows bedecked in Moschino couture.

After shooting street style photography for over three years now, I am simply not interested in attesting to the genuineness or reality of one moment in street style photography's history over another. I am not interested in fetishizing reality as something to be pursued at all costs, as some spark of authentic life emerging from the cold industrial machine of neoliberal capital. I have no stake in making truth claims about my work. I will leave the obsession with truth to the philosophers.

No, I am nostalgic for the 'good old days' of street style blogs, that all-too-brief period between roughly 2005 and 2012, for a different reason: that is the moment in street style's history that I most relate to. It is the period in which bloggers were most performatively autonomous of the fashion industry, when they sought to capture diverse individuals in various cities throughout the world. Such blogs put new cities on the fashion map. They expanded the scope and range of industry representation. They challenged industry aesthetics and standards, featured a variety of body types and age ranges, a number of distinct sartorial sensibilities. And they had the scrappy, threadbare aesthetic of the self-conscious outsider. It is an aesthetic I recognized as kin. It felt immediately familiar to me. It felt like mine.

I share, that is, a politics with the early street style bloggers, as well as an aesthetic, an ideal, and a commitment to street style photography at its most explicitly anthropological. Street style photographers like Hämmerle, Rodic, Obando, Tsitouri, and Jokinen were as interested in people as in clothes. Like Humans of New York, they had an expansive and empathetic vision. But unlike Humans of New York, they made no pretence of featuring *all* kinds of people. They had no interest in capturing the whole of human diversity, creating a museum display of mankind. They photographed – and in fact, continue to photograph – the fashionable few, the stylishly eschew. They photograph singularities and exceptions, rather than affirm massive social categories like 'regular' and 'ordinary'.

The early street style blogs celebrate the inventiveness and artistry of individual style in a way few photographic genres have succeeded at doing before or since. They pick out the unique and the off-type. They challenge trends and conventions. They expand the scope of representational possibility for fashion-related imagery. And 'fashion-related' is the key term here. The lens of street style photography has always been selective, focused primarily on urban dwellers working in largely creative industries, people who have a distinctive style and yet are not easily pinned down, who defy type, flout conventions, and complicate the convenient social categories we attempt to construct around them. Isn't this what we mean by 'cool' in the first place? A stylized autonomy? A 'being such that it is'? And isn't there something valuable – politically, poetically, anthropologically – in documenting cool of this sort? Street style photographers, in the final analysis, take cool pictures of cool people in cool clothes posing in cool locations. That's it. And why isn't that enough already, anyway?

FIGURE C.4 Guido, Walnut St, Philadelphia. Photo by author.

FIGURE C.5 Rachael, off 16th St, Philadelphia. Photo by author.

FIGURE C.6 Julian, Sansom St, Philadelphia. Photo by author.

By way of an ending

In March 2015, three years after my first entry on the Urban Fieldnotes blog, I sat down to compose the following post: 'Back in 2008 or 2009', I wrote, 'street style bloggers would make a big deal out of their final posts. They would thank their readers for following them. They would talk about how much the blog had meant to them'. Inevitably, they would provide some sort of justification for why they would no longer be blogging. 'Too much work', they might say, or 'Life was getting in the way.' 'A new job is taking up all my time', or, like Gunnar Hämmerle, 'I just don't feel it the way I used to.' The final post, I explained, was a genre, designed to fulfil social obligations. It was evidence of the communal spirit of blogs of that time, their dependence on engaged networks of readers, and their culture of mutual support. The final post was not unlike a 'Dear John' letter, a polite but emotionally wrought convention for severing social ties. And also like a 'Dear John' letter, the writers of final posts tended to deny the actual finality of their action. 'I am taking a little break from blogging', they might say. 'Goodbye for now.'

As you have probably guessed, I sat down to write that post because I intended it to be *my* final post. It had been a rough winter, and I had barely been out on the streets for months. I had just finished and sent off to Bloomsbury the first draft of this book, and I had little more to say about street style blogging as a concept or a practice. Besides, I was losing readers. I, like other bloggers I know, had noticed a general trend towards readers viewing content primarily on other social media platforms, rather than visiting blogs directly. While my Instagram and Tumblr followers continued to grow, visitors to my blog were dwindling. Why bother to visit blogs, after all, when you can simply stream through content on some other app? Why go to blogs when blog content can come to you? The end times for blogs appeared already to be in sight. It was time, I decided, to cut the chord. And so I started to compose my final post as a reflection of the social conventions of final posts. It was very 'meta', just like my blog had always been.

I didn't need to write the post, of course. People don't generally compose final blogs posts anymore. The sense of social obligation to do so has faded away, just like old blogs simply fade away. Posts get spaced further and further apart. Months go by with no new updates. And then one day, a 'website not available' message appears across the computer screen when you type their URL into your browser. All evidence of their existence is erased, confined to the virtual vaults of the Wayback Machine. The final post is something of a lost art, like 'thank you notes' or formal emails. I, however, thought it would be a nice touch to complete the blog with a nod to tradition. My intention was to end the post with the following, tongue-in-cheek statement, 'I am taking a break from blogging. Goodbye for now'. And then I would never write another post. The idea made me laugh.

I finished the post and stared at the screen for some time, my cursor hovering over the 'publish' button. Something was keeping me from pushing my middle finger down. Over the course of the past three years, I had made blogging a significant part of my weekly routine. Most weeks, I spent hours on the streets of Philadelphia looking for subjects, and I loved the high I got from finding someone really unique and interesting. I liked the casual interactions between myself and them, the revelations about style and brands that came out of those interactions, and the way we collaborated to produce an image. I liked feeling like a modern-day flâneur, moving through the city without a destination in mind, slinking down alleyways and sidewalks. And I liked how much better my photographs were getting, in both composition and technique. I was good at this, I realized, and I didn't want to stop doing something I was good at. I wanted to cultivate my photographic skills and embrace the label of 'visual anthropologist' even more completely to justify my doing so. Plus, I liked the immediate gratification of posting my research as it happened, rather than having to suffer through the months of waiting typical for other types of academic publication. Blogs don't require peer review. They retain an academic autonomy unlike anything else in scholarship today. Through street style blogging, I felt like I was doing the best, most timely, and most public anthropological work of my career so far.

The blog had transformed significantly since I first started it. No longer was it primarily a methodological device for studying other bloggers. I wasn't doing any more blogger interviews. I was no longer publically reflecting on the experience of blogging. With the completion of this book, I had finished with that aspect of my street style project. Urban Fieldnotes was now just another street style blog. Not that that was a problem. As I have claimed throughout this book, street style blogs, at their best, constitute a popular form of visual anthropology. They document the looks and trends of the moment. They catalogue the varieties of human sartorial expression. They capture the urban fashion zeitgeist, without constructing convenient fictions of sociological categories. Urban Fieldnotes, I believed – and continue to believe – was valuable to anthropology *as* a street style blog, not just as a tool for studying them.

So, instead of hitting 'publish' that day, I found myself moving the mouse over to the 'delete' button instead. Within a few days, I was back out on the streets taking pictures, conducting street interviews, and investing myself in my street style work once again. As I finish this conclusion, I am still updating Urban Fieldnotes, though with somewhat less regularity than before. I still believe in the promise of the blog, as I believe in the promise of street style blogs more generally. And I still find the blog a useful mechanism for furthering my anthropological work. I don't know how long I'll keep doing it – as long as it feels like a productive, viable alternative to academia as usual, I suppose. But I do know how it will end when it eventually does. It will end the same way most blogs end these days, not demarcated by some formalized, antiquated gesture – some denial-ridden, emotionally wrought goodbye to my readers – but by a gradual attrition of posts, until a single date affixes itself to my blog page like an unfinished sentence etched into a sidewalk.

FIGURE C.7 Nijiah, Sansom St, Philadelphia. Photo by author.

BIBLIOGRAPHY

Agamben, Giorgio. 1993. *The Coming Community*. M. Hardt, transl. Minneapolis: University of Minnesota Press.

Agamben, Giorgio. 1998. *Homo Sacer: Sovereign Power and Bare Life*. Stanford: Stanford University Press.

Aristotle. 1999. *Nicomachean Ethics*. Indianapolis, IN: Hackett Publishing.

Aspelund, Karl. 2009. *Fashioning Society: A Hundred Years of Haute Couture by Six Designers*. New York: Fairchild Publications.

Azhar, Rohaizatul. 2013. 'Hunting for the Face: When It Comes to Street Style, Photographer Yvan Rodic Says Nothing Beats Self-Confidence'. *The Straits Times: Lifestyle Briefs*.

Bakshy, Eytan, Winter A. Mason, Jake M. Hofman, and Duncan J. Watts. 2011. *Everyone's an Influencer: Quantifying Influence on Twitter*. Association for Computing Machinery, Pp. 65–74.

Banet-Weiser, Sarah. 2012. *Authentic (TM): The Politics of Ambivalence in a Brand Culture*. New York: New York University Press.

Banet-Weiser, Sarah, and Marita Sturken. 2010. 'The Politics of Commerce: Shepard Fairey and the New Cultural Entrepreneurship'. In *Blowing up the Brand: Critical Perspectives on Promotional Culture*. M. Aronczyk and D. Powers, eds. Pp. 263–284. New York: Peter Lang.

Barthes, Roland. 1981. *Camera Lucida: Reflections on Photography*. New York: Farrar, Strauss, and Giroux.

Barthes, Roland. 1990. *The Fashion System*. Berkeley: University of California Press.

Baudrillard, Jean. 1994. *Simulacra and Simulation*. Ann Arbor: University of Michigan Press.

Bauman, Zygmunt. 1998. *Globalization: The Human Consequences*. Cambridge and Oxford: Polity Press.

Bauman, Zygmunt. 2003. *Liquid Love*. Cambridge: Polity Press.

Benjamin, Walter. 1955. 'The Work of Art in the Age of Mechanical Reproduction'. In *Illuminations*. H. Arendt, ed. Pp. 219–253. New York: Harcourt, Brace & World.

Benjamin, Walter. 2002. *The Arcades Project*. New York and London: Belknap Press.

Berlinger, Max. 2014. *What Happened to Street Style?* http://www.businessoffashion.com/articles/opinion/op-ed-happened-street-style.

Berman, Marshall. 1982. *All that is Solid Melts into Air: The Experience of Modernity*. New York: Penguin Books.

Blackett, Tom, and Bob Boad, eds. 2000. *Co-Branding: The Science of Alliance*. London: Palgrave-Macmillan.

Blumer, Herbert. 1969. 'Fashion: From Class Differentiation to Collective Selection'. *The Sociological Quarterly* 10 (3): 275–291.

Boellstorff, Tom, Bonnie Nardi, Celia Pearce, and T.L. Taylor, eds. 2012. *Ethnography in Virtual Worlds: A Handbook of Method*. Princeton: Princeton University Press.

Bogost, Ian. 2012. *Alien Phenomenology, or What It's Like to Be a Thing*. Minneapolis: University of Minnesota Press.

Bolter, David Jay, and Richard Grusin. 2000. *Remediation: Understanding New Media*. Cambridge, MA: MIT Press.

Bourdieu, Pierrre. 1980. *The Logic of Practice*. Stanford: Stanford University Press.

Bourdieu, Pierrre. 1984. *Distinction: A Social Critique of the Judgment of Taste*. Cambridge, MA: Harvard University Press.

Bourdieu, Pierrre. 1993. 'The Field of Cultural Production, or: The Economic World Reversed'. In *The Field of Cultural Production: Essays on Art and Literature*. R. Johnson, ed. Pp. 29–73. New York: Columbia University Press.

Brooks, David. 2000. *Bobos in Paradise: The New Upper Class and How They Got There*. New York: Simon & Schuster.

Bruns, Axel. 2008. 'The Future Is User-Led: The Path towards Widespread Produsage'. *Fibreculture Journal* 11. http://eleven.fibreculturejournal.org/fcj-066-the-future-is-user-led-the-path-towards-widespread-produsage/.

Chia, Aleena. 2012. 'Welcome to Me-Mart: The Politics of User-Generated Content in Personal Blogs'. *American Behavioral Scientist* 56(4):421–438.

Clarke, John, Stuart Hall, Tony Jefferson, and Brian Roberts. 1976. 'Subcultures, Cultures, and Class: A Theoretical Overview'. In *Resistance Through Rituals*. S. Hall and T. Jefferson, eds. Pp. 9–74. London and New York: Routledge.

Clifford, James, and George E. Marcus. 1986. *Writing Culture: The Poetics and Politics of Ethnography*. Berkeley: University of California Press.

Collins, Lauren. 2009. "Man on the Street: Bill Cunningham Takes Manhattan," in *The New Yorker*. March 16. http://www.newyorker.com/magazine/2009/03/16/man-on-the-street.

Daguerre, Louis Jacques Mondé. 1980. 'Daguerrotype'. In *Classic Essays on Photography*. A. Trachtenberg, ed. Pp. 11–14. New Haven: Leete's Island Books.

Dawson, Dyanna, and J.T. Tran. 2013. *Street Fashion Photography: Taking Stylish Pictures on the Concrete Runway*. San Francisco, CA: Chronicle Books.

Dean, Jodi. 2010. *Blog Theory: Feedback and Capture in the Circuits of Drive*. Cambridge: Polity Press.

Deleuze, Gilles, and Félix Guattari. 1987. *A Thousand Plateaus: Capitalism and Schizophrenia*. B. Massumi, transl. Minneapolis and London: University of Minnesota Press.

Döblin, Alfred. 1994. 'Faces, Images, and Their Truth'. In *Face of Our Time*. A. Sander, ed. Pp. 7–15. London: Schirmer Art Books.

Dorst, John D. 1989. *The Written Suburb: An American Site, an Ethnographic Dilemma*. Philadelphia: University of Pennsylvania Press.

Duffy, Brooke. 2015. 'Amateur, Autonomous, and Collaborative: Myths of Aspiring Female Cultural Producers in Web 2.0'. In *Critical Studies in Media Communication* 32(1):48–64.

Duncombe, Stephen. 1997. *Notes from Underground: Zines and the Politics of Alternative Culture*. London and New York: Verso.

Eco, Umberto. 1972. *Towards a Semiotic Inquiry into the Television Message*. W.P.C.S. 3, Birmingham: University of Birmingham.

Edwards, Elizabeth. 2001. *Raw Histories: Photography, Anthropology and Museums*. London: Bloomsbury.

Ellis, Carolyn. 2004. *The Ethnographic I: A Methodological Novel about Autoethnography*. Walnut Creek, CA: Alta Mira Press.

Entwistle, Joanne, and Don Slater. 2013. 'Reassembling the Cultural: Fashion Models, Brands and the Meaning of "Culture" after ANT'. *Journal of Cultural Economy* 7(2):161–177.

Ferrier, Morwenna. 2014. 'How Street-Style Photography Got Real'. In *The Guardian*, Vol. 12 August 2014. TheGuardian.com.

Florida, Richard. 2002. *The Rise of the Creative Class*. New York: Basic Books.

Geertz, Clifford. 1977. 'Deep Play: Notes on the Balinese Cockfight'. In *The Interpretation of Cultures*. Pp. 412–453. New York: Basic Books.

Gershon, Ilana. 2011. 'Neoliberal Agency'. *Current Anthropology* 52(4):537–555.

Giddens, Anthony. 1979. *Central Problems in Social Theory: Action, Structure and Contradiction in Social Analysis*. Berkeley and Los Angeles: University of California Press.

Giddens, Anthony. 1991. *Modernity and Self-Identity: Self and Society in the Late Modern Age*. Stanford: Stanford University Press.

Gilbert, David. 2006. 'From Paris to Shanghai: The Changing Geography of Fashion's World Cities'. In *Fashion's World Cities*. C. Breward and D. Gilbert, eds. Pp. 3–32. Oxford: Berg.

Graeber, David. 2011. *Debt: The First 5,000 Years*. New York: Melville House.

Gramsci, Antonio. 1971. *Selections from the Prison Notebooks*. New York: Lawrence and Wishart.

Grimshaw, Anna. 2001. *The Ethnographer's Eye: Ways of Seeing in Anthropology*. Cambridge: Cambridge University Press.

Habermas, Jürgen. 2001. *The Structural Transformation of the Public Sphere: An Inquiry into a Category in Bourgeois Society*. T. Burger and F. Lawrence, trans. Cambridge, MA: MIT Press.

Hall-Duncan, Nancy. 1979. *The History of Fashion Photography*. New York: Alpine Book Company.

Hardt, Michael, and Antonio Negri. 2001. *Empire*. Cambridge: Harvard University Press.

Hartman, Eviana. 2006. 'Introduction'. In *STREET: The NYLON Book of Global Style*. M. Pangilian and C. Makita, eds. Pp. 8–9. New York: Nylon LLC.

Harvey, David. 1989. *The Condition of Postmodernity: An Enquiry into the Origins of Cultural Change*. Malden and Oxford: Blackwell Publishers.

Harvey, David. 2005. *A Brief History of Neoliberalism*. Oxford and New York: Oxford University Press.

Hayano, David M. 1979. 'Auto-Ethnogaphy: Paradigms, Problems, and Prospects'. *Human Organization* 38(1):99–104.

Hearn, Alison. 2008. ' "Meat, Mask, Burden:" Probing the Contours of the Branded "Self" '. *Journal of Consumer Culture* 8(2):197–217.

Hebdige, Dick. 1979. *Subculture: The Meaning of Style*. London and New York: Routledge Press.

Hebdige, Dick. 1988. *Hiding in the Light: On Images and Things*. London and New York: Routledge.

Heckert, Virginia, and Anne Lacoste. 2009. 'An Introduction to Irving Penn's Small Trades'. In *Small Trades*. I. Penn, ed. Pp. 9–19. Los Angeles: J. Paul Getty Museum.

Heffernan, Virginia. 2008. *Pop Couture*. The New York Times: 22.

Heider, Karl. 1975. 'What Do People Do? Dani Auto-Ethnography'. *Journal of Anthropological Research* 31:3–17.

Hesmondhalgh, David, and Sarah Baker. 2011. *Creative Labour: Media Work in Three Cultural Industries*. London and New York: Routledge.

Hill, Andrew. 2005. 'People Dress So Badly Nowadays: Fashion and Late Modernity'. In *Fashion and Modernity*. C. Breward and C. Evans, eds. Pp. 66–77. Oxford: Berg.

Hine, Christine M. 2000. *Virtual Ethnography*. London: SAGE Publications.

Hollan, Douglas W., and Jane C. WellenKamp. 1996. *The Thread of Life: Toraja Reflections on the Life Cycle*. Honolulu: University of Hawaii Press.

Holt, Douglas. 2000. *Does Cultural Capital Structure American Consumption*. New York: W.W. Norton & Company.

Holt, Douglas. 2004. *How Brands Become Icons: The Principles of Cultural Branding*. Cambridge: Harvard Business School Press.

Howarth, Sophie, and Stephen McClaren, eds. 2010. *Street Photography Now*. London: Thames and Hudson.

Ingold, Tim. 2013. *Making: Anthropology, Archaeology, Art, and Architecture*. London: Routledge.

Jameson, Fredric. 1992. *Postmodernism, Or, the Cultural Logic of Late Capitalism*. Durham and London: Duke University Press.

Jarrett, Marvin Scott. 2006. 'Forward'. In *STREET: The NYLON Global Book of Style*. M. Pangillan and C. Makita, eds. Pp. 6. New York: Nylon LLC.

Jerslev, Anne, and Mette Mortensen. 2014. 'Parazzi Photography, Seriality, and the Digital Photo Archive'. In *Digital Snaps: The New Face of Photography*. J. Larsen and M. Sandbye, eds. Pp. 155–178. New York: I.B. Tauris.

Johnson-Woods, Toni, and Vicki Karaminas. 2013. *Shanghai Street Style*. Bristol: Intellect.

Jones, Carla. 2007. 'Fashion and Faith in Urban Indonesia'. *Fashion Theory* 11(2/3):211–232.

Jones, Terry. 2000a. 'A Wink's as Good as a Nod'. In *Smile i-D: Fashion and Style: The Best from 20 Years of i-D*. T. Jones, ed. Pp. 9–12. Köln: Taschen.

Jones, Terry. 2000b. 'So Far So Good'. In *Smile i-D: Fashion and Style: The Best of 20 Years of i-D*. T. Jones, ed. Pp. 23–26. Köln: Taschen.

Keen, Andrew. 2008. *The Cult of the Amateur: How Blogs, MySpace, YouTube, and the Rest of Today's User-generated Media Are Destroying Our Economy, Our Culture, and Our Values*. New York: DoubleDay.

Klein, Naomi. 2007. *The Shock Doctrine: The Rise of Disaster Capitalism*. New York: Picador.

Kotler, Phillip. 1986. 'The Prosumer Movement: A New Challenge for Marketers Advances' in *Consumer Research* 13:510–513.

Küchlich, Julian. 2005. 'Precarious Playbor: Moddes and the Digital Games Industry'. *The Fibreculture Journal* 5(25). http://five.fibreculturejournal.org/fcj-025-precarious-playbour-modders-and-the-digital-games-industry/.

Lasch, Christopher. 1979. *The Culture of Narcissism: American Life in an Age of Diminishing Expectations*. New York: W.W. Norton & Company.

Lash, Scott. 1994. 'Reflexivity and Its Doubles: Structure, Aesthetics, Community'. In *Reflexive Modernization: Politics, Tradition, and Aesthetics in the Modern Social Order*. U. Beck and A. Giddens, and S. Lash, eds. Pp. 110–169. Cambridge and Oxford: Polity Press.

Latour, Bruno. 2005. *Reassembling the Social: An Introduction to Actor-Network Theory*. Oxford: Oxford University Press.

Law, John. 2004. *After Method: Mess in Social Science Research*. London and New York: Routledge.

Lazzarato, Maurizio. 1996. 'Immaterial Labor'. In *Radical Thought in Italy: A Potential Politics*. P. Virno and M. Hardt, eds. Pp. 133–150. Minneapolis: University of Minnesota Press.

Leland, John. 2004. *Hip: The History*. New York: Harper Perennial.

Lifter, Rachel. 2013. 'Fashioning Indie: The Consecration of a Subculture and the Emergence of "Stylish" Femininity'. In *Fashion Cultures Revisited*. S. Bruzzi and P. C. Gibson, eds. Pp. 175–185. London and New York: Routledge.

Lipovetsky, Gilles. 2002. *The Empire of Fashion: Dressing Modern Democracy*. Princeton and Oxford: Princeton University Press.

Lipovetsky, Gilles. 2005. *Hypermodern Times*. Cambridge: Polity.

Lury, Celia. 2004. *Brands: The Logos of the Global Economy*. London and New York: Routledge.

Luvaas, Brent. 2010. 'Designer Vandalism: Indonesian Indie Fashion and the Cultural Practice of Cut 'n' Paste'. *Visual Anthropology Review* 26(1):1–16.

Luvaas, Brent. 2012. *DIY Style: Fashion, Music, and Global Digital Cultures*. London and New York: Berg.

Luvaas, Brent. 2013. 'Shooting Street Style in Indonesia: A Photo Essay'. *Clothing Cultures* 1(1):59–81.

Lyotard, Jean-Francois. 1984. *The Postmodern Condition*. G. Bennington and B. Massumi, trans. Minneapolis: University of Minnesota Press.

MacDougall, David. 1998. *Transcultural Cinema*. Princeton: Princeton University Press.

Maffesoli, Michel. 1995. *The Time of the Tribes: The Decline of Individualism in Mass Society*. London: Sage.

Marwick, Alice E. 2013. *Status Update: Celebrity, Publicity, & Branding in the Social Media Age*. New Haven and London: Yale University Press.

Massumi, Brian. 2002. *Parables for the Virtual: Movement, Affect, Sensation*. Durham and London: Duke University Press.

Mauss, Marcel. 2000. *The Gift: The Form and Reason for Exchange in Archaic Societies*. New York: W.W. Norton & Company.

McCracken, Grant. 2005. *Culture and Consumption II: Markets, Meaning, and Brand Management*. Bloomington: Indiana University Press.

Mears, Ashley. 2011. *Pricing Beauty: The Making of a Fashion Model*. Berkeley: University of California Press.

Menkes, Suzy. 2013. 'The Circus of Fashion'. In *New York Times T Magazine*, Vol. 10 February 2013. New York.

Mentges, Gabriele. 2000. 'Cold, Coldness, Coolness: Remarks on the Relationship of Dress, Body, and Technology'. *Fashion Theory* 4(1):27–48.

Merleau-Ponty, Maurice. 2013. *Phenomenology of Perception*. London: Routledge.

Miller, Daniel, and Sophie Woodward. 2012. *Blue Jeans: The Art of the Ordinary*. Berkeley: University of California Press.

Misch, Felix. 2011. 'Weisure, Blurk, Playbor, Lark'. *FUTURIST* 45(3):64.

Muggleton, David. 2000. *Inside Subculture: The Postmodern Meaning of Style*. Oxford: Berg.

Ong, Aihwa. 2006. *Neoliberalism as Exception: Mutations in Citizenship and Sovereignty*. Durham and London: Duke University Press.

Ortner, Sherry B. 1989. *High Religion: A Cultural and Political History of Sherpa Buddhism*. Princeton: Princeton University Press.

Ortner, Sherry B. 1996. 'Making Gender: Toward a Feminist, Minority, Postcolonial, Subaltern, etc., Theory of Practice'. In *Making Gender: The Politics and Erotics of Culture*. Pp. 1–20. Boston: Beacon Press.

Ortner, Sherry B. 2006. *Anthropology and Social Theory: Culture, Power, and the Acting Subject*. Durham and London: Duke University Press.

Ortner, Sherry B. 2013. *Not Hollywood: Independent Film at the Twilight of the American Dream*. Durham: Duke University Press.

Pappademas, Alex. 2012. 'Up from the Streets'. In *GQ*, Vol. June 2012. http://www.gq.com/style/profiles/201206/scott-schuman-sartorialist-gq-june-2012-interview. www.gq.com.

Pettman, Dominic. 2006. *Love and Other Technologies: Retrofitting Eros for the Information Age*. New York: Fordham University Press.

Pham, Minh-Ha T. 2011. 'Blog Ambition: Fashion, Feelings, and the Political Economy of the Digital Raced Body'. *Camera Obscura* 76(26):1–37.

Pink, Sarah. 2006. *Doing Visual Ethnography*. London: Sage.

Pinney, Christopher. 2011. *Photography and Anthropology*. London: Reaktion Books.

Polhemus, Ted. 1978. *Fashion and Anti-Fashion*. London: Thames and Hudson.

Polhemus, Ted. 1994. *Streetstyle: From Sidewalk to Catwalk*. London: Thames and Hudson.

Polhemus, Ted. 1996. *Style Surfing: What to Wear in the 3rd Millennium*. London: Thames and Hudson.

Powers, Devon. 2014. 'Lost in the Shuffle: Technology, History, and the Idea of Musical Randomness'. *Critical Studies in Media Communication* 31(3):244–264.

Pratt, Mary Louise. 1992. *Imperial Eyes: Travel Writing and Transculturation*. London and New York: Routledge.

Reed-Danahay, Deborah. 1997. *Auto/Ethnography: Rewriting the Self and the Social*. Oxford: Berg.

Rocamora, Agnès, and Alistair O'Neill. 2008. 'Fashioning the Street: Images of the Street in the Fashion Media'. In *Fashion as Photograph: Viewing and Reviewing Images of Fashion*. E. Schinkle, ed. Pp. 185–199. London: I.B. Tauris.

Rodic, Yvan. 2010. *Facehunter*. Munich: Prestel.

Rose, Nikolas. 2006. *The Politics of Life Itself: Biomedicine, Power, and Subjectivity, in the Twenty-First Century*. Princeton: Princeton University Press.

Ross, Andrew. 2009. *Nice Work if You Can Get It: Life and Labor in Precarious Times*. New York: New York University Press.

Ross, Andrew. 2013. 'In Search of the Lost Paycheck'. In *Digital Labor: The Internet as Playground and Factory*. T. Scholz, ed. Pp. 13–32. New York: Taylor & Francis.

Rudnyckyj, Daromir. 2009. 'Spiritual Economies: Islam and Neoliberalism in Contemporary Indonesia'. *Cultural Anthropology* 24(1):104–141.

Safe, Georgina. 2012. 'Bloggerazzi are a Street Hazard Outside Shows'. *Sydney Morning Herald*: 12.

Schor, Juliet. 2004. *Born to Buy: The Commercialized Child and the New Consumer Culture*. New York: Scribner.

Scott, Clive. 2007. *Street Photography: From Atget to Cartier-Bresson*. London and New York: I.B. Tauris.

Seigworth, Gregory J., and Melissa Gregg. 2010. 'An Inventory of Shivers'. In *The Affect Theory Reader*. M. Gregg and G.J. Seigworth, eds. Durham and London: Duke University Press.

Sennett, Richard. 1974. *The Fall of Public Man*. New York: W.W. Norton & Company.

Sennett, Richard. 1996. *Flesh and Stone: The Body and the City in Western Civilization*. London: W.W. Norton and Company.

Sewell, William H., Jr. 1992. 'A Theory of Structure: Duality, Agency, and Transformation'. *American Journal of Sociology* 98(1):1–29.

Shirky, Clay. 2009. *Here Comes Everybody: The Power of Organizing without Organizations*. New York: Penguin.

Sontag, Susan. 1973. *On Photography*. New York: Picador.

Strathern, Marilyn. 1987. 'The Limits of Auto-Anthropology'. In *Anthropology at Home*. A. Jackson, ed. Pp. 16–37. London: Tavistock Publications.

Taylor, Astra. 2014. *The People's Platform: Taking Back Power and Culture in the Digital Age*. New York: Picador.

Taylor, Lucien. 1996. 'Iconophobia'. *Transition* 69:64–88.

Terranova, Tiziana. 2004. *Network Culture: Politics for the Information Age*. Ann Arbor, MI: Pluto Press.

Terranova, Tiziana. 2013. 'Free Labor'. In *Digital Labor: The Internet as Playground and Factory*. T. Scholz, ed. Pp. 33–57. New York: Taylor & Francis.

Thompson, Hugh. 1985. 'Media: The Great Style Steal/ Street Magazines'. *The Guardian*.

Thornton, Sarah. 1996. *Club Cultures: Music, Media, and Subcultural Capital*. Hanover and London: Wesleyan University Press.

Tsing, Anna. 2013. 'Sorting out Commodities: How Capitalist Value Is Made Through Gifts'. *HAU: Journal of Ethnographic Theory* 3(1):21–43.

Turkle, Sherry. 2011. *Alone Together: Why We Expect More from Technology and Less from Each Other*. New York: Basic Books.

Tyler, Stephen A. 1986. 'Post-Modern Ethnography: From Document of the Occult to Occcult Document'. In *Writing Culture: The Poetics and Politics of Ethnography*. J. Clifford and G.E. Marcus, eds. Pp. 122–140. Berkeley: University of California Press.

Van Dijck, José. 2013. *The Culture of Connectivity: A Critical History of Social Media*. Oxford: Oxford University Press.

Villett, Michelle. 2007. 'Taking It to the Web: Street-Style Blogs Are Delivering Instant Inspiration – and Democratizing Fashion'. *The Globe and Mail*: L8.

Wacquant, Loïc. 2004. *Body & Soul: Notebooks of an Apprentice Boxer*. Oxford: Oxford University Press.

Wallach, Jeremy. 2008. 'Living the Punk Lifestyle in Jakarta'. *Ethnomusicology* 52(1):98–116.

Warren, Caleb, and Margaret C. Campbell. 2014. 'What Makes Things Cool? How Autonomy Influences Perceived Coolness'. *Journal of Consumer Research* 41:543–563.

Weber, Max. 1978. *Economy and Society*. G. Roth and C. Wittich, transl. Berkeley, Los Angeles, London: University of California Press.

Weinzierl, Rupert, and David Muggleton. 2004. 'What Is "Post-subcultural Studies" Anyway?' In *The Post-Subcultures Reader*. D. Muggleton and R. Weinzierl, eds. Pp. 3–23. Oxford and New York: Berg.

Westerbeck, Colin, and Joel Meyerowitz. 1994. *Bystander: A History of Street Photography*. Boston: Bulfinch Press.

Williams, Raymond. 1977. *Marxism and Literature*. Oxford and New York: Oxford University Press.

Willis, Paul. 1977. *Learning to Labor: How Working Class Kids Get Working Class Jobs*. New York: Columbia University Press.

Wise, Bambina. 2012. 'The Sartorialist Lands in South Africa'. In *Women's Wear Daily*, Vol. 2 November 2012. New York.

Woodward, Sophie. 2009. 'The Myth of Street Style'. *Fashion Theory* 13(1):83–102.

Yarhi, Stefania. 2012. 'How the Poses Were Struck; Stefania Yarhi on the Enduring Art and Artifice of Fashion Week in Street Style'. *National Post.*

Yi, David. 2012. 'Street Shooters During Fashion Week. These Photos Capture the Style Outside the Tent'. *Daily News:* 4.

Zhao, Jianhua. 2013. *The Chinese Fashion Industry: An Ethnographic Approach.* London: Bloomsbury.

Ziv, Yuli. 2011. *Blogging Your Way to the Front Row: The Insider's Guide to Turning Your Fashion Blog into a Profitable Business and Launching a New Career.* New York: Yuli Ziv.

INDEX

Ross, Andrew 218, 221, 240, 243
Rubinstein, Mordechai 118
Rudnyckyj, Daromir 220
Russos, Anna Della 256

Safe, Georgina 68
salvage anthropology 29
Sander, August 34, 35, 47, 296
sartorial creativity 115
Sartorialist, The 8, 17, 23, 46, 59, 62,
    67, 87, 117–19, 135, 137, 247,
    255, 263, 283. *See also* Schuman,
    Scott
Sartre, Jean-Paul 244
Schor, Juliet 150
Schuman, Scott 46, 62, 67, 137, 232, 239,
    255, 281
    on amateur photographers 242
Schwartz, Driely 66f
Scott, Clive 39, 108
search engine optimization (SEO) 221
Seigworth, Gregory J. 125
self-expression, form of 221
Sennett, Richard 19, 25, 27
SEO. *See* search engine optimization (SEO)
Seoul, street style photography in 85–93
serious hobbies 243–6, 258
Sewell, William H, Jr. 127
Shirky, Clay 222
Sinding, Adam Katz 62, 134, 137, 276
    photographs 62–3
    on professional photographers 242
    shooting style of 63
Singh, Preetma 271f
Slater, Don 219
Sloma, Yael 60f, 130, 282
social documentary photography 34–5
    vs. street photography 39
Sociological Quarterly, The 118
sociologists *vs.* anthropologists 77
Sontag, Susan 25, 28, 30, 31, 108, 124
sponsored content 232–3
Stanton, Brandon 295–6
Steichen, Edward 43
Strathern, Marilyn 12
street fashion 67–8. *See also* street style
    photography
Street Gazing (blog) 124, 249
'Street Paver' 38f

Street Peeper (blog) 258
street style bloggers 4, 13–16, 257f, 280f
    business practices of 218
    documented styles 76
    ethnographic study of 18–20
    at Fashion Week 277–81
    as freelance photographers 258
    role of 77
    shooting from sidewalks 260
    stuff of 16–18
    vs. subjects 280–1
street style blogs 4, 32–3, 136
    brand-consciousness of their readers
        150
    competition among bloggers 67
    digital democracy 5
    global popularity of 4
    hustle 249–52
    Indonesian 9
    lines of inclusion and exclusion
        129–33
    plus-size models on 133
    practical, material realities of 10
street-style *habitus* 126–8
street style photography 4, 76
    vs. anthropological photographs
        32–3
    in Athens, Greece 106–12
    in Beijing 96, 99
    in Cape Town, South Africa 101–6
    case of 144
    Cunningham role in 44–7
    definition of 23
    description of 23–4
    domain of 64, 65
    formula for 124
    freelance 235–40
    global 53–8
    internet connections for 67–8
    Jones, Terry 47–51
    Le 21ème (blog) 62–6
    lightings 23
    in Los Angeles, California 106–12
    from margins to mainstream 51–3
    'return to the real' in 294
    Rue Laplace and Rue Valette 26
    rules of 278–9
    scientific realism 24–33
    standards of 115

to street fashion 67–8
subject of 130
tools of 28
Web 2.0 59–62
STREET: The NYLON Book of Global Style 53
street walk, styles of 52
Streetgeist (blog) 106, 121
Streets Walker, The (blog) 60f, 130
stunning 118
Sturken, Marita 218
Sturrock, Alex 294–6
style. *See also* street style blogs
    questions about 144–86
    shared conception of 130
StyleClicker (blog) 129, 232, 281
Style Coalition 232
Style.com 67
style radar, cultivation of 123–6, 130
    by fashion magazines 135
Style Sophomore (blog) 85
Stylites (blog) 93
subject(s) of street style 141–4, 142f–3f,
        149f, 151f–8f, 160f–4f, 170f–2f,
        174f–5f
    attitude of 150
    brands 144–5, 146f, 150
    musical taste of 145, 147f, 148,
        178f–85f
    Philadelphia style, capturing 186–7,
        188f–212f
    quality of cool 176–7
    question of style 144–86
    style inspirations of 145
    visual argument 141–4
    wearing of 148, 160f–4f

Taiwan, street style photography in 85–93
Talbott, Fox 28, 34
Taylor, Astra 222
Taylor, Lucien 19, 144
Teller, Jürgen 42
Terranova, Tiziana 218, 221, 233, 243
Theodore, Ouigi 119
Thompson, Hugh 49
Thornton, Sarah 117
thoroughfares, reconstruction 25
Tokyo, street style photography in 85–93
Tol, Linda 264f

Ton, Tommy 46, 63–4, 67, 137, 237
tools of street style photography 28
TorontoVerve (blog) 145
Tran, J. T. 218
trend forecasting 44
Trés Awesome (blog) 124, 129
'tribal styles' 51
Tsing, Anna 225
Tsitouri, Alkistis 11f, 106, 107f, 109f,
        110f
    Athenian stylistic diversity 108
    Athens style *vs.* L.A. style 112
    on L.A. fashion 112
Tumblr 67
Turkle, Sherry 14
Tyler, Stephen A. 77
TypePad (blogging platforms) 67

urban cosmopolitanism of Helsinki
        (Finland) 71
urban culture 143f
Urban Fieldnotes (blog) 11f, 117, 119, 121,
        150, 301, 302
    Aphillyated Apparel 226f
    case study 121–2, 122f
    digital resources 215
urban individualism 27

Van Dijck, José 17, 59, 62, 223
Verde, Angel David 276
Victoria Beckham show 64
visual anthropologist 302

Wacquant, Loïc 133
Wallach, Jeremy 177
Wang, Alexander 156f, 261
Warren, Caleb 117, 123
Weber, Max 37
Weibo (blog) 96
Weinzierl, Rupert 161
WellenKamp, Jane C. 159
Westerbeck, Colin 27, 34, 40, 108
Westwood, Vivienne 47
'White Eagle and Standing Bear' 29f
Williams, Raymond 5, 187
Willis, Paul 12, 52
Wintour, Anna 275
Wise, Bambina 46
Wixson, Lindsey 63